ESSAYS IN MYSTICISM

Explorations into Contemplative Experience

D1551620

by

Wayne Teasdale

with a foreward by
George A. Maloney, S.J.

Sunday Publications, Inc.
Lake Worth, Florida

ISBN: 0-941850-02-1

CONTENTS

AVUNCULO MEO
JOHANNI J. COSGROVE
MAGISTRI MAGNO BENIGNO
ATQUE PATIENTI
DEI PRAESERTIM VIRO.

FOREWORD

In all of us human beings there is a built-in drive toward mysticism. We desire, when we are able to transcend the pre-conditionings that hold us enslaved to our false selves, to stretch out with the fullness of our being toward union with the Ultimate that we call God. Karl Rahner wrote that the Christian of the future will have to be a mystic or he or she will be nothing at all. Such a person will have had to experience Someone or religion will be meaningless to the one practising any type of formal religion.

Dr. D.T. Suzuki, in his *Studies in Zen*, writes in a similar fashion describing how mysticism saves religion from being empty and devoid of any real enthusiasm:

> Though mysticism has frequently been misinterpreted and condemned, there is no doubt that it is the soul of the religious life, that it is what gives to a faith its vitality, fascination, sublimity and stability. Without mysticism, the religious life has nothing to be distinguished from the moral life, and, therefore, whenever a faith becomes conventionalized, and devoid, for some reason or other, of its original enthusiasm, mysticism invariably comes to its rescue.

We are beginning, in these latter decades of the 20th century, to see a return to mysticism in all religions, especially that of Christianity. It is a phenomenon, however, that is most easily misunderstood, since it means so many things to so many people. A college student freaked out by dropping "acid" talks about his "mystical experience". The business man who sits assiduously each morning and evening for 15 minute periods of "transcendental meditation" talks to his friends of his mystical union with the Unknown. Some Protestant fundamentalists link mysticism with occultism and will have nothing to do with it. A Catholic nun sits in the lotus position and gets on her "level" to meet her healing Savior. Hippies live in communes scattered all over the United States or even migrate to India, the motherland of mystics, to "experience the inner world."

A COMMON ELEMENT

Yet, regardless of the religious form used, there seems to be a common element in all mysticisms. In the Christian East of Pseudo-

Dionysius and the Far East of the *Upanishads*, to be a mystic means to be a fully alive human being. Such a person, through intense asceticism and purification of the body-soul relationship, touches an inner reality that is unchanging, eternal, holy and beautiful. If we call this Reality God, then mysticism seeks to establish between the subject and God, an intimate, immanent union that is experimental and is beyond man's habitual conceptualization and control.

Intrinsic to an authentic mysticism is the accent on the conscious awareness of a subject brought progressively into a more intense assimilating union with God. Pseudo-Dionysius, in his great classic, *The Mystical Theology,* describes it as a leaving behind of the operations of the senses, emotions and intellectual powers in order to "strain upwards in unknowing as far as may be towards the union with Him who is above all being and knowledge. For by unceasing and absolute withdrawal from thyself and all things in purity, abandon all and set free from all, thou will be borne up to the ray of the Divine Darkness that surpasses all being."

Hinduism, with most other Far Eastern religions, follows its basic orientation with the emphasis on the concept of *advaita* or non-duality. The mystic, through heroic efforts over years of yogic self-discipline, breaks through the false dichotomy between a subject and an object to enter into his true self by a process of enlightenment (*Samadhi*) that reveals his oneness with God and with the whole of creation.

The basic stress on the transcendent God as being external to the subject and revealing Himself through the medium of prophets, is found predominantly in such prophetic religions as Judaism and Islam.

CHRISTIAN MYSTICISM

But Christianity seeks through the Incarnate Word of God and Man in one person to synthesize the two seemingly opposing accents. God remains always totally "other" to man, yet through a progressive mystical union, God and man become one via grace, and this mystical grace is God's indwelling life within man, assimilating him into the trinitarian life through love, which does not destroy man's subjectivity and personhood, but differentiates his individuality to the very degree that he becomes aware of his oneness with God.

This is a common element in all of Christian mysticism, whether of the Eastern Fathers or the great mystics of the West such as Meister Eckhart, John Tauler, Henry Suso of the 14th century or St. Teresa of Avila and St. John of the Cross of 16th century Spain or Thomas Merton of the 20th century in America.

What is needed as moderns search for a deeper, more mystical experience of God, is a return to the fundamental doctrine common to all of the great Christian mystics. Still, it is very difficult to understand the writings of mystics that are so embedded in particular cultural aspects not intrinsic to authentic mysticism. We need an articulation in modern terms of the essential elements of true Christian mysticism.

AN IMPORTANT CONTRIBUTION

Wayne Teasdale, in this work, *Essays in Mysticism*, offers us a serious and solid work that contributes much to our modern understanding of what is behind genuine mysticism. His probing, philosophical mind in touch with the great Christian mystical writings, especially those of Meister Eckhart and Pseudo-Dionysius, presents a Christian doctrine of mysticism that we can rely on as being of one piece with a vast and sublime *catholic* tradition of mysticism throughout the ages.

Yet, he is not only giving us a reasoned and orderly presentation that we can be certain is authentic. He evidently is a person who himself has already advanced along the sinuous paths of deeper prayer and speaks very often from an *experiential* point of view. It is this quality that saves his writings from being merely a "philosophy" or mysticism and leads us into a burning desire to follow his footsteps into the arid desert of unknowing where we, too, shall know by not knowing.

This book answers a great need in the field of mysticism and offers us Christians, above all, a safe and orthodox presentation that we can trust as being in the authentic tradition of the best in Christian mysticism down through the ages.

George A. Maloney, S.J.
John XXIII Institute for Eastern Christian
Studies at Fordham University
May, 1980

AUTHOR'S PREFACE

The purpose of this work is to advance an understanding of contemplative or mystical experience as the most important value and activity of man's life in the world. This is crucial, since it is a matter of Truth and of *survival*. For Humanity is threatened at this point in history, and only contemplation, as the basic value of global society, can save it from the consequences of confrontation between two dangerously polarized systems, both of which are based on material values, i.e., having things and power. Neither system is in touch with the vocation of man, which is to realize his relationship with the Absolute, with God. But if contemplation is ultimately to replace consumerism and the ruthless pursuit of power or status, then we must know more about what it is. Thus, it is because the mystical impulse or the contemplative experience *is* the alternative value for man that we must of necessity make some attempt to be open to its truth and to gain an insight into its nature. We have to do this, furthermore, since this is the way to achieve our fullest potential as creatures of God, and because this is the only way that real equality among nations and people will ever come about, thus, making true peace, on a world scale, possible.

There is an important creative tension here in these essays between experience and reflection or, to be more precise, between contemplative or mystical experience and metaphysical reflection, which strives to relate spiritual experience to the whole of reality. Actually, what this tension represents is Mysticism informing or inspiring the structure of metaphysical thought, as the experience of what is ultimately the case has a bearing on our philosophical efforts to give an explanatory system of reality. Mystical experience, that is, what is revealed in this primary avenue of Truth, has momentous implications for our view of reality or for what form our metaphysical reflection will take. This creative tension or relationship should become clear as the reader journeys along through these essays.

These pieces were written during a three year period between 1977 to 1980, and so I have grouped them into three sections of four essays that are somewhat similar in what they discuss or in their approach, in their focus. The reader will find that there is some overlap. This could not be helped given the nature of this book and the order in which the actual writing of the several pieces occurred. The three sections are: **SYMBOLS OF THE MYSTICAL, EXPERIENTIAL**

KNOWLEDGE OF GOD, and **THREE "SPECULATIVE" MYS-TICS.** For the benefit of the reader, a brief but more detailed summary of each article is given in a special section entitled Resume.

In the first section, **SYMBOLS OF THE MYSTICAL,** we try to show how certain experiences *point* to God, the spiritual nature of man, and symbolize the quest, contemplative realization or some aspect of the Spiritual Life. "The Coming Psychic Mutation" focuses on several human experiences that indicate the supra-material nature of man. These experiences include: parapsychological phenomena, the near-death experience, dreams, psychedelic drugs, and mystical intuitions etc. "The Splendor of Chartres" characterizes the quest for God, and so also symbolizes the mystical life. "The Name of God" attempts to show how the sacred name *Yahweh* has something essential to tell us about God as Presence, and so has implications for spiritual experience. "The Spiritual Significance of The Transfiguration" suggests the mystical meaning of this event as constituting a symbolic manifestation of God and as giving us an invitation to penetrate into the contemplative dimension of the Gospel in which the Spiritual Life really comes alive for the Christian.

In the second section, **EXPERIENTIAL KNOWLEDGE OF GOD,** we are concerned to give some idea of what the mystical experience is. "The Contemplative Attitude" follows this theme and discusses the continuity between mystical life and the world or our attitude towards the world, what it is as it is enlightened by contemplative grace. "Mysticism as a Form of Revelation" elaborates the larger notion of Revelation, which is able to accommodate mystical experience as essentially a concrete manifestation of God in and to the soul. "The Source of Being" is a dialogue with the Vedic or Indian Tradition; it is primarily a mystico-metaphysical statement. Here and in "The Mystery of God" one can see the tension we spoke of above and the overlaping effect. "The Mystery of God" considers the two basic approaches to knowledge of God, i.e., the properly philosophical and the experiential, that is, the mystical, and how the latter is superior to the former and, in a real sense, is its origin.

The third section, **THREE "SPECULATIVE" MYSTICS,** presents three figures who have been normative in the Christian Contemplative Tradition. Here again, the reader will see that creative tension between experience of the Absolute and reflection, which develops systematic insights on the nature of reality as a consequence of the mystical intuition. "The Mysticism of Plotinus" centers on his profound discussion of mystical union. This extraordinary and eloquent contemplative has had an enormous impact on many Christian mystics and writers. This influence is quite evident in the Pseudo-Dionysius. "The Mystical Philosophy of the Pseudo-Dionysius" and "The Religious experience of the Pseudo-Dionysius" concentrate on his general metaphysical view, which arose from his mystical insights, and on his notions of the *via negativa* and of 'deification' as the way and the result respectively of mystical union. It also introduces his method of reaching the abode of God. "Eckhart's Mystical Doctrine of The Godhead" tries to get at what Eckhart means by the Abyss, Wilderness or Desert of the Godhead and how this is related to the Trinity. Although this is a metaphysical position, it is nevertheless, a product of a very deep experience of God.

Finally, I beg the reader's kind indulgence if there is some repetition in the text. This could not be avoided given the nature and difficulty of the area and the manner in which these several essays were written. In a real sense, these pieces express something of my own rather limited experiences, intuitions and reflections. And if something of the reality of the mystical is conveyed, then this book will have been a success. I am conscious, furthermore, of the fact that in the Spiritual Life we are always only beginners. And this is true of all the great world religions. The important point, however, *is* to begin, for this is Mankind's final hope.

W.T.

ACKNOWLEDGEMENTS

I wish to acknowledge in a special way my debt of gratitude to my friend, Father Francis J. Lescoe, Ph.D., of The McAuley Institute, who gave valuable assistance in the preparation of this volume, and to Sister Mary Sarah Muldowney, R.S.M. for her unfailing kindness to me. Thanks are also due to Father George Maloney, S.J., especially for his encouragement and his thoughtfulness in agreeing to write the foreward to this book. He is a great contemplative. I also wish to mention Dom Thomas Keating, O.C.S.O., Abbot of Saint Joseph's Abbey, who has often inspired me and who has encouraged me to write. In a special way, I should like to thank Father Aelred Williams, O.C.S.O., of Caldey Abbey in Wales, editor of *Cistercian Studies*, for his many kindnesses to me. Thanks are also in order for Father Bede Griffiths, O.S.B., of Shanti Vanam, India and Professor Ewert Cousins of Fordham University, both of whom have had an influence on me. I wish also to remember my other friends, Father Benedict Groeschel. O.F.M., Cap., Robert Fatiggi, Father John Chethimattam of Fordham's Philosophy Department, the Franciscan Brothers of The Good News, Dr. Raimundo Panikkar, Dr. Stephen Seleman, Anne Purvis, the Musa Family, and the generous souls of The Catholic Worker Movement. I would like to remember all the members of A.I.M. (Aide Inter Monasteres) living in various parts of the world but sharing the same objectives of advancing the intra-religious dialogue, and especially to commend Sister Pascaline Coff, O.S.B., Secretary of The North American Board for East-West Dialog, the American branch of A.I.M. Finally, let me express a special word of appreciation to my friend Msgr. Ettore Di Filippo of the Holy See Mission to the United Nations, and Francis Tiso of Seabury Press.

RESUME

These summaries are offered in order to help the reader by pointing up the essential elements at work in each essay. In this way, the rader will have some concrete sense of what is going on in Mysticism. Of course, these summaries are not and cannot be exhaustive.

I. SYMBOLS OF THE MYSTICAL

1. The Coming Psychic Mutation

This little piece is an attempt to show that the implications of many different fields of research and diverse human experiences sugget that man is far profounder in his mystery than scientism, materialism and atheism have thought. It touches upon mystical intuition, the direct awareness of the Presence of God; the various manifestations of parapsychological phenomena; the near-death experience; the drug experience and the nature of dreams etc., asking what all these experiences indicate about the nature of man. Furthermore, it is an atempt to synthesize these insights into a larger picture of man's nature as a spiritual being, which all these experiences indicate as the case.

2. The Splendor of Chartres

This little article links the Cathedral of Chartres with the theme of pilgrimage and what pilgrimage is. It then presents a meditation on Chartres and indicates the significance of this great church for the spiritual development of the individual who happens to traverse its inner secrets. For pilgrimage in general and Chartres in particular are closely associated with the mystical quest.

3. The Name of God

This very brief essay approaches the "Name" of God, YAHWEH, "I AM WHO AM", in the way of a scriptural exegesis, but then tries to explicate how the meaning presented in the findings of Scripture scholars, that is, as suggesting "Presence" as its essential significance, is consonant with St. Thomas' notion of God as Esse or that the Name of God signifies that God is Pure Act itself, Existence as such; this is his brilliant insight into the nature of Being, the seminal concept that has come to have the name of aseity. Then we take it a step further and consider Eckhart's mystico-metaphysical meditation on the meaning of the Name. All the various interpretations are found to be complementary.

4. The Spiritual Significance of The Transifguration

This piece is an anagogical exegesis that tries to shed some light on the mystical meaning of this very crucial event in The Gospel. It centers on the Mystery of the Divine Light and how, in the Transfiguration itself, something of the Trinity is glimpsed. It then invites us all to that Christian and human maturity that comes when a soul plunges into the embrace of God's love that is at the center of the Spiritual Life.

II. EXPERIENTIAL KNOWLEDGE OF GOD

5. The Contemplative Attitude

This article begins by showing why there is so much confusion and misunderstanding about the nature of prayer. Its aim is to communicate an insight concerning prayer in its highest expression as contemplation, the mystical or "tasting" Knowledge of God. It considers the nature of contemplation, dealing with the **content** of the state of mystical experience. It also delineates the connection between contemplation and the world, explaining how "world" is more a question of our attitude towards it rather than this concrete objective system of facts that we call "the world". This is not the same thing as the assertion that the world is an illusion; it is more subtle than that. What **is** being maintained in this idea of world is the fact that "world", in the Spiritual Life, has more to do with a way of seeing or looking at it, and interpreting it in terms of which we assign it a certain value, or perceive what precisely its value is when rightly understood from the perspective of interior awareness or contemplation. This article also moves to establish that relationship of continuity between genuine prayer, the contemplative experience of God's Presence, and our other activities in the apostolic realm, that the former "energizes" the latter.

6. Mysticism As A Form of Revelation

Here we try to suggest that Revelation, our notion of it, has to be expanded to include mystical experience, since God **is** revealing Himself in a very intimate and special way to a person, whereas, in Scripture and Tradition, which have been the constant emphasis of Revelation's sense in the Christian universe, there is an indirect approach to God via His Word. And yet this scriptural approach has also got to include the mystical, since the mystical has so much to say about God firsthand. Mysticism discloses a profounder dimension to Revelation, which actually completes Scripture and Tradition, and gives us its (Scripture's) meaning in an inner experience of God, a consciousness of His reality. For this reason, we focus on St. Bonaventure's understanding of Revelation as more relevant to making this contact with the fuller sense of Revelation and its nature as manifesting knowledge of the Divine, as God revealing Himself in and to a soul graced with the intimacy of the mystical or unitive life, than St. Thomas' notion of Revelation, which is restricted to the scriptural context. St. Bonaventure, on the other hand, offers a more flexible model that allows us to reach out to the other religious traditions in order to learn from them what God has revealed of Himself to their saints and sages. This is of course what the Church has encouraged us to do in Her conciliar document: Decree On Non-Christian Religions. There is then a discussion of what Mysticism is. The article goes on to present three examples of mystical experience, i.e., that of St. Bernard, St. Francis and St. John of the Cross. Finally, there is a brief consideration of method in the mystical life.

7. The Source of Being

The Source of Being compares some of the chief themes in the Vedantic and Christian Traditions. It focuses its discussion on Raimundo Panikkar's brilliant work, **The Vedic Experience**. And so, we take up the themes of Being and non-being, establishing how it is metaphysically impossible to posit a literal notion of non-being as the origin of Being, which would be totally alien to the Christian Tradition. The article also considers the relationship between the Godhead and the Trinity, and maintains that the Godhead is the undifferentiated unity of Essence of the Trinity and itself. We're not suggesting, however, a Quarternity in the Divine nature. The article also touches upon the role of the Church in the global situation, prayer and Mysticism.

8. The Mystery of God

This essay approaches the reality of God from the philosophical and mystical levels, and serves to emphasize the two primary ways. In the former, it attempts to demonstrate the Mystery of the Divine by presenting certain proofs that establish God's existence, His personal nature and the necessity for Him to be triune. It also treats of the Godhead and the Trinity, especially showing how they are related and are ultimately the same. It also considers God's nature itself, what it is. In the latter case, that of the mystical dimension, it attempts to convey the **reality** and certitude of the mystical experience, giving some indications of what the event is like. In this task, we draw on the utterances of a few mystics, who are characteristic of our Tradition. Again, something is also said about the role of the Church.

III. THREE "SPECULATIVE MYSTICS"

9. The Mysticism of Plotinus

Essentially, this chapter is concerned with the Plotinian insight of mystical union, the ecstasy, the merging of the soul with the One. Plotinus is important because of his profound influence on the Christian Tradition and others, notably Islamic Philosophy and Sufism, the crown of Islamic Mysticism. And this influence, on Christianity, was not simply in the area of supplying Neo-Platonic elements, but also in contributing his own hard won mystical insights on the nature of Contemplation, the process of the soul's return to the One and its consummation in the state of ecstatic union. This union is elaborated, its mystical content, and it is suggested that ultimately, Plotinus can be considered a theistic type of mystic. Of course, this is disputed by some, but we do not take up this controversy, since it is fairly clear from his terms that he is a theist of some sort. For this reason, in addition to his mystical views, he is relevant to Christian Mysticism. This would also explain his great attraction in the Patristic Period, as the Fathers looked to him for inspiration and confirmation of their own experience, as well as to make understandable his pronounced impact during the many fruitful centuries of the Middle Ages on such diverse figures as the Pseudo-Dionysius, Scotus Eriugena, St. Bonaventure, Eckhart and countless others.

10. The Mystical Philosophy of the Pseudo-Dionysius

This long essay presents a general view of the Dionysian system of metaphysics, emphasizing its Neo-Platonic character, but also its decidely mystical content and nature, that the philosophy of the Areopagite is informed by his mystical insights. And so, we enter into the themes of his metaphysics and his Mysticism, which have been formative in the Christian Tradition, showing how the former springs from the latter and is prefected by it. That creative tension between religious experience, in its highest sense as contemplation, and reflection should become clear at this point. Thus, there is discussion of the Thearchy, his term for the Absolute, which is something *analogous to the One of Plotinus, emanation and return, the catophatic and apophatic methods, intelligibility etc., and the nature of the mystical ascent.*

11. The Religious Experience of the Pseudo-Dionysius
This chapter is more concerned with the mystical doctrine proper of Dionysius. And so it concentrates on his concepts of the Divine "darkness", the via negative or the "unknowing", the knowing without comprehending what is being known in the mystical state, and the notion of 'deification', the becoming like unto God as a result of the grace of mystical union, which is a prominent theme in the mystical literature of the Orthodox Church.

12. Eckhart's Mystical Doctrine of The Godhead
This essay centers on a very obscure notion in the tradition of Christian Mysticism, that of the Godhead. There is an obvious affinity between this notion and the Plotinian One, and Pseudo-Dionysius talks about the Godhead at length. The Godhead is the unmanifested, contemplative aspect of the Divine Reality. It neither creates nor acts, but just is this Presence of selfquietude beyond Being. It is the foundation of the Trinity, which is the dynamic aspect of the God-nature. Eckhart is not implying a Quarternity in the Divine nature. Far from it! Eckhart calls the ultimate Mystery of the Divine, the Abyss, Desert or Wilderness of the Godhead. And this is where all difference is transcended in the mystical union. This, however, does not mean identity. This article thus explores a quite misunderstood but very important insight.

ESSAYS IN MYSTICISM

I

SYMBOLS OF THE MYSTICAL

1

THE COMING PSYCHIC MUTATION

Western thought and experience is beginning to expand beyond the limits imposed by an immature scientific perspective. We are waking up from the suffocating nightmare of modern science and technology. Or as one great thinking of our age says: "Humanity is outgrowing the myth of science."[1] The scientific outlook is a myth in the perjorative sense, as it has been conceived for the last two hundred years, because it has been falsely presented as a panacea for all our problems and the answer to every question. This has been the posture of scientism, the popularization of the scientific myth, which has "canonized" the method of science as the only standard of truth. This attitude, however, is dying as we realize more and more the vast extent of this Mystery we call reality. The chief problem of science is that it reduces all thought and experience to the explanatory principles of its own uncritical assumptions. And the most serious flaw of science is its assumption that reality must conform to its expectations, expectations which are too narrow to capture what is ultimately real. It is a kind of reductionism, such as Freud's attempt to reduce reality to libido, as the product of it, and Marx's attempt to reduce it to a byproduct of economics, which are themselves made the consequence of material factors. It seems that it has not occurred to some in the scientific community, with some notable exceptions, that reality as it is does not conform to their perspective or their expectations. For life is too subtle and profound to be captured in a microscope, a test tube or calculated by a slide ruler. Science is basically approaching things from the side of structure rather than from the side of an organic understanding of the fundamental interrelatedness of all things and the Source from which this unity proceeds. The parameters of life are infinite, whereas, those of science have been and still are quite circumscribed. Reality overflows, in an unlimited degree, the categories of scientific intelligibility. Even though science is no longer bound to mechanism and materialism, which are the underlying assumptions of atheism, still an effect remains from these ideas that haunts contemporary life. These ideas, however, must be put to rest, as they are part of man's intellectual adolescence. They began to give way decades ago, but only really began to come apart in recent times.

We began to see in the period of the sixties that something was seriously wrong. The flower of our youth were dissatisfied with the oppressively dull life of prosperity, the result of abundant capital and advanced scientific technology, which served to create the easy American way of life. They saw life in Western society, especially in the United States, as empty, exploitive, lacking meaning and purpose, and terribly complicated. Something was missing. This was perceived earlier on in the century by such visionary thinkers as Bergson, Einstein, Eddington, Heisenberg, Planck, Marcel, Heidegger and countless others. They saw that Truth could not be caught in a finite system, and that science somehow was just scratching the surface of what is essentially ungraspable insofar as the principle behind the real is concerned. The rise of Existentialism was in large measure a reaction against the dominance of scientific, technological culture and the harm it was perceived to be doing to man.

What our youth were groping towards was self-understanding and a vision of their place in the scheme of things. They were seeking the Transcendent of which they possessed an inkling, a vague sense of something Ultimate. Somehow, Western culture must *regain* its sense of the Absolute if society and man in society are to survive. The proliferation of cults, gurus and methods of meditation and spiritual realization are symptomatic of an inherent, universal desire for something beyond this life, for something that explains it all, providing a glimpse of Eternity. This innate, human desire, furthermore, specifies its "object", and the "object" in turn grounds the desire making it constitutional to man's happiness. Thus, this desire itself is a kind of map for exploration into the realm beyond the world. The great spiritual masters of our age have arisen precisely to open the door of the Spirit and to point the way to absolute knowledge, which is not conditioned by the presuppositions of any system, since it is based on direct experience.

The pressing task before us, which grows more urgent with the passing of each year, is that of drawing forth the implications for our knowledge, indeed for our life, and for our view of human nature of diverse experiences and research. There is the fascinating reality of ESP or parapsychological phenomena, which will not go away because dismissed by close-minded scientists. More and more scientists are coming to the conclusion that the evidence for these phenomena can no longer be ignored. What can parapsychology teach us about our nature? What apple carts and other vested interests does it disturb? And is it not to Mankind's ultimate benefit that we advance beyond the limits to our seeing that those with these vested interests would like to maintain?

There is also the extraordinary fact of the so-called "near-death" experience. That it exists there can be no doubt. It has been universally verified as a common happening to people of a wide variety of backgrounds. I remember meeting someone a few years ago, before the news broke about this strange phenomenon, who told me that in the course of working in the intensive care unit of the cardiac arrest section of a hospital, he had encountered several hundred cases of the near-death experience. He had witnessed the responses of all these people as they were brought back and as they confided their experiences to him. I also know of two graduate students at Fordham University, who claim to have gone through this experience as they were presumed to be clinically dead by doctors in the emergency room, where they were brought after supposedly fatal car accidents. What does this say to us concerning ourselves? What is its meaning for the truth of our nature?

We can raise similar questions with respect to the reality of mystical experience. It is interesting how many sceptical writers stand in awe before Mysticism. They seem to know that there *is* something there; they know that it is genuine. Mystical experience is the "laboratory" proof of the spiritual nature of life. It is a penetration beyond space and time to the timeless realm of the infinite and eternal, and it is that Reality which gives the foundation to all existence. In our time, the Church is rediscovering her precious mystical or contemplative tradition, which has been obscurred since the Reformation. In Judaism, the mystical sect called Hasidism, to which Buber himself belonged, is on the rise. And the interest in eastern mystical insights goes back a hundred years or so and has intensified in recent years. In a real sense, we can say the future belongs to Mysticism. People have grown weary of theoretical knowledge and speculation. They will only listen to those who have the experience of which they speak. All the influx from the East in the last several years has an unmistakable mystical thrust in mind. It is answering to that level of reality. This profound intuition, what William James called " . . . the deepest . . . into the meaning of life",[2] must be integrated into our total view of life and human nature.

Then there is the baffling problem of psychedelic drugs. Although this is not a very popular subject, as a consequence of constant government propaganda, which is trying to discredit psychedelics, even in research situations, what they reveal cannot be perpetually swept under the rug. They show us, for one thing, how crude and narrow scientific and technological culture is. The status of this experience in our knowledge must be determined. Like it or not, psychedelics may yet prove to be the best lead we have to the meaning of existence. The government's prohibition against these drugs will not prevent us from asking the crucial question of their implication for our emerging notion of reality.

3

Another area, of which we have little understanding but which may well have important clues to contribute, is that of dreaming. The dream state presents a very serious challenge to the shallow conception of truth. Dreaming has different conditions than does the waking state. For one thing, in the waking state, objects must be a certain distance from us in order for them to be clearly perceived. Similarly, one has to have the requisite sense organs so that one may experience what they are equipped to reveal. In the dream state, however, one perceives without spatial extension, and one sees, hears, tastes, touches and smells without the actual use of the five senses which correspond to these perceptive functions. We are beginning to realize that other cultures, notably certain tribes of North American Indians, possess fundamental insights into the nature and control of dreams. And these insights are far more advanced than those of contemporary psychology. Ironically, it is the unenlightened psychologist who is the primitive in this area. This has undeniable consequences for our future view of what we are. The fact of dreaming and what it means must also be included in any concept of human nature which will surface.

Related to dreams, there is also the whole domain of the unconscious, which is today taken for granted in psychology. Especially relevant to our notion of an expanded understanding of human nature is the seminal work of that great genius C.G. Jung. One of his most remarkable discoveries is that of the archetypes. These are universal models, patterns or images in the collective unconscious. They are something like Platonic Forms, although more imagistic. Jung also discovered, deep in the unconscious, what he calls the God-archetype. He says that it is absolutely ineradicable, nor can it be explained away by an appeal to some reductionist concoction. The way in which he describes this God-archetype corresponds somewhat to the ancient notion of the soul as *imago Dei,* the image of God, which appears in Scripture and is developed at length by St. Augustine and others. The point is *is* that Jung has been able to confirm some aspects of the Ancient Wisdom, even though this was not his intention. His insights and those of countless others must be taken into account in our future concept of human nature.

These and innumerable other experiences, acknowledged and hidden, have to become part of a new *synthesis* in our self-understanding. We are moving into a new age in which the dusty theories of our materialistic past, remnants of Nineteenth Century science and the Enlightenment, will be discarded, because we will have achieved a new,

4

enhanced vision of who we are and of what our place is in the cosmos. We are being born into a higher understanding of Truth and discovering our real identity. A crucial psychic mutation is struggling to surface in human consciousness. When it dawns, humankind will be the richer, for then we will have finally understood the meaning of the Delphic Oracle's exhortation to Socrates twenty-five centuries ago: "Know thyself."

* * *

2
THE SPLENDOR OF CHARTRES

There is a primordial desire of every soul to find the spiritual center of one's being where God dwells in secret and silence. This center is untouched by the world. This represents the great quest to return to the *centre,* as Father Bede Griffiths puts it,[1] to find and maintain a vital contact with the Divine Life welling up within each one of us in "the cave of the heart", to use a metaphor popular in India, one that Father Bede is fond of using in his public talks. We must all make this inward journey in our own way and in our own time. We must enter the silence alone to discover God, as *silence* is God's language, indeed, His very abode. Some progress faster than others, depending on the willingness, seriousness, effort and generosity that each person brings to the quest.

In the West, we externalize the search for God. For God is out there or so transcendent that we say "He is above us," and He is. The East of course follows a more immanent tendency[2] and proclaims the God Who is within the soul, and surely He is as all the mystics in the West have also acknowledged. And Christ tells us that the Kingdom of God is within us. The truth is that God is both within and beyond us. He is both the immanent Source of our life and being and the transcendent end of our search. Now it is quite striking to discover that pilgrimage, the traveling to a holy place or from one sacred place to another, exists in both the East and the West. It is a universal activity of the serious seeker after Divine Wisdom. Pilgrimage is, furthermore, an ancient occupation, or shall we say, preoccupation, perhaps, as old as Humanity itself. Even in Islam it has a place. Mecca attests to this. And in India, there is the long pilgrimage to the sacred source of the Ganges, the great mother of rivers. This arduous journey, a labor of the heart, is made by millions every year. Similarly, people go in large numbers to the many shrines associated with the major events in the life of the Buddha, particularly where he achieved enlightenment. Pilgrimage, thus, is not an exclusively Western phenomenon; it illustrates an essential longing of the heart, of the deepest intention of the soul, for a taste of the eternal or the beatific. Something very profound is happening in the minds of pilgrims, something necessary to their spiritual growth. Are we not all pilgrims and is not life itself a great pilgrimage? Does it not constitute our long search for the Divine?

Christianity has always had holy places where supernatural power seems to emanate in a special way. From antiquity this has been the case. Consider the many shrines that commemorate aspects of Our Lord's life in the Holy Land, an area also charged with enormous significance for Jews and Moslems. Has not Rome always been a place of pilgrimage? And in each Catholic country, there are special places made so by Our Lady (Walsingham in England and Lourdes in France as well as Fatima in Portugal, to mention a few), tributes to her, or by some saint, who is especially revered by a particular Christian people.

Of course Chartres is one of the most sacred places of Christendom and has been so since the Eighth Century. People flock there from many lands and faiths to gaze upon its more than earthly splendor. For this grand church is and always has been connected with the Virgin, much as Notre Dame in Paris. It has inspired numerous poets, artists and writers through the ages, even of different faiths, e.g., Henry Adams, the American figure at the turn of the century. And we may wonder what it is that Chartres possesses that so attracts the multitudes to its door?

There can be no doubt that it has something to do with the nature and purpose of pilgrimage. In a certain sense, a pilgrimage is an extended prayer in which the soul opens herself up to God, becomes receptive to His action, by way of a spatial act, which is the taking of a pilgrimage itself. It also symbolizes the inner journey, the interior longing for and finding God. It is a kind of contemplation, employing images, those found in the particular holy space, a place set apart. And Chartres' are breathtakingly beautiful. It is a contemplation in which the affections of the ardent pilgrim are awakened. The images of Chartres or any such place important to the faith of any people, arouse profound acts of love toward God within the heart of the person. Thus, sacred spaces like Chartres provide us with concrete content for a deep spiritual movement, an interior happening within the life of the soul. They are externalizations of our faith, monuments to its depth and power to inspire us. But more importantly, such places and particularly Chartres, reflect the authenticity of an ineffable spirituality, an attribute that cloaks itself in the terms of Divine beauty, in the signs and symbols of an aesthetic mysticism somewhat like that of St. Augustine's, which was very Platonic in spirit.

For Chartres evokes the deepest stirrings of the soul and awakens that restlessness that seeks to find fulfillment in the Vision of God in His incomprehensible glory. Beauty, furthermore, as the Greeks knew so well, lifts the soul to the contemplation of the Divine. All the elements of Chartres, the architecture, the shape, the statues of the saints with their serene look of holiness, the lighting, the stain glass (especially this), the atmosphere of the interior, the music, the liturgy, all contribute to that inscrutable mystery that this great church harbers.

And in its mystery, Chartres reflects the far greater Mystery of the Universal Church herself.

When one enters, one notices immediately that it is darker than most churches, and this assuredly lends itself to the brilliance of color, a veritable symphony of varying hues unified in a common theme, that streams in through the stain glass windows. These windows have an olympian quality of supra-human charm, which, like a magnet, draws one to their presence, and yet only as symbols of something far loftier. Aldous Huxley says that the stain glass of Chartres and other churches symbolizes and evokes visionary experience.[3] The quality of darkness in the interior of the church receives the inconceivable richness of light that pours in from the sun. The inside of Chartres then becomes bathed in this extraordinary radiance that manifests, in an unutterable way, an eternal truth, especially is this so as the sun begins to set and the mystery of Chartres deepens, as the ages seem to lend their weight to the venerable, solemn stillness of this magnificent church.

Chartres is one of those places in which a person must just be, simply allow yourself to rest in its unspeakable glory, a representation of God's. As one gives oneself to the contemplation of its majesty and beauty, in a passive way, slowly one is uplifted by its spiritual power. It is also helpful to move around and then to sit, seeing this holy place from many vantage points. Everything in this church, one discovers, is directed to the center, to *unity*, which symbolizes God.

The great rose window in the front of the church, which brings together all the important events in the History of Salvation, also represents, it would seem, in a mandalic fashion, the very unity of God Himself and of creation in Him; it seems to signify how all things come together in Christ, the perfect Icon or Image of the Divine glory. For Christ gives us a glimpse of God's unsearchable nature. He is at the Center of the Godhead as well as at the center of the cosmos. He unifies all things in the Father through the inwardness of the Holy Spirit. The splendor of Chartres' stain glass, especially the rose window, graphically portrays this mystical truth.

A saintly monk at Ealing Abbey in London once spoke to me of his impressions of the stain glass in a particular cathedral in Europe. It was not Chartres' glass. He said that he stood on the outside and regarded the church, and saw nothing, but the moment he went inside, it lit up with such heavenly color and light. And then he said to me, "but isn't this the mystery of faith itself? From the outside (unbelief) a person sees nothing, because this is the state of ignorance, but from

the inside, from the advantage of faith, one begins to understand."
This is a truth the Middle Ages knew so well. For the mystery of
Chartres is the mystery of *faith,* which in turn grants us a momentary
look at our future glory in that great promise of eternal life that this
splendid church represents and to which the life of the Church herself leads us.

* * *

3
THE NAME OF GOD

The name of God, YAHWEH, whose meaning was revealed to Moses, is a difficult issue to resolve. It has been given various interpretations ranging from its designation as symbolizing *absolute existence,* that God is in Himself the pure act of TO BE (the notion of *aseitas*), to the idea of the "Present One" of contemporary biblical research. In the former, He is the One Who *is,* and in the latter, He is the One Who is *there* (present) for His people. The former is the thrust of the Tradition, which is clearly expressed in the thought of Moses Maimonides and St. Thomas Aquinas, culminating in Eckhart's mystical exegesis of the Tetragrammaton, as the name is called. There was also considerable reflection on the significance of the name in the Patristic Period, but considerations of space do not permit us to treat of these early attemps to get at its meaning. The interpretations of the name range from this Greek metaphysical refinement (Maimonides, Thomas and Eckhart, who use Greek metaphysical categories mixed with those taken from our common tradition) to the findings of modern and contemporary biblical study, which puts the stress on the *language* itself and especially the context of the statement. Thus, the latter represents a method that is more empirical than the former, with all the attendant assumptions that this implies. It is concerned with an analysis in the terms of what is contained in the written text of Scripture. Although we see and acknowledge the important value of this approach to the Word of God, still we do not think that this method should be or can be justified in an exclusive sense, that is, as the sole criterion of scriptural research.

The reason why we cannot limit ourselves to this modern approach alone is because there are other levels of *meaning* that are grasped with different methods. The modern approach places the emphasis upon the meaning intended in the passage, that is, from what the biblical writer commited to parchment. But we must remember that the biblical writers were the instruments of the actual Author, Who is God. The modern method seems to put the weight on the side of the human or the instrumental cause of Scripture. Whereas, God also tries to say something through the pen of the biblical scribe, but what God intended is oftentimes unknown to us and hence also to the one who wrote under the influence of Divine inspiration. This indeed presents a serious problem for biblical scholars. After all, Scripture only makes sense as a vast metaphysical statement of the object of faith's consent, and this statement is conveyed in the limited expressions of the Hebrew habit of mind and language. Furthermore, ultimately, Scripture's meaning is also mystical, since it is a meaning which comes from God.

It is because this passage of Scripture is so central to the meaning of Israel, her faith and purpose, and is, thus, the *key* to Jewish, Christian and Islamic Philosophy and Theology that we are so concerned with it here in this chapter. There is a Mystery signified in this sacred name, and this Mystery is the foundation of our common heritage.

It is interesting that the Old Testament, as well as the New, constitutes a unique metaphysics, that is, has one and elaborates it, although not in a systematic way. The general outlines of this metaphysics are well known, that God *is* and is the Origin or Cause of the universe, man and life itself, that He or His will, His Purpose is the meaning of existence. For He made us to have a relationship with Him. YAHWEH *cares* for us. These themes and many, many others are constants in the Bible. The point is *is* that these motifs reflect metaphysical Truth, even though some biblical scholars would not want to put it quite this way.

For Metaphysics as such is concerned with ultimate principles and insights, such as where it all has come from, why and so forth. Scripture is a record of answers to metaphysical questions that human beings are accustomed to ask themselves quite by necessity of their nature. And these are perennial questions. Does not Scripture suggest that God's Law or Truth is written in the heart? or in more contemporary language, that the human psyche has a very definite God archetype, which is the imprint of the Divine Law within the very structure of the soul's psychic life? But Scripture is also a metaphysics divinely instituted. It did not arise from man's speculation alone; it arose chiefly from God's intention and movement towards us, His revelation to us that He is. Sacred Scripture is, thus, also the record and plan of our relationship with God, and it has mystical teachings that are beneficial to the soul's spiritual growth.

We would like to enquire, in this chapter, into what the name of YAHWEH or "I AM WHO I AM" means in the light of biblical research and in the light of the Tradition. We believe that they are not mutually exclusive interpretations, but that one entails and completes the other. We will consider the philological, historical and theological questions[1] through the medium of contemporary methodology and then suggest how God as Presence, which modern scholarship emphasizes, is in essential harmony with and implies God as the fullness of existence or Being, as Existence or Being itself, which the Tradition holds. In other words, the actual implications of what is being said in the Tetragrammaton is revealed in the Tradition, even though Scripture does not use the terminology of Greek and Christian Metaphysics. The Tradition has been able to draw forth God's intended meaning and what it reveals of His ontological nature. It is evident that this must be the case, since what is Present (YAHWEH) must necessarily *be*. That is why there is no real antagonism between the modern approach and that of the Tradition. This Tradition includes both metaphysico-theological reflection and a contemplative or mystical dimension.

The Philological Question

The Divine Name of YAHWEH was Israel's banner of faith. To the Semitic mind, it was necessary to know God's name in order to have and maintain a relationship with Him. The name designated the essential characteristic; it was basically descriptive, giving an insight into the nature of God. And this was generally true of names. For the Jews, "the revelation of the divine name was in some way the revelation of God Himself. It was the revelation of His Person", so says Plastaras.[2] Nor is there any evidence that this name was ever used to designate God in any other tradition,[3] though its root may be derived from other languages.

The etymology of the name YAHWEH is the content of the philological question. This aspect of the question also has diverse opinions represented. It is such a primordial consideration that it is difficult to find substantial agreement.

Yah might have originally been an interjection, which was associated with the moon cult. The name YAHWEH might then be this exclamation affixed to the third person pronoun. If we follow this view through, however, we cannot explain the religious significance that is connected with this name, that is, that it is the denomination for the God of Israel, and we cannot understand why it has power to reveal something about God.[4]

Furthermore, the name is probably derived from the root HWH, which came into Hebrew via Aramaic or Amoritic; it means "to become". This word would signify "He causes to be", because it is the third person, having the causative form of the verb. Other sources (i.e., the Akkadian documents), parallel with the biblical tradition, suggest that the name YAHWEH was part of a divine title, i.e., Yahweh-Saba'oth or "He Who causes the armies (of Heaven ?) to be".[5]

The Historical Question

The question here is whether or not the Divine Name YAHWEH was new. It seems that two views are evident in Scripture. On the one hand, the Elohist tradition (Exodus 3:13-15) and the Priestly (Exodus 6: 2-4) assert that the sacred name was revealed for the first time to Moses. Both of these traditions emphasize the *newness* of the name, particularly the Elohistic tradition. On the other hand, the Yahwistic tradition indicates that the name was far more ancient than thought, that it went back to the early times of Salvation History, long before the time of Moses. In this stream of tradition, the name is found in Genesis. "At that time men began to call upon the name of YAHWEH" (Genesis 4: 26).[6] Abraham is recorded as having built an altar to YAHWEH and prayed to Him (Gen. 12: 8).

Bernard Anderson holds that the account of the revelation of the name to Moses, which the Elohist and Priestly traditions relate, is substantially accurate, and that the Yahwist tradition is simply trying to make a theological point, i.e., that YAHWEH is the Lord of History. To make this point, it identifies the worship of YAHWEH with the very early beginnings of the biblical narrative.[7]

Plastaras believes that theological differences between the Elohistic and Priestly traditions on one side, and the Yahwistic, on the other, cannot alone explain the discrepancy concerning the origin and use of the name. He is convinced that the name was known to the Kenites, Jethro's clan, who were celebrated for their dedication to the YAHWEH cult. Evidence for this view is suggested by the story of Cain. It is said that Cain was the ancestor from whom the Kenite tribe descended. Genesis 4: 15-16 says that Cain was marked with the sign of YAHWEH. Also, Enosh, who is called the father of Cain, is portrayed as the first follower of YAHWEH. Again, this is recorded in Genesis 4: 26: "To Seth also a son was born, and he called his name Enosh. At that time men began to call upon the name of YAHWEH.[8]

. Evidence, thus, points to the Kenites as the first to worship YAHWEH as God. Although this is perhaps true, the Kenites did not have the same awareness of YAHWEH that Moses had. What Moses revealed to Israel about YAHWEH was quite different from what the Kenites knew of Him. Moses did not preach a new God but a deeper appreciation of the God they already knew.[9]

The Theological Question

The most important aspect of this issue is the theological dimension, which attempts to elucidate what precisely the name YAHWEH could have meant to Moses and to Israel. This is not an easy matter to determine. Moses did not just hand on a revelation of God's name but also a theological tradition regarding its significance.[10]

The Amoritic root HWH in time became associated with the Hebrew verb HYH, which carried the connotation of "being" or "becoming". But this had a dynamic sense to it and this is how Hebrew employed it. This dynamic sense emphasized the meanings of "come to pass, take place, become or be present".[11]

Thus, the name YAHWEH indicates a dynamic Presence. This is generally the accepted view today, although there are some (notably L. Koehler), who would hold that the Tetragrammaton is a reprimand to Moses, telling him to mind his own business. This position may be reasonable in the light of the ancient significance of names and naming, but the context of Exodus 3: 13-15 does not seem to support this interpretation.

Plastaras feels that the name of YAHWEH, the "I AM WHO I AM" is an exegetical gloss intended to explain the association of the name with the verb HYH for those who may not have known it. He maintains that the real answer to the question of Moses (Exodus 3: 13: "If they ask me, 'What is His name?' What shall I say to them?") is given in Exodus 3: 15: "Say this to the people of Israel, 'The Lord (YHWH), the God of your fathers . . . has sent me to you': this is my name forever, and thus I am to be remembered throughout all generations."[12]

Hence, the name of YAHWEH indicates that He is a God of *Presence,* of dynamic relation to His people; it is a definition of God in terms of active Presence. The whole context of the passage supports this interpretation. "Ehyeh" means God is there and ready to respond or act. YAHWEH is "He Who Is There".[13]

This is also the view of Brevard Childs. Following Vriezen, he says that verse 14 *"Eehyeh ser Ehyeh"* is a paronamastic use of the verb HYH (hayah) indicating and emphasizing God's reality or actuality, but His actuality is His Presence for Israel. "I Am Who I Am" means: "I Am there, wherever it may be . . . I Am really there!"[14] Childs establishes this view by recourse to a very persuasive parallel in Exodus 33: 19 in which YAHWEH is speaking to Moses: "And He said, 'I will make all my goodness pass before you, and will proclaim before you my name 'The Lord' (YAHWEH), and I will be gracious to whom I will be gracious, and will show mercy on whom I will show mercy."

Notice that the grammatical structure and context are the same, indicating a similarity of meaning. "I AM WHO I AM" or "I AM PRESENT to whom I AM PRESENT" involves the same insight as "I will show mercy to whom I will show mercy." Jacob says that this is a way of intensifying the meaning for the sake of emphasis.[15] Plastaras says that the name was a way of saying "He Who Is Present (in power)" or "He Who Is Present (to save)"; for the name of God, YAHWEH, was for Israel "a *promise* of Salvation."[16] Also, the name of YAHWEH contains the action or the verb that indicates His Presence; the name, as a consequence, has a dynamic quality.[17] It is at once a proper name and the designation of one of His characteristics, namely, His Presence *for* those who are faithful to Him. The name also conveys a sense of God's power or communicates the idea that His Presence is powerful.[18]

It is also possible to interpret the Tetragrammaton in a *causative* sense. This is the approach of Foxwell Albright, who maintains that the primordial meaning of the passage *"Ehyeh- Asher- Ehyeh"* is: "He causes to be what comes into Existence".[19] Thus, God would be designated by His essential *sourceness* as the One Who causes existence. This approach is obviously closer to the interpretation of the Tradition. Plastaras says that Albright's position cannot easily be dismissed. Still, he feels that the text does not as such support Albright's contention, since Hebrew verbs did not have a causative sense.[20]

Because of the grammatical construction, which has a number of parallels in the text of the Old Testament, and because this structure indicates the dynamic, active Presence of God, Plastaras would not agree with Albright. The grammatical structure, characteristic of the Tetragrammaton and its parallels, always seems to be used to convey a *sense* of uncertainty and indetermination. One parallel, which we have already mentioned above, that is, Exodus 33: 19, " . . . for I will be gracious to whom I will be gracious, and I will show mercy on whom I will show mercy", since it has nearly the same grammatical structure and the same basic meaning, would seem to establish the interpretation of God's name as essentially "the One Who is Present to save" etc. Furthermore, included in the statement of His name, God also revealed His sovereign freedom.[21]

Jacob holds that, whereas, "El expresses life in its power, YAHWEH expresses life in its continuance and its actuality. YAHWEH is indeed He Who Is."[22] Although Jacob accepts the interpretation of the name to denote the Presence of God, he yet issues a warning not to assume that because the Jews did not have a propensity for metaphysical language that they did not understand the actuality of Being. He does not think that it is attributing to them a too highly developed metaphysics to hold that they could "define God as 'He Who Is' ". After all, the Jews had a sense of His eternity.[23]

But he points out that the Hebrew concept of existence always includes *relation* and so also existence. YAHWEH is the One Who is with someone. "*Ki' ehyeh 'immak*" (Exodus 3: 12) means "for I will be with you". The emphasis is upon *Presence* rather than Being. Hence, the vocation of Moses was to make people "aware of the Presence of YAHWEH in their midst . . ."[24]

It would seem that the Presence of YAHWEH metaphysically entails His existence, even though the biblical mind took His existence for granted. To be present means by necessity also to exist, to be. Moreover, it would seem that the repetition in the Tetragrammaton is the Hebrew way of emphasizing the Presence and, thus, of attempting to express what they lacked in the clarity of a precise language, since they did not have the technical terms to do so nor a sophisticated grammar. They were perhaps trying to say that YAHWEH is the *most* present One, the *plenitude* of saving Presence, because He is also the fullness of Existence. He does not have Presence or existence; He *is* Presence and He *is* existence.

Furthermore, to be present is to be *there* and to be there is *to be* in the fullest sense. Thus, when we think it through, the metaphysics of Presence necessitates the metaphysics of existence, and this is true for the sufficient reason that Presence *is* existence and vice versa. As a consequence, both the approaches of the Tradition and that of modern biblical scholarship seem reconcilable.

Moses Maimonides, the great Jewish philosopher, theologian and biblical exegete of the Twelfth Century says that the sacred name was not pronounced because of the great power associated with it. All other names of God in Scripture are derived from His actions; they are not actual attributes of the Divine Essence. Pseudo-Dionysius makes the same point five centuries earlier.[25] Maimonides goes on to say that: " . . . the Tetragrammaton, in the way it was pronounced, conveyed the meaning of 'absolute existence' (yod, he, vau he). In short, the majesty of the name and the great dread of uttering it, are connected with the fact that it denotes God Himself, without including in its meaning any names of the things created by Him."[26] Hence, Maimonides gives a very strong endorsement to the Tradition, which claims that the name refers to God's Esse, His pure existence. For because God is one, as Scripture tells us, He is also a simple unity, and being unity, His essence or nature and His existence or Esse are the same. Thus, He *is* existence because there is no distinction in His nature. To say that "God is the One Who Is Present" is really to say, equally so, that He is the *only* One Who really IS in the ultimate sense. All else is derived from His creativity.

Eckhart, referring to the mystical significance of the name, holds that the Tetragrammaton is not itself the Divine Name but a circumlocution for God's name. This is true because God's name is an absolute *secret*, and like the Divine Essence itself, is inexpressible since beyond form and concept in God's own hiddenness.[27] Eckhart feels that the name signifies a self-sufficiency to God, a unity holding itself within itself. He says:

> It also indicates a certain reversion and turnback of His being into and upon itself, and its abiding or remaining in itself; also a sort of boiling up or giving birth to itself, an inward glowing, melting and boiling in itself and into itself, light in light and into light wholly penetrating its whole self, totally and from every side turned and reflected upon itself.[28]

Perhaps, we will not know the true meaning of God's name until we are with Him in Paradise, but, in the time between, the above are a few indications. It will become clear how *presence* and *existence* are essential to the mystical experience.

4

THE SPIRITUAL SIGNIFICANCE OF THE TRANSFIGURATION

Of the events in the life of Our Blessed Lord recorded in the gospels, the Transfiguration stands out in bold relief as actually bridging the ontological gap between the finite and the infinite, the temporal and the eternal, and between earth and Heaven. In its profound meaning, it is one of the most important occurances in the Gospel and is at the center of Christian Life in its supernatural or mystical dimension. For it is essentially a mystical event, which at once brings together or sums up the Wisdom of the Old and the New Testaments. It does this of course in and around the person of Christ. It is a very strange or unusual event, and it is difficult to locate its meaning in Christian experience. Whereas, the Resurrection signals Our Lord's victory over death and rightly establishes an order in human life in relation to Him, which is the Church and her sacramental life, and the Ascension records His departure from this existence into the glory of Eternal Life with His Father and the Spirit, the Transfiguration represents a glimpse of the Divine Light shining through Christ's human nature and shows us His Divine truth, communicating to us a sense of what is behind the scenes of this life. It signifies our true origin and our destiny for future Beatitude. It grants us a momentary picture of the actual relationship between created being and Divine being, and manifests how the latter gives existence to the former as its constant Source and its ultimate telos. The Transfiguration, in this sense, is like the sun at its brightest shining through the forest, revealing the trees in its radiant splendor.

It has a key place in the Gospel narrations since it bears a message of great hope and expectation, which presents, for a brief instant, a vision of Truth insofar as Christ is the Truth as the Second Person of the Blessed Trinity, and it also presents an image of Eternity and Christ's place there. It puts everything into its proper ontological focus, for the Divine glory, in its deifying Radiance, is at the center of Reality and is this Reality itself. The Transfiguration at once deals with the Trinity in a symbolic way, Eternal Life, the role of Christ and the Church in the Divine Order, but it is primarily a *call* to contemplation and the mystical life, having its attention on the *Lumen gloriae*, the Thaboric Light, which is the Presence of God in His Spirit transfiguring the Son and creation as well.

This lofty perspective on the Transfiguration is not new, at least generally so. For the Greek Fathers, and the Latin Fathers as well, were keenly aware of its anagogical or mystical truth, what God is saying in this event. This is especially true of such Fathers as St. Athanasius, St. Gregory of Nyssa, St. Clement of Alexandria, Origen, St. Basil the Great, St. Gregory of Naziansus, St. John Chrysostom, the Pseudo-Dionysius, St. John Damascene and St. Andrew of Crete, to mention a few in the Eastern Christian Tradition in which it finds its most conscious and eloquent expression. For each of these figures reflected on this crucial event. In fact, the great patristic scholar Georges Habra says that for all the Fathers in the Greek Tradition, the Transfiguration was primarily a contemplative reality; it consisted in a certain mystical perception of Christ's divinity. This is how the Fathers interpreted it.[1] The accent is decisively on the adjective *mystical*. Let us consider the scriptural, metaphysical, theological (Cosmic) and mystical aspects of this very inspiring event, one which has been the subject of many works of art, especially the iconographic variety.

Scriptural Basis

The Transfiguration is described in the three synoptic gospels, i.e., in Matthew,[2] Mark[3] and Luke[4]. This is curious as John was one of the three witnesses, and yet he does not mention it in his gospel. Presumably, this is the same John. The three accounts record essentially the same fact, that is, that Jesus took Peter, James and John up a high mountain and was transfigured before them. His face became as bright as the sun and His clothing became whiter than wool, to use the same metaphors. Our Lord is then seen conferring with Moses and Elijah, who stand for the Law and the Prophets. They are apparently discussing Christ's approaching passion. The three Apostles are of course terrified, a quite natural reaction to so extraordinary an event. At the same time, they are fascinated; they feel a certain irresistible attraction. And then a cloud hovers above the head of Jesus, and a voice says: "This is my beloved Son; He enjoys my favor. Listen to Him." When the three look up, they see only Jesus, and He admonishes them to keep quiet about the vision they have seen until after His Resurrection.

Now, Peter does something characteristic of man, especially of religious man. He tries to preserve the moment of vision by way of his suggestion that he be allowed to pitch three tents, one for Jesus, Moses and Elijah. This reveals one of the chief structural habits of *homo religiosus*, which is his tendency to institutionalize religious insight. It is a dominant trait of the human psyche, which seeks contact with the changeless Reality of the Divine. When we are fortunate enough to see something of this Reality, we naturally wish to hold on to it, especially is this true when everything else is in a state of constant change.

There is a great deal contained in the structure of this supernatural occurance. Let us look at some of its many elements before proceeding on to a consideration of the metaphysical, theological and mystical significance of this happening and its meaning for Christian Life.

The first point is that Jesus chooses only a few for the vision. In this instance, Peter, who will later lead the infant Church, James and John, the one Our Lord loved. We cannot know what was in His mind when He chose them, but we can see one of the clear implications for the Spiritual Life. And that is that mystical experience or vision is for the few, not because it is a form of elitism, but because only a few aspire to it and also because there are comparatively few teachers who have the requisite experience, knowledge and holiness. This is the paradoxical state of the Church in our time, as in other ages, insofar as Spiritual Life is concerned. As Abbot Thomas Keating says in his brilliant tape on contemplation: "The Church has been in a spiritual desert since the Reformation."[5] Surely one reason for the spiritually impoverished condition of the Church today is that we are too much up in the head and not enough in the heart. This is true even of prayer, which is often much too discursive.

The next thing that the Apostles notice is that Jesus's face becomes radiant with a praeternatural brilliance, a common form for many theophanies, and His garments become whiter than snow. Here is the reference to the Thaboric Light, the Light of Divine glory, which we will have more to say about further on. The fact that Moses and Elijah appear in the vision is important since they represent the Law and the Prophets. Jesus tells us that He has come to fulfill them. They are symbolic of the normative religious values of Israel, and Jesus, in His Transfiguration, is seen to be greater than they. He is the focal point of the Old and the New Law and the realization of the prophetic function that finds completion in His mission, for everything converges on Christ. The true prophet is simply one who represents God, and who speaks for Him, because inspired to do so.

Now, the appearance of the cloud and the voice of the Father, along with the *Lumen gloriae* transfiguring Christ, and the Person of Christ Himself, express the living Truth of the Trinity. The voice in the cloud is the Father, creative Source of existence and of Christ's mission to the world; Jesus of course is the Son, the appearing Image of the Divine Wisdom, and the Thaboric Light, being the very Light of God's inner life, is the Holy Spirit. To be sure, this is a *symbolic* revelation of the Trinity.

The awe, confusion and fear which Peter, James and John experience is typical of the human reaction to a supernatural event. For the three represent the Church; they are the incipient Church's members, at least some of her members, and their reaction is, in a sense, what our response would be, our initial reaction. In a special way, the Church is present at this event, and she participates in it. Christ mediates between the Church and His Father, Our Father, insofar as He is the Redeemer of mankind, but He is also the Mediator of the Divine Light itself. For its impulse transfigures Him, and in the event of the Transfiguration, we see Reality for the first time, since we see who Christ really is. He is the One Who makes God's Light, in its Mystery, to shine upon us. He gives us some idea of how the Father as Source is or He shows us something of the Divine and what it is like in its hidden life. Let us now turn to the central metaphysical point of the Transfiguration, i.e., its mystical and theological significance as a revelation of the Trinity.

The Divine Light

As a metaphysical and mystical event, in a definite theological setting that is consonant with the images and symbols of the Old Law mixed with the New, the Transfiguration is for man an invitation to advance into spiritual maturity, an invitation to pass beyond the faith of childhood to that faith enlightened by Divine grace on the contemplative level of experience. Thus, the Transfiguration is a call to a greater awakening in our awareness of God's Presence dwelling within the soul as the Trinity and without as the vivifying force behind the cosmos and its laws. It is a summons to a special relationship with God, Who, as the Apostle says, "dwells in an inaccessible Light.[6] It is this Light that was perceived somewhat by Peter, James and John, for this is the *Lumen gloriae.* It is that Light which is God Himself. It seems that in the Transfiguration, God allowed His glory to burst forth. For He is "Light in Whom there is no darkness",[7] as St. John says. Let us now digress awhile on the ontological reality of this Light.

In the mystic Light, what is real shines forth, and that is God in His infinite Truth, the deifying splendor of His Presence. He makes Godlike that soul who chances upon Him in grace. The deifying Light of His Presence makes the soul like unto God because she is united to Him, to that which is always deified since it is God Himself, for that which is so deified has always been so. God is God in the great luminosity of His ineffable being, which is eternally a generating, dynamic Light emanating from the Triadic Center of Pure Unity grasping itself in its act of

21

Identity with itself in which it is the Trinity. The pure and eternal generation of the Light in itself, in its differentiating of the Persons, *is* the Trinity, and the Light is its eternal result. Reality is pure Light, because that which has the fullness of Being, since it *is* Being itself, is open to what it is. Everything that it is or knows is evident to it all at once. Nothing is hidden from its comprehensive gaze. Thus, it is Light, a total purity, in which is contained the plenitude of Reality itself in its dynamic generating Source, the Trinity, as its ontological structure, if we may use the term structure. In the Trinity, there is no thought, if we mean by thought a rational, discursive mode of intellection. God does not have to think since His Truth is known to Him in just being Who He is in His triune act of self-communion. He eternally intuits from His inner life the content of His nature as pure unity in triadic relatedness to the same essential Identity, which permits Him to know Himself and all things, but God knows Himself through a form of intense and complete "vibration". In this "vibration" He grasps Himself, for the "vibration" is the Trinity playing its eternal harmonics, in three ultimate relations, which are infinitely fecund in their actual thematization.

The Divine Light, which transfigured Christ on the mount, the Thaboric Radiance of the *Lumen gloriae,* which penetrated Christ's being, because He is it, has a triadic Source, and this we call the Trinity. The Light of Divine Splendor is the eternal result of the three Persons of the one Divine Essence. Light is the spiritual content of their living reality and truth. The Light, in the event of the Transfiguration, yet manifests three forms, i.e., the voice from the cloud, the glorified Lord Jesus and the Light which glorifies Him. The Trinity generates its Light, which is because the Persons are. The Light reveals the eternal radiance of the triune Godhead. For the Light is the Godhead self-illuminated in itself, and this is its essential intelligibility, which bears for it its actual meaning in its Identity. In so being, it knows itself and everything else as well. For everything is revealed to God in the Light of His being and Consciousness, but this Light is the *openness* of all things to Him. Furthermore, pure luminosity is pure openness of Being and a grasping of its infinite possibilities. The Divine Light is not static, rather, it is dynamic, and this is its triadic Identity. The Trinity is, thus, a dynamism in God's nature.

The Transfiguration casts into the Light of Truth the eternal Reality of God's being as the simple structure it has in its Identity as Trinity. Because everything is clear and manifest to it, it is pure luminous truth. Light is the revealed as well as what reveals, and they are the same.

What makes the Light to be is itself, which eternally resolves itself into three essential relations, conscious functions, poles of inseparable Identity, three actual Persons, Who eternally work out among themselves the *secret* of Who God Is. They are this Mystery in being the functions they have. This trinitarian process has no beginning except the ontological priority of the Godhead's unity. The unity is always first, and that is why the Godhead is also three, since the triadic inner life *is* the very nature of the unity self-comprehending, its act of being and knowing, which are the same.

God receives the impulse of His being in an eternal self-relating within the unity of His everlasting situation. The Trinity is like a perpetual dance that takes place within the unity of the Persons. For the Trinity generates the Light because it manifests in being What It Is, the very fullness of Truth, the pure awareness of What Is. Light again is the revealed, and what it most of all reveals *is* itself as well as its basic structure. This is the triadic dynamism of the Divine Presence in its process of self-relating and self-knowing. This is God as such, the One Who generates everything that is or can be. The Light reveals the Trinity, because the Trinity *is* the Light being eternally "created" in itself. It always is this threefold Light, but is such because it is one-in-three or unity comprehended in Trinity. And this Light, Who is God, is also the great "Father of Light."[8] Is this not the same Light that Plato refers to in his vision of the Sun,[9] which also reveals to the soul a certain immutable content, the Form of the Good, and which Plotinus shows us has also a triadic structure in the three principles of the One, the Intelligence and the Soul? It is true of course that the Plotinian notion is a subordinationist doctrine.

The Cosmic Dimension of The Transfiguration

In the *Paradisio* of Dante's *Divine Comedy*, that great mystical work, the coming of the soul into the Presence of the Divine Light is a gradual process. One cannot come into the Divine fullness all at once; it is too intense to be perceived. Preparation is needed. It has to be a slow process of knowing, a seeing of more and more, a progressive revelation to the soul of God's ineffable Light. The soul then comes to a point where she sees everything in a flash, but the distance to this point, not in spatial terms but spiritual, is great. In this understanding, Dante is following his own experience, although he is, perhaps, also following the structure that the Pseudo-Dionysius pursues in his work, *The Celestial Hierarchy*. This is the book where the famous stages of *purgation, illumination* and *union* are elaborated. Although they were known in more ancient times having been discovered by Plotinus in the West, they were not really well received until popularized by St. John of the Cross in the Sixteenth Century. Again, one gets to God slowly through a series of mediations, which *purify* the soul, in which the Light of God's being is made more intelligible to the mind. In human life, as in Paradise, Christ *is* the focus. He is the Cosmic Mediator, and it is in Him that we see the Father, the Source, in the spiritual understanding given in the Holy Spirit. Christ is the Mediator in God, because He reveals to the Father His truth, which is their relationship to and in themselves, and this is the Spirit, the bond uniting them in the conscious content of their nature.

Just as the Son is the focus in the Godhead insofar as He is the Logos, God's self-understanding and the ground of all things, He is also the focus in the creation, on the cosmic level of Being. He is the Supreme Meaning, the intrinsic Archetype of universal order, which in being Who He is, unites it in Himself and in reality, making it to be. He is the Cosmic Center of creation, since He is the *meaning* of Who God Is in the archetypal Image of the Divine nature that Christ exemplifies.

The Transfiguration is also a cosmic event, since it signifies the Presence of God within created being itself. This is the *immanent* side of His nature, which is the implicit foundation of all existing creatures. It is in the sphere of Divine immanence that the Transfiguration becomes intelligible as a cosmic happening. Bilaniuk, in his profoundly beautiful essay on the Transfiguration, which has been somewhat inspired by Teilhard's vision of the Cosmic Christ, says that God's transcendence means that He can also be and must be immanent, that immanence is an expression of transcendence. Bilaniuk says that:

> By denying formally and materially all sorts of pantheism and by affirming the infinite immanence of God in the created extra-divine reality, we are affirming divine transcendence or at least we are pointing out one of its aspects, because it is true to say that God is so perfectly and infinitely transcendent, that even His infinite immanence does not diminish it, but on the contrary, heightens it . . .
>
> God is transcendent, not only because He stands infinitely above, apart and outside created, finite, and relative extra-divine reality, but also because He can by His infinite immance penetrate, put Himself-in-the-presence-

of, sustain, govern, this extra-divine reality to such an infinite extent, that on the one hand, He does not destroy created beings, and on the other hand "immanates" them so infinitely that He reaches into the core of their existent being to spheres where they are no more and where He alone, the infinite God, can extend His infinite transcendence. Humanly and figuratively speaking, God is infinitely transcendent not only towards the "above", but also towards the "below": "within" and "through" creatures.[10]

The Transfiguration allows us to see with earthly eyes the dynamic Light of the transcendent God in His Immanent act in things as that which constitutes them in being and maintains them in their existence. What Bilaniuk is trying to say is that God's transcendence moves in two directions simultaneously, i.e., beyond the cosmos, as the Absolute One without limitation or definition, and within each particle of the created reality, as the very power which makes everything to be. In the Transfiguration, that is what the three disciples witnessed, the revelation of Christ as the Center even of the universe's being, the realization that everything, in a sense, "leans" on His being in order to exist. For the spark of Divine Life is in each thing, else it would not be.

The Thaboric Light revealed the central truth of the Mysterty, that everything *is* established in Christ as the Logos, as having the form of all things in His function of being the Divine Exemplar of Being and intelligibility. Existence and the cosmos itself are gathered up into the Christ of History and Eternity. As Bilaniuk points out, Christ is also *Christos Pantocrator,* Christ the Ruler of all things. This is the Christ of glory, Who, thus, transfigures all things[11] in Himself. He is at the center of every atom, because He is the focus of the Father's Love, which is expressed in the Spirit, and which pervades all things. The cosmos itself is one great act of Divine contemplation, which happens between the Father and the Son in the unifying Love of the Spirit.

The Transfiguration stands at the center of Cosmic History as the *key* to this history. It tells us that Christ is the Way, the Way to the Knowledge of the Mystery of God, which leads to the Father in the dynamic movement of the Holy Spirit. The Thaboric Light shines forth in Christ as a *sign* and a beacon leading Humanity *home* to the glorious Source, Who is the Father.

It is because of the great importance of this event in Christian Life that it has been given such a prominent place in the sublime liturgies of the Orthodox and Eastern Catholic rites as well as in the Christian Art of the iconographic tradition, which is gaining in popularity today in the Catholic Church. For the Church is coming more and more to re-cognize her common heritage with the profoundly mystical tradition of the Eastern Church, which has been handed on from the Fathers. The Church is beginning to realize that we *are* one Church but with diversity of liturgy, emphasis and discipline. We are one in the Mystery of Christ, which is the Mystery of the Blessed Trinity, and this unity is made the more urgent in the breathtaking theophany of the Trans-figuration, which urges us on to do God's will in our time. Hence, the Transfiguration is an invitation to the Churches to see and express their unity in Christ. Let us now take a look at the Transfiguration as it bears on our growth in God-consciousness, that is, as it prompts us to spirit-ual realization insofar as we may be assimilated to the Divine Life in the grace of mystical prayer and the divinizing Union. We must have some perspective here and keep firmly in mind that what is said here is a glimpse; it does not exhaust the depth and vast extent of mystical experience. And this is true of the entire work.

The Mystical Dimension

The Transfiguration shows us the possible, since it is actual for God, and so it can also be actual for us. Each soul is invited to be one with the Divine Light. The soul can be one with God, and because so, it *must* be one with Him. This is where true happiness is to be found, to which the saints and mystics of all ages attest. Because we love God we are children of the Light. This love reveals itself, its great intensity of truth experienced, in the longing of the soul for God, to be united with Him. Is not the desire for God an invitation to seek Him? This is surely a sign that we are on the right road. A pure desire for God must reach Him as a river finds the sea. God comes to the one who seeks Him, and this expresses itself in everything such a soul says, does, and most im-portantly, is.

A pure desire for God is the path that leads to a mystical life that has to be nourished in contemplation, in the fertile garden of medita-tion, in the effortless awareness of God's Presence. This is not a refer-ence to discursive meditation, i.e., with images, but to a meditative process that concentrates on "the poverty of a single word", to use an expression popularized by St. John Cassian in his Tenth Conference, which takes the mind beyond images, thoughts and the body-con-

26

sciousness, and brings the soul into an awareness of God's Presence within. If God should show Himself in His Light of glory could the soul withstand this grace? God is immensity of Light and Truth in Himself as His own awareness, and also for the soul, but only to the degree that she can receive His gift of Himself. God is also infinite compassion.

The soul has a certain capacity for God, but this must be developed in *prayer.* Prayer is the activity of seeking God, and of resting in Him when He is found. Then it becomes a receiving from Him. The soul is brought into the luminous Presence of God and is illumined in Him; she is transfigured in the simple act in which God subsists, in the Trinity itself. Pure intelligibility that is boundless, immeasurable in its Light and Truth is found there. "Come and be transfigured in God" is what the event of the Transfiguration is suggesting in its spiritual or mystical significance. It is essentially a summons to maturity in contemplation, in this loving relationship with God. Christ has been given to us as the Way to this transfiguration in the Divine Life. As St. Paul puts it: "For God, Who commanded the light to shine out of darkness, has shined in our hearts, to give the light of the knowledge of the glory of God, in the face of Christ Jesus."[12]

II

EXPERIENTIAL KNOWLEDGE OF GOD

5

THE CONTEMPLATIVE ATTITUDE

Contemplation or prayer is one of the most misunderstood of human activities, and yet it is also the chief function of the person that defines the fullest measure of what it means to be human. It is the profoundest expression of the individual's *authenticity*, that which comes from the "cave of the heart". For it is in prayer that each person truly finds himself or herself; it is an activity of seeking God, and this is the only way that we are going to discover who we really are individually, as a self in God, and collectively, as a community united in our experience of God in that attitude of enlightened faith, having had some direct contact with the Divine Life there in the darkness of the "cave" where God dwells, a "place" beyond the world, our thoughts and beyond the imagination, in the Silence of the Presence. Furthermore, prayer is man's *vocation* insofar as it is directed to the knowledge and love of God. Indeed, it is supremely the vocation of man to be united to the Source in this life and in the bliss of Eternal Life. Since prayer is the central activity of man's vocation, it is also that which makes him to be the most human, as it constitutes the means of fulfilling the divine call to perfection, which can only come in relation to God. And is not true perfection a state in which the individual soul is Godlike? But this can occur only to the degree that the soul is assimilated to the Divine Life by way of *participation* in It. And this participation in God's inner being, the trinitarian life, this living and resting in God, is *contemplation*.

Let us consider the nature of prayer in its highest sense as this contemplation, the loving *awareness* of God's Presence, the content of this precious knowledge, and then show how this is related to our other many activities, wherever they may be, and let us, moreover, consider what implications it has for our understanding of the world. Let us first, however, take a look at the contemporary situation.

The State of Prayer In The Church

There is quite a marked confusion about the nature of true prayer in the Church and in society. Prayer is misunderstood, because, as it is generally practiced in the Western cultures, it is infected by the limited scope of Western man's values, which are primarily orientated to security in the material realm. Now with this kind of a disposition, we can well understand why the experience of prayer has suffered and why there is so much confusion about what prayer actually is.

Many events in History have contributed to this impoverished state of prayer in the Church, i.e., the great Schism, the black death and other plagues, the Hundred Years' War, the Reformation, and especially the Counter Reformation, which at the initiative of the Jesuits, reacted against personal revelation and mystical inspiration common up to this time, because of apprehension at the possibility of serious error and counterfeits. The heresies of Jansenism and Quietism also took their toll. These two movements were a kind of false mysticism. Again, these factors and others have led Abbot Thomas Keating to remark, in his tape devoted to contemplation, that: "The Church has been in a spiritual desert since the Reformation".[1]

Given the many historical causes that have contributed to the present spiritually diminished condition of the world, and have shaped the general view and practice of prayer, it is not difficult to appreciate how these events and circumstances, when informed by a secular culture with its concentration on *having* things instead of *being* and realizing our vocation in the activity of prayer or contemplation, have produced a society in which most people are basically ignorant concerning the nature of true prayer. Since there was a vacuum of genuine spirituality, with the exception of monastic life, the externals came to be emphasized, and the focus of prayer became supplication, which of course has a place but should not take center stage. And this happened because, on the one hand, the Church had virtually lost sight of her contemplative dimension, the depth experience of God, that which we all long for, and, on the other hand, because the evolving secular mentality, from the Nineteenth Century on, held out the promise of concrete materal goals that were achievable with the requisite effort. But this was at the expense of man's interior life, and it filled a vacuum or so it seemed. If the Church's inner spiritual life, as reflected in her vital mystical tradition during the first fifteen centuries of her history, had held sway from the advent of the modern world, the state of society and the practice of prayer might have been in a much healthier condition. Because it was not, the rising secular mentality became more pronounced and even influenced the very life of prayer, oftentimes making it too shallow and much too preoccupied with the vocal level and its supplicatory orientation. Hence, prayer is misunderstood because we have practically lost contact with the Church's tradition, which was only kept alive in monasteries and convents dedicated to contemplation.

But this impoverished state of prayer is now beginning to give way to a new movement towards greater *interiority*, and this is happening on a global scale. This has arisen primarily as a result of contact with the East and its ancient methods of meditation. These methods have always been rightly ordered to a mystical consciousness of life and reality. Also, Thomas Merton and other writers have greatly contributed to this genuine *renaissance*, to this vibrant reawakening in the Church and the world generally, encouraging a rediscovery of our own profound tradition of contemplation and the mystical life.

Contemplation

But what is the reality of contemplation, and what is the content of such experience and knowledge? So many today are talking about it, thus, it becomes more and more urgent for us to try and acquire a better understanding of its nature. Now, the constant Tradition of the Church is that contemplation is the loving awareness of the Presence of God. The emphasis is on being *with* God in *silence* rather than a vocal level of prayer. God is the focus or "object" of contemplative prayer. It is not an activity of discursive reason, whether speculative or practical. In fact, it has very little to do with thinking. For contemplation and mystical experience are pre-eminently involved in the hidden life of God in Himself, in His glory as well as in the soul's very being, her *esse*, and this also issues in the awareness of God in creation. This is the basis of nature mysticism, which is popularly associated with St. Francis, although this did not exhaust his experience of God, for Francis was a great contemplative saint. Nature mysticism is a primitive level of contemplative experience. Every mystic experiences the Divine in nature, but no authentic one stops there. This is what often happens to poets, surely this is what happened to the Romantics. Contemplation, furthermore, is the seeking and the *finding* of God in silence and solitude united with the realization of His wonderful love for us and our love for Him.

It is a progressive clarification of our knowledge of His life within us and in everything. Contemplative prayer has a single-minded intention: to love God. We may try to reach Him with lofty conceptions, which are valuable in their place, but these alone cannot attain to Him, Who is hidden in His own divine solitude. The author of *The Cloud of Unknowing* tells us, as so many mystics do, that God cannot be grasped by thought, for thought is unable to comprehend Him. "God will not be man-handled", as Thomas Keating is fond of saying in this regard.

It is rather by *love* that He can be known. *The Cloud* puts it this way: "By love He may be touched and embraced, never by thought."[2] In this teaching, to some extent, i.e., the *apophatic* aspect, the idea of unknowing with the mind, the author of *The Cloud* is following the doctrine of the Pseudo-Dionysius, especially the latter's *Mystical Theology*.[3] The emphasis, however, on the primacy of love in *The Cloud* is new, although it also appears in the doctrine of St. Bonaventure, who was also influenced, like *The Cloud*, by the Dionysian notion of negative theology.

The Cloud says that all thought and conception and the mind as such must be covered "over with a cloud of forgetting."[4] The *way* to God is through a pure, sustained desire of love directed to Him. *The Cloud* puts it this way: " . . . beat upon that thick cloud of unknowing with the dart of your loving desire and do not cease come what may."[5] Hence, contemplation requires a waiting for God in the silence and darkness of one's own heart, where God's eternal Silence envelops the soul and carries her into His inner life hidden from all things. Contemplation is, thus, as Thomas Keating says, "a tasting knowledge of God."[6] It is a *direct* knowing by not knowing (a paradox indeed), a way of knowing that God is because one encounters Him, but also a not knowing, since one does not comprehend His mystery nor penetrate His infinite intelligibility.

True contemplation or mystical experience occurs when the mind is *quiet* of all content, whether thoughts or images. The inner noise must cease just as the outer. "Be still and you will know that I am God", says YAHWEH in the Old Testament.[7] This is the way or *method* of mystical truth, a way of meditation in the Eastern sense. It is a dark, obscure knowledge that has many dimensions and approaches. As a way, it cannot be forced, for one comes upon it through determination, long practice requiring great patience and suffering, and above all, *grace*, since it is a gift, but one which God desires to give to everyone. It happens when the mind gives way to the Spirit and just lets go. And that is the essential meaning of contemplation, a letting go into God. But how difficult it is to trust God and let go, especially to let the ego die. William Johnston, commenting on the following passage from the Song of Songs (5:1), "I slept, but my heart was awake", says that: " . . . the mystics, interpreting these words quite differently from the exegetes, declare that the mind is asleep, the mind is silent, reason and imagination and sense are quietly lulled to rest; but the heart is alert and awake."[8] In this mystical state, reason, imagination and the senses are suspended, but the soul has entered into a greater *consciousness* that is not circumscribed by the limited parameters of normal, everyday thought and experience.

In contemplation, when the soul has been elevated into an awareness of God within her, He floods her being and all of her faculties with His ineffable Presence and overwhelms her with His embrace. He comes "like a thief in the night", and takes hold of the soul uniting her to Himself. So intense is this experience that, although every faculty of the soul is affected, none of them can perform their usual function, since they are all drawn together in a loving act of attention to His Presence. All is at rest as He takes control. This occurs in His time, which is eternity and in His space, which is His very being. George Maloney describes this experience in a very striking way:

> This loving God truly invades us, no longer an idea or a thought, but as the Source of all life. He drives out of our hearts all vestige of sin and darkness and transforms us into His loving light. As we get caught up inside of God's invading energies of love, we find ourselves gradually being consumed by the Trinity's mutual love for each other and for us. We become a prism by which God can radiate His love to all that we touch. We become a magnifying glass, to use the example of the Gorlitz shoemaker and mystic, Jacob Boehme, that allows the rays of God's warm love to burst into flame and to enflame the world with godly love.[9]

The Content of Mystical Light

This invasion by God's energies, His very being, which stream into our life in these precious moments of extraordinary grace, into the most secret core of the soul's being, brings with it a certain mystical realization of God's nature. This is the crucial area of the content of the mystical truth. Aside from the obvious problems of interpretation, which are subject to a linguistic, cultural, historical and theological framework, there is the added difficulty of rendering into language what is actually beyond the competency of language to express. For contemplative knowledge or experience is essentially ungraspable in the immediate, living experience of divine union itself. Neither is there anything to hold on to in the experience, nor can the faculties work in their normal mode of operation. It is only as we reflect on this experience or unitive contemplation that we can attempt to reconstruct something of the content of God's ineffable intelligibility that allures us deeper into His unfathomable Mystery. We can call this function of looking back to the *reality* of the mystical encounter an exercise in speculative mysticism, which attempts to capture the metaphysics of the content, as best as this can be accomplished. Any such attempt always falls far short of the Reality, because the inner truth of God is so luminous and untouchable, for it exceeds the capacity of the intellect to know in the infinite extent of its *simple* unity and the inscrutable mystery of its *triadic* theme. Here we see that creative tension between experience and reflection showing itself.

Now, contemplation is an awareness of God in a pre-eminent way; it is an intimate knowledge of His Presence to the soul within and also a perception of that same Presence in all created being. For every bird that catches our gaze on the horizon is a shining forth of His Presence in a natural event in creation. And behind, in, without, below, above, around, between and beyond, God *is* the center of it all. In the highest mystical state, the soul is drawn into the Trinity's essential being, which is the Godhead's contemplation of itself.

The first contemplation happens eternally as the Father arises from the Stillness and the Silence of the underived nature, the formless form of the Godhead and utters His mystery into the Son, Who embraces all that the Father is and yet is the One Who receives the Father's love and His eternal gift of Divine Life. The Son is the Fahter's self-contemplation in which He beholds His nature and knows Himself. The Father has His identity in the Son, and the Son has His truth in the Father, for He manifests Him in His own being and also to the Father, as well as to creation. The Father knows Himself in His Son (and perhaps only in this way), and this knowledge, impregnated with unspeakable love, *is* the intimacy between them that can only be expressed in another, and that is the Holy Spirit. At the center of the Godhead is the Father as uttering the dynamic life of the Trinity in His Word, the perfect imaging of His nature. The generating point of all things in God is a simple but totally incomprehensible *unmoving-movement*, which eternally resolves itself into three essential "graspings", and these are the Persons, the divine relations within the Godhead's unity. We will come back to this theme again and again in order that it may be conveyed in its profound power, the great truth that is present in this statement. The Persons are, in their nature as related functions of identity to the one Ground of their same or identical essence, relations within the being of God eternally attempting to hold on to the Mystery of the Godhead, the Mystery of Who He is to Himself and Who they are in Him.

On this plane, we are beyond thought and form as well as the world itself. The only form there is *is* the three-fold structure of the God-head's dynamic subsistence. The Father merges into the Son, the Son into the Father, and they mutually merge into the Holy Spirit. The Father's contemplation is the Son and the Son's contemplation is the Father and Himself reflected in the Father's being and love, and this eternally results in a third contemplation, which happens as a consequence of the sheer intensity of presence to each other; this is the Father and the Son welling up eternally into the Holy Spirit, Who unifies them in Himself in the very act of arising.

At the center of the Godhead is this Mystery that eternally resolves itself into the triune, dynamic relatedness of each-in-each, the Trinity. The Persons work out God's Identity; this has always happened, and is the basis of all reality. For this is the truth of the trinitarian Mystery. In these three ontological acts-in-one, mutually related to each other, God posits His being, and this is why His being is actual. He is pure relation to Himself in His Mystery, and this relation is the *impulse* of the triadic dynamism in which is present the fullness of His being, infinitely playing its pristine harmony. The Persons are the three enduring elements of the Divine harmony, and this harmony exists only because they are in tune with each other, from which proceeds the great song of creation, the outpouring of their harmonious love. This constitutes a perfect balance that holds the everlasting Secret, and that is the eternal Secret of Who God is in Himself. And this inner life of the Godhead, the Trinity, is the Kingdom of God mentioned in the Gospel.[10]

The Persons of the Trinity are essentially a perpetual, primordial searching of the Godhead for the intrinsic foundation of its being; it seeks to establish itself, and it succeeds in this act of establishing its Identity in a ceaseless, dynamic contemplation of its three immutable "movements", which are not tied to any thought-content. The three Persons are the very life of God as He knows and loves Himself. They are the dynamic of His inner being and truth. They are the three aspects of God's contemplative nature, which represent His Identity in act and in knowledge. They dramatize the attempt to capture His Mystery, for they are the very grasping of what to us will always be Mystery. This is true even in the Beatific Vision or mystical experience.

What we do know from the experience and from Revelation is that God pours forth His love in Christ, the perfect Image or Icon of the Divine glory. God gives us a *glimpse* of His Mystery in His Son in the great Cosmic event of the Incarnation, which is the projection of the Father's love into the concreteness of His Son here in this world. In this event, the Son takes human form, the One Who is from eternity formless, because He is the fountain of all form as the Logos, puts on the form of a man and gives us a "picture" of God's love for us. Christ is the link between the inexpressible truth of the Godhead in its dynamic life as Trinity and human life. The Son stepped into our condition so that we could have some idea about God, and to free us from sin and from our ignorance, the chief effect of sin. Christ is the Way, the path to the glory of the Father, which we must traverse in the Spirit.

Contemplation is simply a *participation* in the triune life of the Godhead that is always going on, an eternal happening, to which Christ has come to pave the Way in order to invite us all into this Mystery of the Divine Life where we have a place. He shows us the Way, which is Himself, since He is at the center of the Godhead, as He is also at the center of the Cosmos and History, and as He is the very life and being of His Church.

This experience of God in mystical prayer has implications for our other activites and for our attitude toward the world. Let us now explore these.

Activity and The World

It is only in and through a very profound and continual experience of prayer, of contemplative life, which is the mystical life of the Trinity going on within the soul, that the person's other activities have any actual meaning. The contemplative experience affects our perception of reality. It purifies our understanding of things and rightly orders our relationships with others. It awakens *compassion* in us for all people, the compassion of Christ, since we see the Divine Life in them, and we perceive them in God. We are aware of God's invitation to us to respond to each person who comes into our life, especially the poor and homeless, the hungry, the needy, the oppressed, the ill, the lonely, alienated and the despised of society. These are the ones Our Lord called "the least" of His brethren.

Contemplation not only allows us to "taste" God, but it also permits us to see reality correctly for the first time, as God wishes us to see it. For it helps us to recognize that God is at the center of all things and is present in every person, no matter how unattractive the exterior appearance. Contemplation "energizes" our apostolic activity, whether in the cloister, the home or in the marketplace, since, from the reality of prayer, of a mystical nature, we are given the ability or impulse to love all of God's creatures in an unselfish way. Clearly, this is the work of the Holy Spirit in the soul. Prayer is the very *energy* of our actions, for they flow forth from it. Prayer also purifies our motives. Our life is made *one* with Christ's and through Him, *one* with the Trinity. As a consequence, we live in Him and He lives in us with the Father and the Spirit. Our actions become His actions and our will becomes His will. Prayer makes us instruments of His mercy and *signs* of His love, a love that no mere human affection can ever equal. It is only because we have an intimacy with God, which is contemplation, that our apostolic pursuits are fruitful, since they arise out of an intense spiritual fecundity, which is the result of prayer and the workings of grace. Prayer colors our labors and lightens our burdens; it also helps us to understand and rejoice in our sufferings.

Because of contemplation and the glimpses it affords us of the mystical heights, we are able to regard the world with the proper attitude. For the world is not simply the area of our life and activity. It is not merely the vast realm of nature opening up onto the boundless horizon of the Cosmos. It is not just the hustle and bustle of urban life, the place of commerce and economic labor, nor is it only the stage upon which we live out our lives. The world is all of these, but it is also and more fundamentally an *attitude.* And like all attitudes, we can have the right one or the wrong one. The wrong one is the one that the Church has always been on her guard against and concerning which she has repeatedly admonished her children in every age. It is the selfish attitude of ego-centricity, a conception of living that seems to dominate these anthropocentric times in which we live. It is a ruthless pursuit of self-gain at the expense of the helpless, the poor, and also at the expense of self-truth or inner knowledge. In the Middle Ages, this egocentric view was held in contempt. This is the real meaning of the term "worldly".[11]

The world, as a misplaced attitude, is nothing other than pride unleashed, manipulating and exploiting the weak, using them as a means to selfish ends. And this is surely to misuse people and things. It is a shameful attitude of hedonism that leads to a disregard for the precious *dignity* of each person, including the individual who has this outlook. This pejorative attitude of world, which prevails (or seems so) in our troubled times, is a godless disposition; it originates in arrogant self-will, which abuses the priceless gift of freedom that God has given to each one of us. This negative attitude is the cause of dangerous strains in the planet's ecological cycles and processes that are subjugated to exclusive economic advantages for a few, without regard for the rest of Humanity. Such an attitude toward the world disorders man's relationship with God, to nature and to one another. And so God, nature and other people react from time to time with their own upheavals, and this is a response to the violence and evil of this misguided attitude. This negative attitude towards the world of course has its price; for those that have this disposition, peace eludes their grasp, and the world seems to them a hostile place, but this is a reflection of their disordered relationship to it, to God and to others.

Only a contemplative vision understands the world, and only contemplative values can *save* Humanity. The world is not a hostile place for the children of God. Neither is it here to be exploited for profit, to the detriment of others. The world exists for all of us to enjoy its many fruits and to be sustained by its benefits. When the world is seen through the eyes of faith, ordered by love and related to in prayer, especially the *intuitive* understanding of mystical prayer, which helps us to see our oneness with nature and our *solidarity* with the rest of Humanity, then it is understood to be a place where we are at home, since we are at peace with God, with ourselves and with His creation.

To the contemplative, nature is not an alien presence, but a *friend.* We are not estranged from it, for we are in *harmony* with its ceaseless cycles. God is at work in His creation; it serves His purpose. Each aspect gives Him glory, because it fulfills its function. His world, in its naturalness, has great beauty, and surely this bears a mark of His Presence. We need not be poets and artists to appreciate this beauty that no poet or artist can equal. Contemplation allows us to see the world as the place of God's gracious activity, as the fertile field of His constant care, bounded by His Mystery, a Mystery of love and *concern.* The contemplative understanding of world is an attitude that is in *continuity* with prayer, an extension of it, and the inner, dynamic life of the Blessed Trinity. The world, in the contemplative view, is a reflection of God's immeasurable glory and an unmistakable *sign* of His Providence insofar as it sustains us in our life. It is also a mystery in its own way, which has a relation to God's Mystery. The contemplative sees the Mystery of God in nature, in the mystery of its various elements and laws, in its ever-flowing processes. This is the mystery of birth and death, growth and decay, of the rising and the setting of the sun, the endless rhythms and cycles of nature, the unending flow of time, the rotation of the seasons, and the boundlessness of the stars and the heavens. Everything in nature works in harmony with God's laws. He it is Who grounds those laws and makes them to necessarily hold true. Even human life has certain laws that only the wise can perceive. The contemplative is lifted to *joy* at the song and flight of birds; he is reminded of the divine power. Such a one is awed, inspired and humbled by the lofty heights of the mountains that symbolize God's dwelling place and the process of the soul's ascent in the Spiritual Life. The contemplative is moved by the power of the sea, which reminds him of his feeble creaturehood. Because the contemplative soul is united to God in prayer, he or she is also united to His world. For contemplation is also a relationship with nature and world as well as with God. It is all a unity to which God, in His triune act, holds the key. And so the world is not a strange and inhospitable place, but home, for God has transformed it in His Son and has set its laws in harmony with His plan, a plan that also serves man's needs. The world flows forth from the super-abundant love of the Trinity, a sharing of the Divine Life with creatures. The world is an act of love for us, and every flower is a contemplation, a way in which God tells us how much He loves us. It is an outpouring of God's goodness. The intense love of the Persons, in the dialogical act of the Trinity's being, is so great that it projects itself outwards and creation occurs.

Neo-Platonism, from Plotinus to St. Bonaventure, was keenly appreciative of this metaphysical truth: that the Good, Who is God, is necessarily self-diffusive. It shares itself; He shares Himself, since the intensity of the trinitarian life has a fullness that can never be depleted, and so it spills into creation and the realm of creatures as an act of love. It is a call, an invitation to us to participate in God's life. Nature shows us this divine economy at work in a masterful way. It is only in a rightly ordered relationship to God, nature and to world that we are enabled to understand our noble place in the Divine scheme of things, that we are called to share in the Trinity's act of love at the center of the Godhead. The contemplative attitude aids us in this quest, since it brings us in prayer to the threshold of absolute Truth, God Himself in His unutterable glory. Contemplation extends our understanding of the world and nature so that we are more conscious of the divine life in them; we see how nature and the world are extensions of God's love, and how creatures have a share in this great cosmic drama. Although we are distinct in being from God, we nevertheless participate in the same system of ontological Mystery that we call the Trinity. Contemplation allows us to be at home in the world because we perceive His Presence in it, perceiving also its being in Him. The contemplative attitude is, thus, a perfect circle, which draws the soul into God's being, illuminates her in the act of the Trinity in the unitive Vision of the Divine essence, and also enlightens the soul's perception of the world and nature, allowing her to see it *in* God, and then to understand that it is all a *vehicle* for the soul in her return to Him when life has been born into eternity and the soul has found her Source.

6

MYSTICISM AS A FORM OF REVELATION

Mysticism has often been a thorny issue in the history of Western Consciousness, unlike the East where it has always been the norm. It has usually been regarded with a great deal of caution in the Church, especially since the Sixteenth Century. This is also true, and to a greater degree in Islam and Judaism. For in orthodox Islam, dominated as it always has been by the theologians, and its extreme transcendent orientation, there has been unremitting hostility to Sufism, the flower of Islamic Mysticism. Likewise, in Judaism, there has always been suspicion of mystical tendencies, as the Jews also have been careful to guard the transcendence of God.

This attitude of Western religious consciousness has had an impact on the view of what constitutes the nature of revelation. Here we will present two perspectives on revelation, that of St. Thomas and that of St. Bonaventure, which we could call the technical, in the narrow sense for the former, and the existential view in the latter case, St. Bonaventure's approach being more ecumenical than that of St. Thomas. The latter view should make it clear that mysticism, is *central* to revelation. In this chapter, we will also show mysticism's influence on the development of religion. Finally, we will introduce some examples of mystical experience from the lives of St. Bernard, St. Francis and St. John of the Cross, who are important figures in the spirituality of the Church, for all three have had a significant impact on Christian Mysticism. It will also be helpful to bring in the insight of the Pseudo-Dionysius on method in Spiritual Life in relation to the goal of the unitive Vision of the Divine essence. In this way, a contribution can be made to the practical demand for some direction in learning the approach to contemplative experience.

Revelation

Rene Latourelle, in his *Theology of Revelation,* calls it the most basic and all-embracing category of Christianity.[1] He sees it as essentially the way that "God comes out of His Mystery" and communicates Himself to Humanity. This communication happens through the inspired word of Scripture.[2] Thus, for Latourelle and the school of which he is a member, revelation has the precise meaning of designating Scripture as such as the authentic record or document of God's self-manifestation to the Human Race, and this alone, strictly speaking, is called revelation. To be clear, however, the Bible records God's revelation of Himself to man. Scripture, thus, is an instrument of revelation.

Now this position has its origin in the very technical language of St. Thomas. Thomas maintained a strict hierarchy in divine matters. In this, he was following the lead of the Pseudo-Dionysius, who taught such a hierarchy in his great work, *The Celestial Hierarchy.* Thomas held that there are three degrees in the soul's knowledge of God. The first and the most common level is that of the unaided reason, which by reflecting on God's effects in nature, order, harmony, beauty etc., comes to acquire a very abstract knowledge of the Creator. The intellect, in this stage, which is purely philosophical, sees the necessity for there to be a God. The second degree of divine knowledge occurs when God enters into the historical process and man's situation, and this is detailed in the Old and New Testaments. This is precisely what St. Thomas means by revelation, this entrance into our history and life by the hidden God Who reveals Himself to us in this way. Because of its restricted range, we call it technical, since it is in fact a technical distinction when viewed within the hierarchy of the three degrees, which Aquinas elaborates. Now, the third and highest degree of divine knowledge is *mystical experience* and the Beatific Vision, which both occur in an elevated state of the mind as a direct consequence of divine grace.[3]

In relation to the present situation of Humanity and the continuing *dialogue* of the world religions, Aquinas' position becomes problematic. This is true because it excludes the possibility of revelation in the other great traditions by virtue of the limited scope of the Thomistic definition. Bede Griffiths, on the other hand, holds that God has revealed something of His Mystery in all religions, and this is quite clear in Hinduism.[4] Before the covenant with Abraham, there was the Cosmic covenant with Adam. From this commenced a Cosmic Revelation in which all the peoples of the world shared, and evidence of this Revelation is found in all religions insofar as they have some definite knowledge of the Divine. Bede Griffiths feels that we must be open to what God has taught, about Himself, to people of other traditions, but which are expressed in their own cultural forms. He says very eloquently that we have to:

> . . . discern this essential Truth, this divine
> Mystery beyond speech and thought, in the
> language-forms and thought-forms of each reli-
> gious tradition, from the most primitive tribal

traditions to the most advanced world religions.
In each tradition, the one divine Reality, the
one eternal Truth, is present, but hidden under
symbols, symbols of word and gesture, of rit-
ual, dance and song, of poetry, music, art and
architecture, of custom and convention, of law
and morality, of philosophy and theology.[5]

Thus, we see the need of a more flexible notion of revelation that can
accommodate the profound insights of the other traditions, as well as
our own, insights which are primarily *mystical* in origin. It is these
mystical intuitions that we have to get at in all the traditions. There is
such a rich experience of God, and we must make this knowledge more
available to the Human Race. We desperately require a larger notion of
revelation that will allow every experience of God to be included in it.

For this reason, it would be wise to follow the tradition of revelation, based on experience, coming from the Greek Fathers, which
passed into St. Augustine's thought and on into the Middle Ages, and
which received its most eloquent articulation in St. Bonaventure and
the Franciscan School of Scholasticism. This tradition allows for the
possibility of a genuine ecumenism in such a way that we see the truth
in each religious tradition.

In this regard, Ewert Cousins, an authority on Mysticism, Bonaventure, and the dialogue of world religions, has important insights. Cousins considers Bonaventure's notion of revelation to be the one best
suited to the needs of the dialogue. In this sense, Bonaventure is cur-
iously modern. Cousins thinks that Bonaventure's sensitivity to the
"depth and nuances of religious experience" and his unique synthesis
of the philosophical, theological and mystical dimensions of consciousness, make Bonaventure significant in relation to other religious traditions,[6] particularly because of his enlightened view of revelation, which permits a more sympathetic approach in the appreciation of other traditions. This makes it possible to sustain a fruitful dialogue, since there is common ground.[7]

Bonaventure's idea of revelation centers around the self-diffusiveness of God the Father in generating the Son as the perfect *exemplar*
of creation and of all things. In this, Bonaventure is clearly in the Neo-
Platonic Tradition coming through the Pseudo-Dionysius. The Son expresses the essence of the Father's being, and creation reflects the
Son.[8] Thus, the entire cosmos is *theophanic,* reflecting the Divine.
Everything is revelational. Cousins maintains that *theophany,* as the
essential experience, touches the core of metaphysics and theology.[9]

42

Bonaventure speaks of revelation as having three modes, which he calls the book of creation, the book of Scripture and the book of life. Now, the Trinity, as the essence of Truth, experience and reality, is revealed in both the book of creation and the book of Scripture. And through Scripture, the book of nature is understood.[10] In order to supplement man's knowledge of the divine in creation and in His Word, however, God has also given that special knowledge of Himself, which arises in human experience, and this is the book of life.[11] And this is actually the area of mysticism.

Thus, Bonaventure has a very profound and expansive conception of revelation which embraces the vast variety of theophanies and shows how all of life and reality is an *epiphany* of the Divine. Hence, mystical experience, located in the realm of the book of life, is also the highest level of revelation, because it is nearest the Divine essence. This is why we call Bonaventure's position on revelation *existential*, since it encompasses the whole of reality and includes the most essential dimension, the *mystical*, whose insights, intuitions and glimpses, again, James called the "truest insights into the meaning of life".[12]

Mysticism

Mysticism is, thus, a form of revelation taken in its larger sense. It is also true to say that revelation can be, in some of its instances, a form of mystical experience. Many narratives in the biblical writings refer to contact with the Divine that transcends mere reason, sense experience, or revelation in its strict, technical interpretation. The experience of Moses and his encounter with God in the guise of the "burning bush", where God tells Moses His name,[13] is a clear example of a mystical experience occurring in Scripture.

This is also an indication of mysticism's influence on the development of religion. Although it would not be accurate to say that mystical experience has inspired all forms of religion directly, still it is certainly true that it is the origin of many types that religious consciousness has assumed in history. This is undoubtedly the case in Hinduism and Buddhism as well as in Taoism, Zen and Shamanism. For, if we take mysticism as normative in Eastern religion and some animistic varieties, then we can see in Hinduism, Buddhism, Zen, Taoism and some of these Shamanistic religions, in their structures and emphasis, a reflection of an original intuition or insight which had its beginnings in the mystical experience of the founders. In the case of Hinduism, it would be the mystical utterances of their sages dwelling in the forests of India, who embodied a Wisdom from *experience* and who handed it on to their disciples. The *Vedas* and *The Upanisads* are the principal sources of this tradition, recording these initial and indeed, perennial intuitions. These early experiences of the founders gave rise to the institution of the guru-disciple relationship, a very human as well as spiritual relationship, which is the methodological basis of handing on the tradition, in the sense of a mystical teaching, in Indian Spirituality. In the instance of the Buddha, the structures of the faith have their origin in his experience of enlightenment, which was assuredly mystical.

Often, the structures of a religion develop as an attempt to institutionalize a mystical insight. For the human psyche, belonging as it does to the Eternal from Whom it has sprung, has a propensity, almost a passion, for the permanent and, thus, tries to fix or hold on to unusual experiences as a matter of course. Again, we can see this tendency at work in the event of the Transfiguration, when Peter wanted to pitch three tents in order to preserve and contemplate the moment of vision. This tendency is true of much of religion and politics, although it is, perhaps, least true of Christianity insofar as Christianity is not directly based on mysticism, and yet it is clearly mystical in what it promises and in what the great mystic-saints were and are privileged to witness. We must also remember that the Gospel has many mystical teachings, inner meanings, that convey the anagogical signifance, to use Patristic language. Let us take a look at the experience of three such saints, Bernard, Francis and John of the Cross, who may be said to have penetrated and lived the mystical dimension of the Gospel.

St. Bernard

St. Bernard of Clairvaux, a pillar of the Twelfth Century and a great monastic theologian, who virtually directed the course of the Church from his monastery, like St. Teresa of Avila and St. John of the Cross, expresses his mystical insights in profoundly *personal* terms. Thus, Bernard has an intimacy with God, but it is also an awareness of God's utter transcendence, which manifests itself, in Bernard's doctrine, by an accompanying sense of Mystery. The experience of God is bounded by this Mystery.

He speaks of the mystical union, or a stage thereof, as a self-forgetting. For he says: "To lose yourself as if you no longer existed, to cease completely to experience yourself, to reduce yourself to nothing is not a human sentiment but a divine experience."[14] The Sufis also mention this self-forgetting and call it "extinction" in the Divine. This may well be the deep meaning of Christ's sober exhortation "to despise oneself",[15] that is, in the mystical sense, to free oneself or be freed by grace, coming from a pure desire and prayer, of ego-centricity, which must occur in *humility* of heart and in the *unitive* experience, both of which, working together, liberate us from ourselves and from the world.

Mystical experience radically changes the person; it is a total transformation, a steady process of becoming godlike. This is what "deification" means in the Eastern Orthodox Tradition. We will have more to say about this when we come to consider the mystical doctrine of the Pseudo-Dionysius. Bernard says of it: "It is deifying to go through such an experience"[16], such a transformation in God. This Divine love, furthermore, cannot be attained by human effort; one can prepare for it. It is a precious gift which God gives to whomsoever He chooses.[17] And this gift *is* contemplation, a flying away to the Divine.[18]

Coming to the essence of this contemplation, Bernard speaks of God entering his soul. He says that this is a very mysterious happening, so much so that he could not determine when God had actually entered or when He had departed.[19] God "touches" or takes hold of the soul; He invades one's being. This is the well-known *Divine touch* to which mystics often refer. In this sense of unknowing, it is a dark knowledge because of so many obscure elements. Both the Pseudo-Dionysius and John of the Cross also emphasize this point. For, all that Bernard knew was that God had become present to him in a fuller sense than usual or that, in grace, he had become more aware of God's Presence within his soul, within the "cave of the heart" where God and the soul meet in His Mystery.

Bernard uses the terms of marriage, like John of the Cross, Teresa of Avila and countless other mystics, to express the mystical union, this intimacy between God and the soul. And all throughout his *Cantica Canticorum*, he calls God or Christ the Bridegroom and the soul the Bride. This also suggests, although not explicitly, that the soul is *always* passive in relation to receiving from God. God, the Bridegroom, leads His Bride, the chosen soul, into the "bedchamber" of mystical love. This emphasis on love is quite characteristic of Christian, Judaic and Islamic Mysticism.

St. Francis

St. Francis of Assisi is perhaps the greatest saint ever to live and certainly one of the most extraordinary mystics of all time. His appeal is universal, for everyone loves him. Francis was so completely united to God, and had become so totally Godlike, "deified", if you will, that he was at peace with himself, that Divine peace, the world, God, nature and others. Every one who ever met him could perceive so clearly the Presence of God in his face, manner and his actions.

Francis' spiritual life was filled with long hours of prayer, sometimes lasting all night. He was often caught up, carried out of himself and absorbed into the Divine Light. His intellect was elevated, and he experienced mystical union.[20] Francis penetrated to the very center of God's being. He describes, to Brother Leo, the extent of his contemplative experience: ". . . and then I was in the light of contemplation, in which I saw the infinite depth of the Divine Godhead and my own wretched abyss of misery."[21]

The climax of the mystical life of Francis came upon him when he had the vision of the six-winged Seraph on Mount La Verna, his hermitage. It fittingly occurred on the feast of the Exaltation of the Holy Cross as Francis knelt in prayer on the side of the holy mountain. In the midst of the winged Seraph, he beheld Christ on the cross. It swept Francis into ecstasy and when he came back to himself, he noticed that the sacred wounds of Christ's passion had been imparted to him in his hands, feet and side. Thus, his identification with the Lord was total.[22]

Francis was also a great nature mystic. This is, perhaps, one of the chief reasons for his enormous popularity through the ages. He somehow represents a perfection that is more than human. His life was a miracle of grace. For we see ourselves as we could be in his profound example. He was so utterly joyful, because he saw God in everyone and everything. In this, he was similar to St. Ignatius of Loyola, or is it the other way around? He had a natural sense of his unity with all creation without being a monist. He was far too conscious of the radical distinction between the Creator and the creature, between the absolute perfection of God and the sinfulness of man, to make such a bold assertion of identity between the two.

His poverty, which is intimately related to his spiritual vision, was probably a profound form of humility in which he saw his absolute dependence upon God. It was an acknowledgement of our ontological condition, that we have everything from God, including our very lives. Francis was attuned to the Divine Harmony. So sensitive was this great and gentle little man that he could perceive the workings of Providence in all the situations of life. He refused to play the ego game, the game of status and position to which the world is addicted. Consequently, his poverty, celebrated and romantized as it is, was really an act of self-defacement. His exterior was not pleasant to behold; he was so overcome by his long fasts and endless hours of prayer that poor "brother ass" became too frail to bear the strains of his many mortifications. His unattractive exterior, however, cloaked one of the greatest souls ever to walk this world. This was evident in his luminous eyes. Oh those eyes! Francis is a mystic who went all the way, and that is, perhaps, a further reason why he is so much loved. Very few souls, including all of the saints of all ages and traditions, can equal the brilliance of his spirit that shines with such radiant sanctity for all the ages of history and Eternity.

St. John of the Cross

Some of the most beautiful descriptions of the mystical life are given by John of the Cross in his sublime poetry. John, like Bernard before him, uses the symbolism of love in his mystical works. This permits him to convey the intimacy existing between God and the soul in the unitive relationship. For instance, consider the tender tone of his famous poem entitled "The Dark Night", and then, let us try to reveal its transcendental meaning.

> 1. One dark night,
>   Fired with love's urgent longings
>   —Ah, the sheer grace!
>   I went out unseen,
>   My house being now all stilled;
>
> 2. In darkness, and secure,
>   By the secret ladder, disguised,
>   —Ah, the sheer grace!
>   In darkness and concealment,
>   My house being now all stilled;
>
> 3. On that glad night,
>   In secret, for no one saw me,
>   Nor did I look at anything,
>   With no other light or guide
>   Than the one that burned in my heart;
>
> 4. This guided me,

More surely than the light of noon
To where He waited for me
—Him I knew so well—
In a place where no one else appeared.

5. O guiding night!
   O night more lovely than the dawn!
   O night that has united
   The Lover with His beloved,
   Transforming the beloved in her Lover.

6. Upon my flowering breast
   Which I kept wholly for Him alone,
   There He lay sleeping,
   And I caressing Him
   There in a breeze from the fanning cedars

7. When the breeze blew from the turret
   Parting His hair,
   He wounded my neck,
   With His gentle hand,
   Suspending all my senses.

8. I abandoned and forgot myself,
   Laying my face on my Beloved;
   All things ceased; I went out of myself,
   Leaving my cares
   Forgotten among the lillies.[23]

In the first stanza, the soul is longing for God and she has *quieted* her senses and the reason; her house is at rest, at peace. All is prepared. In an *unknowing knowing*, which is darkness, because the soul does not fully grasp God, but she knows that He is there, and this is a secure knowledge, since it is *certain*, for it is known in a *direct* manner, the soul ascends to God by the secret ladder of contemplation. This is hidden from the world, existing in a mystical state of consciousness and knowing, but the soul does not apprehend the full range of the encounter. Again, the soul is hidden from the world, and she does not desire it or any creatures; she is joyful unto bliss because she is returning to the Source. The Light of God directs her from within, guiding her to a place where He waits, a place beyond this universe and beyond the mind. This Light leads the soul into the Presence of God, to Whom she is united. He leads her to a place where they are completely alone. This mystic night is more lovely than the dawn, for God and His beloved soul are united in a mystical way. She is transformed in His being without losing anything. They are a long time together there. The mystical union suspends all of the soul's senses and faculties, as she is drawn into the Unity of God. The soul is made one with Him, and she forgets her very existence, finding Him, thus, and leaving her "cares forgotten among the lillies". The soul then transcends with God.

John of the Cross goes on to describe this Presence of God dwelling in the soul as it reaches the heights of an intense, constant love and becomes, from a beginning as a little spark in the soul, the "Living Flame of Love".

1. O Living flame of love
That tenderly wounds my soul
In its deepest Center! Since
Now you are not oppressive,
Now consummate! if it be Your Will:
Tear through the veil of this sweet
    encounter!

2. O sweet cautery,
O delightful wound!
O gentle hand! O delicate touch!
That tastes of eternal life
And pays every debt!
In killing You changed death to life.

3. O lamps of fire!
In whose splendors
The deep caverns of feeling,
Once obscure and blind,
Now give forth, so rarely, so exquistely,
Both warmth and light to their Beloved.

4. How gently and lovingly
You wake in my heart,
Where in secret You dwell alone;
And by Your sweet breathing,

Filled with good and glory,
How tenderly You swell my heart
with love![24]

God, the 'Living Flame of Love', wounds the soul in her deepest Center, in the "cave of the heart", because of the Power of His loving Presence, taking His abode secretly in the soul. The Divine touch has become a permanent dwelling within the being of the soul and this is a *taste* of eternal life. God wakes the soul to His Presence within her and wells up into this flame of love that totally absorbs her into its absolute Reality. For God becomes the Supreme Center of the soul's attention and longing, filling her with the *glory* of the Divine Life. And in his poem entitled "Stanzas Concerning An Ecstasy Experienced In High Contemplation", John of the Cross says that contemplation gives the *highest* knowledge possible, a knowledge of God's essence, which is a transcending of knowledge as such as "an understanding of not understanding".[25] Here again, we have the Dionysian theme of *apophatic* or negative theology, which is inspired of a direct Vision of the Divine essence and is less concerned with a speculative knowledge of God's being, since this is impossible to begin with. We will have more to say about this *via negativa* of the Pseudo-Dionysius when we come to consider his religious experience. For John of the Cross, as for most mystics, we *can* receive some knowledge of God's essence, but it is a dark knowledge that cannot be understood. We understand by not trying to understand, since this knowledge is *ineffable*. Although we can have it, still we cannot express it or adequately grasp it in the mode of a rational knower, because its Meaning is boundless. It transcends the entire range of our categories and the parameters of our ordinary and our metaphysical consciousness. Such is the vision of St. John of the Cross.

Method In The Mystical Ascent

The method and the stages of the soul's ascent to God, which John of the Cross elaborates in his works, are essentially the insights of the Pseudo-Dionysius, though the experience, content and stylistic expression are John's. Let us look at the Dionysian method, one which also bears the mark of Plotinus, of which we will have more to say later.

The Pseudo-Dionysius says that all Being, Truth and Love are hidden "in the dazzling obscurity of the secret Silence. . . "[26] This is the Godhead in underived Unity and in the Trinity, which is the Divine essence knowing itself. The *way* to union with the Divine is through complete *renunciation* of the selfish designs of the ego and a withdrawal from all perceptions of the senses, from images, notions, concepts and thoughts of the mind.[27] In this way and in God's time, the soul finds "Him that has made Darkness His secret place."[28] The soul comes into the luminosity of His Truth as it exists in Him as pure essence, the perfection of *esse* as the infinite Meaning, unified in the Consciousness of its act of being that which it is. God being simple, His essence and His existence are the *same* and, thus, He *is* Existence itself. He holds the eternal moment of TO BE in His infinite act of being. All existence comes from Him because He is the very *reality* of what Is in the sense of a Divine Plenitude. He is the pure Meaning of Holy love. Thus, the intellect is blind before the diaphanous splendor of God's Presence. For, He dwells in Darkness, which means that, the Light of His being is so luminous it *seems* as Darkness to the mind; the intellect simply cannot understand. One has to pass beyond all things in order to be united with Him Who is totally transcendent to all things insofar as His inner Mystery is concerned.[29] The soul comes to know God when the mind is *still*, and in unknowing is "united by his (the soul's) highest faculty to Him that is wholly Unknowable, of whom thus by a rejection of all knowledge, he possesses a knowledge that exceeds his understanding."[30] We, thus, can and do have Vision of God, but we cannot really reconstruct it in our refelctions. There is near-total intellectual poverty in relation to the Divine Light. We can know it, and know that we know it subsequent to the encounter, but it is a private knowledge insofar as we are unable to actually show others what we mean, what God *reveals* to us of Himself and His Mystery.

Mysticism is the most essential form of knowledge, and as direct experience of the Ultimate Truth, of God in His glory, it is also the most precious form of *revelation*, since it is the highest kind of knowledge of the Divine that the soul is capable of in this life. The Beatific Vision alone is higher. To see this, we need, first of all, to have a larger persepective on the nature of revelation, like that of Bonaventure, and more importantly, this being the point, we *must* have this mystical *encounter* with the Divine Source in the conemplative state, above the mind and beyond the ego, where we understand first-hand that God *is*. For mysticism is the revelation of God, the Absolute in a direct experience. It is, thus, the *primary* dimension of existence and of God's self-communication of His being and Reality. Let us conclude this essay with a poem that, like John of the Cross and others, conveys the mystic theme.

The Celestial Rose

O mystic night
awaiting Dawn's Light,
in the center of the soul
a brilliance so intense,
a million stars shine
with floods and flashes of brightness,
a vibrating Radiance immense
in still recollection of Something
essentially Divine.

In the soul's garden,
place of a place far beyond the mind,
dwell flowers magic untouched by time
in simple attention to the Sun,
life-giving and warm, a gift.
The Light reveals that Vastness,
supra-Olympian creativity
hiding everywhere.

In this secret garden
in solitude as the soul her vigil keeps,
a Divine suddenness opens from that Light;
in that mystic night,
a star shone in the soul's sleep.

In the garden's twilight
stream serene beams;
into the soul such loving rays
pierce that darkness of her night.
She in that supreme moment rests
as He plays in her waking sight.

In the mystic garden's Light
the soul a flower is before the Sun;
so good to be in that delight,
a mere flower in the ceaseless
quiet of a mirth-filled night

while angels sing so sweetly
as their solemn gaze points
to the Living Fount.

How that flower has a place
a spiritual fight she makes
against the weeds of earthly merriment.
In the garden's mystical glow
a joy anticipates that coming **Dawn.**

A star shines in the soul's center
lighting her way till morning,
in that garden's unearthly radiance,
guiding her within
to a place beyond the world
into Eternal Streams of illumination
more splendorous than Spring's early dream,
awakening her to the Presence,
inexhaustable Fount of form and kind.

A gentle walk reveals
in that walled-garden's Light,
a path leading Somewhere
to a Mystery within,
living in secret and Silence,
while flowers sway in Summer's breeze
harmonizing with rays of Dawn,
colors and patterns
taken from some Ageless Form.

The Light in the soul's cloister
more intense grows,
aflame with Love most sublime,
grows more immense,
radiating energy Divine,
greater than the Cosmic psalmody,
then, turning on the flower's way,
lets go a flood into the soul's interior,
illuminating her in those
radiations of the Celestial Height.

In that peaceful soul
where night has gone,
having fled the onrush
of a cosmic joy,
the blossoming soul,
transfigured in Beauty eternal,
becomes like a mere feather, helpless
floating, ever floating in Divine Immensity,
being ever drawn by some unspeakable
  attraction,
ever towards the Center of it all.

O luminous night
arising in a feeble heart
touched by mystic grace,
the fullness of that joyful height
traces in the soul's delight,
a picture, obscure at first, but wait, see
it is a Celestial Image
that transforms the face.

The flower becomes in that Light
glorified in an ineffable Bliss
that IS what Dante knew
in our Heaven beyond the sun,
in that Love Threefold
that 'moves the stars'.[31]

THE SOURCE OF BEING*

The following reflections bear on some of the cruical issues involved in Vedic Thought, the origin of the Indian Tradition. We are concerned here with Being and non-being as they are related to the Divine. We also touch upon the Godhead, the Trinity and the Incarnation. In addition to these, there is a brief reflection on prayer, mystical experience, and the role of the Church; it is from these considerations that our ultimate concerns should become evident. In these musings, we have not stayed close to Panikkar's text, but we have at least addressed a few of the important issues, especially as these are central to the dialogue between Christianity and Hinduism. To take up all the questions occasioned by Panikkar's brilliant, but massive book would require an equally large volume, a task this author has neither the time nor the energy to accomplish, let alone the ability. In this essay, again, notice that creative tension or dialectic between religious experience and metaphysical reflection.

Background

Vedic consciousness seems to be the product of a synthesis consisting of the mythological, metaphysical and mystical impulses of its inner life. These impulses may have occurred in one conscious being, a soul or they may have existed separately as different levels of awareness, situated in diverse mements of history, in a variety of saints and sages. They may also have existed simultaneously in a number of spiritual masters back in the primeval period, the time of the forest sages.

The concepts of mythological consciousness, are perhaps, ontologi-

* This essay was written for the occasion of a conference held at Shantivanam in South India (August, 1978), to which the author was invited by Bede Griffiths. Unfortunately, I was not able to attend, but did send this piece. The Conference had as its theme: "Personal Reflections on God in Light of the Vedic Experience". The conference was organized around Raimundo Panikkar's work, *The Vedic Experience, Mantramanjari: An Anthology of the Vedas for Modern Man and Contemporary Celebration* (London: Darton, Longman and Todd, 1977). Father Bede and Dr. Panikkar ran this interesting East-West meeting.

cal insights, and in some notable instances, mystical intuitions expressed in language. The problem with myth is that the poverty of its terminology limits the cogency of the insights as they are given expression
in the language of mythic thought. But we must keep in mind that
these people, these forest seers had a very deep experience of God;
there is no doubt that they were seeking knowledge from contact with
the Divine.

All traditions reflect on *origins*, and they are forced by circumstances of culture to use the poor tools they have, the concepts on hand in
their experience. Each tradition tries to reach and convey the same
Truth but from different perspectives. Terms can and do constrain
insight. The task is to refine the terms in the light of the experience so
that they become reasonably serviceable in communicating and representing the Mystery of the Absolute. This is, perhaps, what happened in
Indian speculation, and they were quite sophisticated at it.

The early mythological thought of Hinduism, lacking the refinement of latter ages in its tradition, had to rely on terms taken from the
concrete human situation. Some would call this the influence of the
fertility cult on Indic consciousness, but such an assessment is too superficial. Any cosmology, developed from the limits of a mythos taken
from human experience, usually labors under an *anthropocentric* reduction, so that the ultimate principle must reflect the human. This is a
serious problem for Hinduism. It is unwittingly an attempt to shape the
ontological reality in the terms of the human, rather than seeing the
human in the underived categories of the ontological, its Source and
ground. There *is* a real difference, and Indian Thought has had moments in which it saw this truth. The human, whose enduring category is
the finite, cannot approximate the Divine, whose category is the infinite, beyond form, even human form and conceptualization. It is even
beyond Being and non-being.

The sages who went to the forests, withdrew into contemplation and
reflection, turning their attention to the insights and intuitions embedded in the myths. They combined their own *mystical* awareness with
the early mythological speculation. Slowly, they refined the language of
myth and produced a metaphysical terminology. At the same time,
through their meditative experience, which was actually contemplation,
they had realization of God or this inner enlightenment, this *samadhi*.
They did not just talk about Him, which is the predominant flaw of
much of Western theology, they also *experienced* Him in the intimacy
of mystical prayer, in meditation. They also discovered *techniques* of
contemplation, which they passed on to their disciples. They were able

to *translate* their awareness of God, of Brahman into metaphysical categories, and they applied these to the contents of the cosmological myths. Slowly, they recast these myths anew in the terms of their own insights and experiences of the Ultimate being. As a consequence, they expanded these mythological, cosmogonic stories and clarified the profound truth in them. This does not mean that their metaphysics was a perfect expression of the ultimate structure of the real, for that can never happen in any system. There can be no doubt, however, that they were living on a very high plane of metaphysical and mystical consciousness.

Now, the starting point, ontologically, of all reality and truth is the mysterious realm of the Godhead. How the Godhead is conceived, subsequent to enlightenment, in any tradition is indeed problematic, for it has to be sifted through the language and mentality of a culture, which has its own limits arising from experience, cultural presuppositions and habits of mind. These limits conspire to obscure the insights on the Divine that a particular people have. As this is quite true of Christian Thought, it is no less true of Vedic Speculation. Before considering the Godhead, we must look into the relationship of Being and non-being. The reason for this will become clear.

Being and Non-Being

It seems that Vedic Thought begins with non-being as the *source* of Being or reality. Somehow Being and non-being are conceived to be equally essential to the Divine. In the *Taittiriya Brahmana*, which Panikkar quotes, the emphasis is on non-being. For it says: "In the beginning, to be sure, nothing existed, neither the heaven nor the earth nor space in between. So Nonbeing, having decided to be, became spirit and said: 'Let me be!' "[1] What does this mean? It cannot mean that nonbeing is the absolute beginning of reality, that it is the source of Being. This notion Western Metaphysics would reject as impossible and inconceivable, perhpas, because we are so dominated by the principle of Being coming from the Greeks. Panikkar himself recognizes this truth and reiterates it in the Greek formula: "Out of nothing, nothing can come."[2] In the West, the emphasis is on Being. Panikkar does say in the same place, however, that Being and non-being are "coextensive."[3] This is surely a debatable statement. Hegel attempted it in a different way. He conceived of the original state of the Absolute as one of an exclusive struggle between Being and non-being[4] rather than a mutual coexistence in the same unity of essence. But Hegel saw this struggle as the birth of becoming; he was concerned with the origin of existence on the earthly plane, and this is how he thought of it in metaphysical terms. Hegel, furthermore, only saw this struggle as the origin of becoming. He did not conceive the Absolute, as Panikkar insists Vedic Thought does, as a relation, whether mutual or exclusive, between Being and non-being. For the struggle between Being and non-being arises from a temporal dimension of the Absolute that requires the existential plane in order to actualize potentialities that are inherent in it. The Absolute itself is beyond the categories of Being and non-being.

What this statement of the *Taittiriya Brahmana* must actually mean is that in the beginning there was "no-thingness", that is to say, no form or no manifestation. Non-being is equal to non-appearance of form. Who could doubt that non-manifestation (non-being) preceded manifestation (being or appearance)?

Furthermore, the concept of non-being as such or nothingness, if asserted to be total negation of Being, is a pseudo category. There is no non-being or nothingness. Nothingness is precisely *no-thingness* in its etymology, not "nothing" but *no thing*, and "thing" is understood as an object capable of perception by finite consciousness. Thus, the connotation of the term itself does not support an ultimate negative meaning. To put it another way, there is no such thing as non-being. For because *somethingness* is, nothingness, as negation of Being, is not and cannot be. The very existence of something, which is the *given* of our experience, negates the possibility of nothing. The clue to all of this is in our existential situation. We exist, therefore, the question of Being receives an implicit answer. Being has *priority* because it *is*, whereas, non-being is a mere rumor of weak metaphysics. That must be the actual starting point, for that *is* our experience of life and reality.

We can speak of non-being but it does not have the meaning that some have thought. It cannot be used as a serious challenge to Being. On that level, it is indefensible, as Panikkar in his wisdom has himself admitted. Yet, even though he admits this, nevertheless, he does give the term "non-being" a negative connotation in the firm sense. This is a very subtle question. How, we must ask, can non-being be "the gravitational center of Being"?[5] Panikkar suggests that this is one of the essential points of Vedic speculation. The question cannot be answered by assuming that Being and non-being are coextensive. What Panikkar's metaphor implies is that at the generating center of Being there is non-being as its ground or that non-being is itself this center. It all depends on how this is meant. If it is meant in the sense of non-being understood as the pure negation of Being in being non-being, then the statement cannot stand, metaphysically, for the sufficient reason that non-being is not an actual possibility of the ultimate state of the Divine. Again, at the center of all things we can experience or perceive, that which makes them to be *is* something in the truest sense. In a way, matter or the material element is nearest to non-being in our experience, because it is always striving to be, which is apparent to our perception in that it is constantly changing. It is always striving to find its foundation, its metaphysical ground, that which is, and does not change, since it has the fullness of existence in that eternal moment in which it *grasps* the TO BE and *is* this TO BE. We have indicated why above. At this point, an alternative to the Vedic assumption can be presented, one which Panikkar would probably agree to, and one which is, perhaps, nearest to his own position. We begin by accepting his basic premise that "neither an affirmation nor a negation is capable of carrying the weight of the ultimate mystery."[6]

The Godhead

What Panikkar's principle actually seems to say about the Divine is that we cannot conceive it in its essence. We are reduced to *apophatic* language. There is, however, another meaning that we can glean from Panikkar's statement, and, I believe, it is one that bridges the gap. We can say that the Divine Mystery is itself beyond the categories of Being and non-being. This is nothing new. It has been said by many in the Western Tradition and is probably what is meant in the Indian Tradition. The Good of Plato and the One of Plotinus are both beyond or *prior* to Being. Being comes forth from the One. The Pseudo-Dionysius says that the Godhead, the One, is as such totally "beyond Mind, beyond Life and beyond Being", and that it is the Formless Form of all form.[7]

Now, Being, as the basic category of Metaphysics, the heart of it, and the all-embracing unity of existence, is yet finite, because it is actually that which bounds the living, what constitutes the limits of the cosmos, and, thus, as such cannot be made to represent in any way, the Divine. There is without question (unless we have misunderstood) a tendency in the Vedic Tradition to do precisely that. For again and again, Panikkar defends the essentially *anthropocentric* thrust of his interpretation. Whether or not this is his own position is quite another matter. Somehow, representing the *Vedas*, he seems to be saying that the Divine has got to come to terms with the human, whereas, we are saying the opposite, that is, that one comes to know the Divine, in the mystical sense, and this is also what Dionysius is saying and countless others in the Christian Tradition, when one lets go of the human, as the human is fulfilled in the Divine. If we talk about God as masculine or feminine or the relation of both, then we miss the point concerning the Absolute. For God cannot even be symbolized by these terms. The masculine and feminine are ontologically reflected in the Divine nature as a give and take, but as such, God, being infinite and beyond form as well as Being, cannot be spoken of in these human terms. Let us now return to our intuition that the Godhead is beyond Being.

When we wish to refer to all that is manifested in the cosmos then we use the term *Being* as the principle that allows existence and holds beings, as well as all form, in manifestation. That is the proper extent of Being and the only domain of its influence. Being is that which makes the manifested to be, to appear. But when we wish to refer to the Divine, to the Godhead and the Trinity, then we *must* pass beyond this finite principle of metaphysics, and in this way point to God Himself.

The Godhead is, as Dionysius says, a pure, undifferentiated Unity.[8] It is unmanifested in Itself. The Trinity is the manifested dimension of the Divine. If we want to use the confusing concept of non-being, we could say that the Godhead is "non-being", meaning that it is not itself Being or the manifested; it transcends Being. Its meaning is infinite and cannot be expressed in or by anything comprehended under the category of Being, except, perhaps, as reflected in symbols, but in these most imperfectly. The symbol in some unique way possesses a *sense* of the Absolute, and its power is in its capacity to convey this sense. For instance, the Sun, as a symbolic representation of the Divine, gives us some idea of God as pure illumination of Truth in Himself, Goodness and Light, for He is the Source, but it does not convey the essential intelligibility of the Divine essence itself, which is totally ineffable.

This Ultimate, Divine subsistent Unity beyond Being and even consciousness, as we know it, resting in its eternal Stillness is, as Eckhart says, free of all activity. In this sense, it is "non-being". For it does nothing. It neither creates nor sustains.[9] It just is. The very nature of the Godhead in itself is the *Stillness* eternally grasping itself. Eckhart says of it: "The Godhead in itself is motionless Unity and balanced Stillness and is the Source of all emanations."[10] It is this ultimate state of Divine Quietude, of pure Unity that Eckhart calls the Abyss of the Divine or the Wilderness of the Godhead; this is what appears to the intellect as "no-thing", since the mind cannot comprehend it.[11] The Godhead is the Divine Solitude and this is, perhaps, Panikkar's meaning when he refers to the initial state of the Divine as being one of soli-tude.[12]

There are two essential dimensions to the Ultimate Mystery. These are Unity and Trinity. And these, incidentally, are the two issues, per-haps, to which the dialogue of world religions will ultimately be resolv-ed, in a metaphysical sense. That is of course providing the dialogue reaches this level of substance, something for which we can only pray, hope and work.

These two dimensions are not exclusive but subsist in the same Unity of essence. We have a good symbol of the relationship between Unity, the Godhead as such and Trinity, its dynamic comprehension and inner truth, in the Taoist symbol of yin-yang. For in this symbol, which is a passive-active relation or tension, we can see that the eternal Mystery of God flows back and forth between rest and "motion", between pure Unity in Stillness and its eternal grasping of itself in what we call the Trinity. The Taoist symbol can also stand for the Trinity proper. Yin-yang would be the Father-Son relationship and the Holy Spirit would be the Unity upon which the relation is predicated.

The Godhead eternally rests in the self-quietude of its essential Presence in which it is this great Silence, a flowing Presence of its Ident-ity in the act of its coming forth eternally from itself. The Godhead grasps its Identity first in the flowing Stillness of its nature where its threefold subsistent way of its inner life is hidden. The Identity of the Godhead is forever posited in the Stillness which permits the Presence to shine forth; for the flowing Stillness is the self-positing act of God's *Esse* in the eternal stability of that dynamic self-relatedness in which He *is* the entrance to total Meaning as Existence itself.

These two dimensions exist eternally in the Divine Life; both are necessary to God. They are, if you will, the "structure" of His actual-ity, for it is what constitutes God as actual. The Godhead and the Trinity are the *same* Reality.

The Trinity

In the Solitude of the Godhead there is yet a deep stirring, an echo of its ultimate truth, its Identity in that *community* of relatedness that is the Trinity. The Trinity is not just theological speculation but *is* the ultimate basis of all reality, actual and possible. Given the experience of God in the mystical state, the Trinity can be deduced and from this we can also deduce the Incarnation, which is the necessary consequence of God's Love within the triune Life of the Source and its outpouring into creation and creatures. This Love is the Son, the perfect expression of God's Love, Truth and nature in the Spirit.

The Godhead flows eternally into itself and from itself captures its threefold Identity in an implicit impulse to know itself, to grasp its everlasting Mystery. This impulse is the eternal Origin of the Father, Who rises in the Divine Stream as the Godhead's venture at comprehending its intelligibility. But the Father, as this impulse to know the inner Reality and Truth of the Divine Life, is not sufficient of Himself to reveal the Mystery in its infinite extent to the Divine Ground. But the Father, in His deeper truth, *is* the Godhead. The Godhead is a name for the Father as rest and as Origin.

When the Father comes forth eternally from the Godhead, He carries with Him the implicit, infinite Meaning of the Divine nature. But the Father of Himself cannot make this Meaning explicit. When the Father surrenders Himself to His essential nature, which is Love, then the Son is eternally generated as the being of this Love. This is much like what Panikkar says about the Divine Love. This Love or *kama* is the source of the energy of God, the *tapas*, which help to bring the world into existence.[13] This is the primordial love that is at the origin of the cosmos.[14] The Father lets go into Himself, and gives in to His essential impulse of Love, and the Son arises as the perfect expression of it, the One Who is there when the Father lets go, because He is the eternal result of the Father's act of Love. The Son is the concentration of God's inner being, this Love, which is also, in the Son, Knowledge and actuality in an Image that everlastingly reflects back to the Father the Reality of His nature. In this dialogical relationship or tension all truth is constituted and God's Knowledge and His Mystery are also eternally established. In the Father, the Source directs its implicit reality, which is undifferentiated. In the relationship of the Father and the Son, the reality of the Divine nature becomes explicit. For the Son grounds all Knowledge, Love and actuality in that metaphysical function of providing a "mirror" in which the Father may behold all that is in God's eternal Now.

The intensity of the relationship of the Father and the Son is too great for them to hold on to in themselves, thus, it overflows eternally into the Spirit Who unifies them in Himself and completes the Mystery, being the One Who resolves it for them and in them. There is no temporal beginning to the inner dynamic of the trinitarian Mystery, for it is always this ungraspable community of inter-relatedness at the Center of God's being.

We try to form an image of the Reality of the Trinity. And whether it is "pictured" in a mythic image or in theological "metaphors" or even if it is expressed in the most eloquent language possible, to the point of awakening the intuition of the Divine Triad, still it remains inaccessible to the human intellect to conceive and convey in language the absolute Reality, which is experienced in mystical consciousness, the Reality of the Divine that a soul may glimpse.

The Trinity is, furthermore, *Someone* Who happens eternally in Himself. The Divine Unity reflects itself in this essential happening within the Unity, an ultimate act, underived in itself, of *inter-relatedness* that makes God to be. For again, God is Trinity from an ontological necessity that is the fundamental law which eternally establishes Him as actual in Himself, in His Knowledge and in His Love.

The Trinity is the *key* to all reality. That is why it is found practically everywhere in either an incipient, intuitive form or in a more conscious theological formulation. For in Judaism, it is perhaps expressed as YAHWEH, the Eternal Torah, which is equal to the Word, and YAHWEH'S Spirit. Also, the *three* Angels, who approached Abraham, seem to symbolize the Truth of God's threefold nature; this is the anagogical meaning, the Truth that God wishes for us to realize.

In Hinduism, the intuition of the Trinity takes many forms, chief of which is the formulation *Satchitananda. Sat* is Absolute Being, equivalent to the Father; *Chit* is Absolute Consciousness or Knowledge and is equivalent to the Son, the Logos, and *Ananda* is Absolute Bliss, equivalent to the Holy Spirit. Of course the terms are different, but the insight approximates that of Christianity, because based on a contemplative experience. There are similar such insights in other traditions. We have already mentioned yin-yang in Taoism. The point is made, thus, it is not necessary to belabor it further in the traditions.

Panikkar also throws out a few ideas on the necessity of the Trinity in itself and as the *meeting* point of the future convergence of world religions in his little book, *The Trinity and The Religious Experience of Man.*[15] So we can go on and on discovering its traces everywhere. The real point is the *mystical* one, that is, to realize the Trinity in its own truth, in its indwelling within the soul, in that infinite happening in which God is this threefold Something. That Reality is beyond us in terms of understanding it in its Living truth. We can see it but we cannot hold on to what we see.

The Word

The Word

The Word, as the intelligibility of the Divine Life, is also the dynamic relation of the Son to the Father. The Word is the term of the dialogue that the Father addresses to His beloved Son; the Word, Christ is the expression of the Father's entire being and the most hidden secret of the Source. Panikkar, although in a slightly different context, speaks of the Word as the rational aspect of the Divine, what reveals its intelligibility to us.[16] Somehow, the Son draws into Himself the very substance of the Divine Impulse and becomes eternally that mystical point in which the Source, as Godhead via the coming forth of the Father, differentiates itself and beholds itself in the infinite categories of Divine Understanding unified in the Logos as Word. The Son, the Word articulates in Himself the entire extent of God's Wisdom, Knowledge and Love. As Panikkar says: "'. . . the Word is the first offspring of the Absolute and sprang from it in a peculiar way. In the last analysis God *has* no name because He Himself *is* Word."[17]

When the Trinity outpours its Love creation is the result. And all creation occurs through the principle of Divine intelligibility, that is, through the perfect Image of the Divine essence in which all form is eternally actual, and this is the Logos. Creation comes through the Son, the Logos. The exemplars of all things are grounded in His function; He sorts it all out in just being Who He is. His relation to the Father and to the Godhead gives form to all things. The dynamism of Love, in the inner Life of the Trinity, when it outflows, gives being to all that can, does and will exist.

Thus, the Incarnation was a supreme act of Divine Love. The Son entered our condition to give us the possibility of mystical Life in the Mystery of the Trinity and in the ineffable contemplative state of the Godhead. Christ came to reveal to us the Reality of God and to show us the Way to Divine Knowledge, and He *is* this Way. He came to share with us the Secret of God's inner truth. Panikkar puts it another way: "Man is Word shared . . . Man is by participation in the Word."[18] Again, the Son came to redeem us from the chief effect of sin —ignorance for there is only one ignorance as such and that is ignorance that God is. In the same way, there is only one true Wisdom, the Knowledge of God, the realization that God is and the mystical awareness of His Presence. But what is the role of the community, especially the Church in spiritual existence?

The Church

God has raised up the Church in history and in our lives to be the communal focus, in the sacramental life, of our journey to Him. For she is the Divine Purpose unfolding itself in time and space. The Church is the universal structure through which all people will ultimately be *reconciled*. Her function is to gather all peoples together who seek the Truth, and to facilitate their growth in the Knowledge of God; she also bears the *responsibility* in charity to address herself to the cries of the poor and the starving of all nations. In this, she must continually do what she can to meet these needs, especially to constantly remind those who are better off of their absolute *duty* to feed the starving of the world, to make substantial and lasting contributions to the material and Spiritual development of the oppressed. The Church is God's Purpose unfolding in her members, for the members are the Church, but the Church also transcends the members. The Church is also history, the vast array of the saints in all ages. We are all *one*, because we have all come forth from the same Source. One day, we will be judged on this very question of our response to the needs of those who daily face the prospects of starvation. The saints in every period have always tried to meet the needs of the poor. The Church must also lead the way for Humanity's *survival*. Whe must *seize* the *initiative* of history and suggest an alternative to the two political ideologies that have brought the Human Race to the point where man is threatened in his very existence. Furthermore, given her universal extent, in the possibility of a global confrontation of nations, she holds the *key* to *reconciliation* and peace.

God has formed His Church from His everlasting Word, and she is the future for Humanity here and in the Eternal Kingdom. For Mankind's evolution will converge into the Church and she will be the "place" where the Spiritual development of Humanity will intensify to the point of a great psychic leap, a quantum leap in consciousness. This is the implication of the convergence of world religions. The Church is from eternity directed to the unification of human consciousness in the global dimension of a higher Purpose, which is the Divine Purpose.

Prayer and Mysticism

Prayer, contemplation or mystical experience is what constitutes us as fully developed human beings in the profoundest sense. It is important, thus, to reiterate this point. Panikkar attests to this great truth when he says that: ". . . prayer considered as man's authentic act (is) the act by which he reveals himself as he really is, and through which reality is revealed to him".[19] The desire of the soul to return to the

Source is a much deeper desire than even the erotic. Prayer is man's reaching out to God as well as his quiet attention to the Divine action within his being, at the core, in the "cave of the heart" where the soul meets God.

When prayer passes beyond words, images, the senses and the reason and enters into the Silence of the Divine Presence, when it becomes a "loving gaze at God through the will",[20] to use Thomas Keating's expression taken from the tradition of St. Gregory the Great, then it becomes *contemplation* and the beginning of the *tasting* knowledge of God that we call the *mystical*.

Mysticism, the final term of contemplation, in its fuller sense designates that ineffable opening up of the soul to the Impulse coming from God, to that absolute reality of being drawn into the blissful embrace of the Divine Unity in which the soul knows nothing except the inscrutable Mystery of the Source. The soul is united to the celestial Stream that flows into the Presence of the Godhead's Desert, where all is Still in God's fathomless inner truth. For the soul is like a tiny island in God's boundless Sea. It reveals a knowledge whose parameters are infinite, embracing a Meaning that has no limits. God is this Meaning, and it is so luminous that it cannot be described or grasped; it can only be known *in* and through His very Life. In the future, as Thomas Keating says, people will no longer be satisfied or impressed by theory; they will *only* listen to those who *know* from a direct contact with the divine.[21]

8

THE MYSTERY OF GOD

When the mystics, theologians and philosophers say that God is ultimately incomprehensible, ineffable and indefinable, they are really saying that He is a Mystery. God is a Mystery, because the human intellect cannot conceive of Him or when it does encounter Him, understand what it experiences. Thus, the question or the *certainty* of God's being begins and ends in Mystery. One might well ask, why then write on the Mystery of the Divine? That God is inscrutable or incomprehensible does not mean that we cannot have some knowledge of Him, even though such knowledge be constricted in range and content. What we propose here is to approach God mystically, and this is what we have been doing in the preceding chapters, and is essentially what we will do in the subsequent ones. Before we do this, however, let us make some philosophical preparation in order to justify our move into the unfathomable realm of Mysticism. It is important to remember that the focus of this essay is God's Mystery, His unknowability for us in this life insofar as reason is concerned, hence His Reality in its mystical dimension, which is God in Himself, though communicated by the poor instrumentality of concepts. This chapter is, thus, metaphysical insofar as we consider God philosophically in the way of a preparation for the event of the absolute mystical state, which we shall attempt to describe (though most inadequately), and is mystical insofar as we try to give some insight into God's actual being in its inner nature as it touches the mystical heights of the absolute experience. The thrust of what we are trying to say gropes toward the communication of the inexpressible. The point is that we wish to convey something of this Mystery, something of its meaning precisely as it is a mystical event. The emphasis is, thus, the *mystic* glance into Truth, or the product of such a glance, the vital Truth of the actual, living experience of God in Himself. Here we are considering the most quintessential intuitions and experiences, beyond the familiar world, plunging into the Divine darkness, where, as William Johnston says: "...when the eye of love becomes accustomed to the dark, it perceives that the darkness is light and the void is plenitude."[1]

In the way of building a foundation that philosophically justifies our procedure toward the supernatural (as if it needed justification, as it is its own justification), we will attempt to establish God's existence; to prove that He is personal and this necessarily, showing what this term signifies when referred to God. We will also attempt to establish that God is Trinity from the intrinsic necessity of being constituted eternally as God. It should become clear that philosophy or metaphysics contributes something essential to the structure of our knowledge of the Divine Mystery but as such barely touches the content of this knowledge. This will give us a better understanding of the limits of reason and of the boundlessness of Mystical Wisdom. It is also crucial to remember that philosophical demonstration only establishes the necessity for God to exist as the Ground of Being, intelligibility and order etc.; it does not give absolute certitude. Certitude must rest on the concurrence of the intellect and the will in the act of assent, and absolute certitude usually results only from the intensity and luminosity of mystical experience itself, which cannot be doubted or denied.

There are countless ways to establish God's existence, but the way of *necessity* is one of the most straightforward. That is to say, the consideration of the question of necessity leads to an awareness of God as the essence of Truth itself. It is one of the doors (a sure one) to metaphysical consciousness, to that absolute science and *seeing* of first principles as they are the ground of reality. For Metaphysics *is* actually a question of seeing with the intellect and not essentially in the form of ratiocination, which is an extremely primitive stage of metaphysical thought, the level of elements patched together, rather than genuine insight. The act of the intellect in which true Metaphysics occurs is a *sudden flash* of understanding or intellectual vision in which the mind just *sees* the absolute structure of reality. Metaphysics is not something that can be learned from books. In books, we learn only the concepts, notions and movements of the intellect in the metaphysical process. When we know Metaphysics, then we can proceed through the movements and capture the truth that transcends the words. Metaphysics is fundamentally a question of a pre-rational (though not an unintelligible) *act of Being* in which the intellect sees how reality is constituted in this act as a process of the Absolute. It is extraordinarily *simple* but takes great effort to retain; it must be worked at constantly. It is a very precious knowledge. Metaphysics is really a higher form of consciousness; we may even call it, in the act as such of the insight into Being, a kind of speculative mysticism.

Now in relation to necessity, the most basic question we can ask about anything is: why is it? When we ask this question, it shows us the object's radical contingency. For what necessity allows it to be? What necessity allows anything to be? As an example, what necessity is there for gravity to hold true? Other than God, what inherent necessity is there for it? Probability is no answer, since it is a disguised form of necessity and because, as conceived in mathematics or philosophy, it cannot explain the required neceesity in cosmological law, nor the necessity operative in biological processes. Indeed, it is one thing to insist on a "fortuitous" arrangement of the material elements of creation (which is most dubious at best), but quite another to elicit the required structure of say, a flower from the simultaneous gathering of the events (chemical and otherwise) that are involved in the development of a flower. The flower is a creature having perfection of form. Where is the necessity that would move a blind process to make the judgment that the perfected form of the flower is preferable to a haphazard from? We can perhaps account for the elements coming together, but what decrees that something as beautiful and as ordered in structure as a flower should arise? It is, thus, all a question of necessity, and God is the Source of that necessity required for anything to be.

We can also offer a cosmological proof. The universe in its material element — matter is — finite, which is self-evident upon reflection when we consider the meaning or role of space in relation to matter. (If one were to give an answer to this from Idealism or Rationalism, we will remark, yes, but even if space, time and matter are mind-dependent, still a ground of necessity *must* found the mind's grasp of intelligibility and its very existence.) Of course this argument presupposes Realism. Space as such represents the container and the limit of the material aspect. Because space is a real element of the staging or props of existence, one is able to sit and write, read, talk, pray, or do whatever we are doing. Space allows us the "place". But space is also the *limit* of matter and as such constitutes the negation of matter's absoluteness. Space prevents matter from being infinite or unlimited. This has important consequences. One of which is that because space is or exists as actual (a factor in the cosmic order), matter is, thus, finite. And because matter is finite, it must have a limited or finite number of causes in relation to time, since a finite degree of magnitude cannot sustain an infinite series of cuases, as a finite universe lacks the necessary ground to posit the intelligible laws that operate in the cosmological rendering of order in the universe. Nor can a finite series originate the chain of causes. The finite number of causes *must* ultimately be traceable to a First Cause, and this is God. This builds on St. Thomas' approach.[2] It is clear that these arguments do not elucidate the Mystery of God; they at least, perhaps, establish that there is indeed such a Mystery.

That God is personal and loves and cares for His creatures can be seen in His regard for and attention to the vast detials of creation and life. From His intimate knowledge of detail we can know that He must be personal, but we cannot conceive what it is for Him to be personal. Certainly, it is different for Him, since He is personal in His own unique way, in an unlimited degree and much greater in its depth of intimacy. For us to be persons automatically indicates limitation, since we are bounded by the parameters of space, time and the condition of corporeality, but for Him, it must mean the actualization and perfection of His love for His cratures. In the long run, God's Personhood means that He *cares*, that He is not impersonal, a mere blind force, but an intelligent being Who is concerned for His creation. And His concern is precisely revealed in His attention to the details, even though they may seem to us as petty. Nothing is petty or insignificant to God, for he beholds it all in His eternal Now.

The Godhead

The eternal starting point of the Divine Mystery is, again, the obscure role of the Godhead. A few mystics in the Christian Tradition make constant reference to it (and this is true of many other traditions as well), but its place within the Divine nature is as much of a puzzle as is God himself. The Godhead as such seems to be the foundation of God's essence; it is the bottomless well of God's being. Somehow, it is central to the Mystery itself. The Godhead seems to be God in total self-contemplation. In this contemplation, God is aware of His Mystery as Silence and Divine Stillness. This Stillness is the infinte Presence of God in Himself. It is a flowing Presence, dynamic, grounded on the absolute immutability of God's being. It is a pure *thereness*, a *dwellingness* fully present to itself as actual, totally self-luminous. This dwellingness of God is the unlimited Mystery of His absolutely definite Presence to Himself, in His own translucent Reality, a Presence that proclaims itself as that which it must and can only be. This Presence is God's home; it is His very self. The Godhead, as Ground of the Divine Life, is again, as the Pseudo-Dionysius says, the unmanifested or undifferentiated "side" of God's nature.[3] As unmanifested Ground, the Godhead is the nameless form, because free of all form and concept in itself. As the Ultimate Form it is above apprehension, ungraspable in itself. Everything dwells in the Ground of the Godhead in a state of essentail *implicitness*.[4] But this implicitness is more than mere potentiality; it is the state of reality in its eternal contemplative rest, before creation, in the Divine Fount of Unity, actual but secure in the Absolute Beginning, in that "place" where it always IS. This means that the Godhead is ontologically the Immovable Center, the rest from which all motion comes forth, whether metaphysical or local. For motion presupposes rest as its necessary condition. The Godhead is the Quietness of Being, the contemplative gazing at all possibility, the disinterested, passive awareness of the full range of all Being. And Being is that which keeps reality in act. In the Godhead, the Divine is pure Unity of essence grasping itself in the flow of its Presence, in the Stillness of its infinite Stability, grounded on the absolute necessity of its existence as the Eternal Center, underived in itself, of all reality in itself. It so fully is that nothing can hinder it. As St. Thomas says, the essence of God, and we can also say, of the Godhead itself, is to be, to exist;[5] He *is* Existence. In this notion of *aseity* of St. Thomas, what we have just discussed, that God is Pure Act in Himself (aseitas), we can see something so fundamental to God and the Godhead, that is, the absolute possession of *esse* as the essential nature of the Divine insofar as its being is concerned. God is the very act of TO BE in Himself, because He alone possesses the act in His Unity which flows from His Simplicity. Again, since God is simple in being, His essence and His existence are *one* act, thus, He *is Esse*, the very source of it, that which makes existence itself to be.

The Godhead as such is complete self-repose, free of all activity. The Trinity is the *active* dimension or "side" of the Divine Life. The Godhead is, as Eckhart says, *unnatured nature*, because it does nothing (it natures nothing), neither does it create nor maintain anything in being, although all things are because it is. Creation and maintenance in being come through the Trinity, and especially through the Word. The Godhead just is.[6] It is self-sufficient contemplation of itself, unconcerned with what is beyond its inner truth. This is God before He creates but also as He is simultaneously active or Trinity. The Divine Ground of the Godhead, the Abyss and the Desert or Wilderness is ontologically prior to the creative, dynamic dimension, as unity is prior to Trinity, even though the passive aspect dwells in the same unity of essence with the active, dynamic aspect which is called the Trinity. Eternally, God is Godhead and Trinity in the identical, changeless act in which He is God.

The Godhead is the Center, radiating point of all reality and being; it is the seedbed of all essence. In its profound Stillness of Unity it makes all things to be possible. It gives them their foundation in the life-giving Center of all actuality that it is in itself. For the Godhead is the complete authenticity of existence in the intrinsic point of its Unity, grounded in its absolute holding of the eternal moment of existence, which is necessary, in that fecundity where all possibility dwells. IT is the eternal wellspring or underived Origin of its Absolute Truth. It holds on to existence insofar as it *is* Existence in its very Center of Unity. God eternally becomes what He already and always is. His being is becoming always what it is in itself, ever anew and yet unbegotten. For His becoming is not a process of development in which He adds reality to Himself (that is the illusion of Process Thought); it is the eternal realization of what He has always been and always will be. Eckhart says of the inner truth of the Godhead that:

> The Godhead in itself is motionless Unity and balanced Stillness and is the Source of all emanations. Hence I assume a passive welling-up. We call this first utterance being, for the most intrinsic utterance, the first formal assumption in the Godhead is being: being as essential Word. God is being, but being is not God.[7]

Eckhart is saying that the Godhead rests in the Unity of its Stillness, which is the balance of a unity that comes forth from the Stillness as the Presence of God in the Mystery of His existence as He is self-possessed in Himself. The Stillness, as His living Presence in the identity of His act, is balanced in relation to the motionless stability of His eternal essence which is founded upon His Unity, and is actually balanced in relation to the dynamic aspect, the Trinity. Thus, His Presence to Himself must conform to His essential Unity, which is to say, His Stillness as His Mysterious Presence to His act of being must be a *flowingness* of His undiminshed energy that is yet encompassed by His Unity. Hence, His Presence, as the Stillness, the fount of Being and Truth, is balanced in its flow in order to embrace always the Unity that makes God to be the Absolute Identity that He is, and the triune act that comprehends the Unity.

Now, insofar as the Godhead is beyond Being, even though Being arises from it, it is of a different order. God is Being in His act of existence, but Being or existence does not exhaust the Mystery of His inner truth, that which is His underived nature. Being is not God, since it comprehends that which is not God. For God transcends everything in His Truth, but Being comes forth from Him as a free expression of His *Esse*, His act of TO BE. We participate in His act. His first utterance is the Word, which is the Father seeking the Mystery's resolution in the Son, and this constitutes the possibility and actuality of Being. The passive welling-up is the Father bringing the Mystery eternally into manifested Being.

Insofar as the Godhead is beyond form, concept, activity, it is precisely no-thing in particular. This realization is what prompted Eckhart, following the Pseudo-Dionysius, to speak of the Godhead as nothing, meaning the absence of all form, concept and activity in His Presence, in HIs inner life.[8] This is what Eckhart means when he refers again and again to the Abyss,[9] Desert, the Solitude or Wilderness of the Godhead.[10] These conceptions, which we will have more to say about in the essay on Eckhart, are attempts to express the contemplative Center that is the Living Fount of the Divine Reality and creativity, that essential rest from which arises eternally the act of dialogical unity that is the Trinity as well as the gift of creation.[11]

We can make two observations about the Godhead at this point. First, the chief importance of this notion, in relation to the *synthesis* of the various world religious traditions, is that it presents us with a *bridge* to Buddhism. For the notion of the Godhead approximtes that of the Void, and the content known in the mystical state of Nirvana. The second observation is that the Divine is an Absolute Unity, and when we try to assert one dimension as superior to another, we are actually impoverishing our understanding of the Mystery of God, which somehow in truth requires and harmonizes in itself both dimensions. But in terms of human life, the Trinity would seem to have greater significance, providing we remember that it rests on the Immovable stability of the Ground, which is the Godhead, and this permits it to be, while the Trinity permits the Godhead to know itself. The Godhead is, as Panikkar says, "a sort of bottomless interiority, infinitely interior to itself."[12]

The Trinity

It is clear to those who have been exposed to the issue, that the Divine Mystery possesses an inherent dynamic aspect, which constitutes God as God, since it grounds Him in His self-knowledge and in His being, as has been indicated above. For the Godhead would not be if the dynamic Trinity were not, as the Godhead is known and *is* only in relation to the pure illuminating knowledge and being of the Persons in the Trinity, Who reveal the Divine Ground to itself and take their being from it, since it is the secret of the Trinity as such, just as the Trinity is the condition for it to be known. There is, thus, a mutual give and take between the Godhead and the Trinity, which necessarily establishes both aspects of the Divine Unity in this relation of Abyss to Trinity or Ground to functions. Indeed, the Persons are ontological functions in the Divine Life, which establish God eternally as God. St. Augustine calls the Persons relations, thus, he was aware of their eternal constituting role, that in some crucial way, they are necessary to God's actual existence. These three relations share the same substance and yet the relations are not accidental to God but necessary.[13] Augustine says, furthermore, that what is predicated of the Persons is not predicated of them in themselves but only in relationship to each other and in relation to the creation, and this includes creatures.[14] The relations that the Persons are in the Divine act or *dialogue*, a community of Persons, are what distinguish them ontologically from one another and what prevents them from being reduced to each other as functions.[15]

The functions, relations or Persons are eternally generated from the Abyss of the Godhead, in which the Father stirs as the essential longing of God to know Himself. For there is in the Godhead, in its Stillness, an implicit Divine Meaning, the Secret of how God is, and this attempts to express itself in order that it may grasp its (the longing of the Father) intelligibility and permit God as such to know Himself and, thus, to be Himself. For the Father *is* the Voice of God crying in the Wilderness of the Divine Ground, in the Desert of His own being. The Father eternally prepares the Way for the Son and for the absolute grounding of the Divine nature, all knowledge and of creation in the Son.

This does not mean that Being and intelligibility are interchangeable in God's Mind, but it does mean that an aspect of the Divine Mystery is that it is intelligible to God, Who is Supreme Meaning in His act of existence as well as in His Awesome Holiness. Because God is meaningful in Himself, Being is intelligible, and because Being is intelligible, knowledge is possible.

When the Father stirs in the Godhead and comes forth eternally as the Meaning or Mystery seeking understanding, He everlastingly generates the Son as the concentrated Center of this Meaning or Mystery, the Image of it, and hence the *key* to the Mystery. But the Father is as such, as Rahner says, "the unoriginated Who is essentially invisible and Who shows and reveals Himself only by uttering His Word to the world."[16] The Son is the one Who, in His eternal function, permits the Meaning to be grasped in the Mind of the Father. The Father in and through the Son, as St. Hillary says, is the Source of Truth and of all things.[17] But, again, the dialogical relationship existing between the Father and the Son is emphatically necessary for anything to be, including the Divine Mystery itself. For that relationship is the essence of the Mystery. In concentrating the Divine essence, the Secret of God's being in the Son, a vital and necessary *contrast* is struck between the

Father as knower and the Son as known (and vice versa), but the moment, which is eternal, that the Father sees His Son as His Meaning, the Son in turn sees the Father as His own Meaning. Together, they realize that they are one and the same Eternal Meaning, sharing the same intimate essence, that is grounded on an infinite Mystery, which the Holy Spirit alone completes in their understanding. The Holy Spirit eternally illuminates the Mystery for them. The Son is the medium of the Father's knowledge, Who in knowing the Word, knows Himself and all things. St. Hillary states that between the Father and the Son there is a perfect, mutual knowledge,[18] which exists precisely because of and in their relationship.

The contrast between the Father and the Son is what makes God's knowledge to be eternally understood, since it is, thus, manifested from its undifferentiated universality and revealed in the medium-reflecting function of the Son. In this contrast there is an intensity that is too great for them, and this intensity of their unutterable communion overflows eternally into the Spirit, Who unifies them and also Himself with them in the inner life of the Trinity. For the Holy Spirit *is* the Divine intensity of Love, which is the mutual affirmation and recognition of the Father and Son. The Holy Spirit *gathers* up the Father and the Son and unifies them eternally *in* Himself as Trinity, in such a way that He is the absolute bond that constitutes the Trinity in its Esse and in its content, which is the Mystery of the Holiness of God. We will return to this theme again.

In an attempt to catch a glimpse of the essential activity that is present in the relations of the Persons, to get at that primary *unmoving-movement* that establishes all Knowledge, Being and Love, Eckhart describes the inner reality of the Trinity as similar to a play, always going on, in which the play, the players and the audience are the *same*, and the script is known before hand.[19] We will come back to this interesting point in the chapter on Eckhart.

For what is the Trinity but God knowing and loving Himself eternally in the simplicity of an act which establishes distinction in function in order to behold the Unity and the Meaning of the Mystery as it exists in God. This is the precise reason why God *must* be Trinity. The Trinity, furthermore, as a set of relations or functions within the Divine Nature, constitutes God as God by establishing eternally His self-knowledge and His very being. This point cannot be emphasized enough. The essential reality of God and of His self-knowledge is grounded on the dialogical contrast between the Father, as Source and the Son, as Word, Logos or Meaning of God, which permits the Father to know Himself and the Son to know Himself in the Father. Both are forever held together in being in the Spirit, Who is their relationship (its content) as Conscious of itself, aware that He is them also, and is, thus, the foundation of their mutual self-donation. From this three-fold [20] movement all reality is born, for creation proceeds from it. The first movement is from the Father to the Son. The second is from the Son to the Father, and the third *is* the movement* of the Holy Spirit proceeding from both, to both, in both and unifying them both in Himself as witness and essential content of their essence. For God to be and to know Himself, He must be dynamic; He must be two. But for the contrast to be, which is what allows Him to know Himself in the Father and the Son, it has to be *unified* and eternally witnessed to. This is the crucial function of the Holy Spirit. Thus, God *is* necessarily Trinity. Hopefully, the above comments have reasonably established this very important point.

To get an inkling of this, an intuition of it is to see that what the Trinity is, is not some decorative piece of Medieval speculation, like the illuminations on a manuscript, but is, metaphysically, the very basis of reality; it is the heart of the Christian Mystery. For in these three basic ontological movements, relations, functions, Conscious "graspings", which are like a mystic dance at the Center of the God-head eternally happening, all reality arises and comes forth. It is the "simple", Absolute Beginning of all things. This is one reason why Panikkar remarks that: "The Trinity, then, may be considered as a junction where the authentic spiritual dimensions of all religions meet." [21] Why is this so? First, because it integrates the three different spiritualities that Panikkar discusses, and secondly as well as more importantly, because it reflects the most essential, far-reaching and truest insight into the structure of Being and the dynamic inner life of God.

We often hear the expression today "God as mother", which has its origin in the Indian Tradition. It is important to realize, however, that in God there is no gender, and that what is gender in created being, in this life, is ontologically polarity in God. God in Himself is neither male nor female, and yet we speak of Him as He. Why is this so? We do this because it designates that God is pure activity in Himself and that He is purely actual in His essence, thus, we refer to Him as He. We also refer to God in this way because this is the way He has revealed Himself to us in the Old and New Testaments. Jesus spoke again and again about His Father. We must also remember that in God there is a constant give and take, which finds its expression in the dialogical, inner relations of the Trinity. In the Trinity, it is a passive-active or active-receptive polarity. If, however, we must speak of gender in God, we could say that passivity in the Divine is *like* the feminine element and activity is *like* that of the masculine. In order to avoid misunderstanding, we have to keep in mind that we are not predicating gender of God, nor do we have any sympathy for such a notion. We are simply saying that human gender has its ontological basis, its origin in God's necessary polarity of activity and passivity. Furthermore, we have to be very careful lest we reduce the Divine to the *anthropocentric*, which is one of the tendencies of our age. To suggest such a reduction is a great error, because God in Himself is totally Other than the human. Such an assertion would destroy His Unity in our knowledge and degrade His Mystery, dragging it down to the merely human level, something which might give comfort to a few, but at the price of Truth. God's being is *sui generis*, unique, for He is His own Absolute Genus and Species, and His Difference makes Him infinitely greater than we. This is one reason why many mystics insist that He is even above or beyond Being. They say this because Being is not a term that can capture the human and the Divine in one and the same category. The Divine is its own Reality. It is not that the mystics wish to deny Being to God, but rather to say that Being in God or as God is wholly different from created Being. To return to the immediate issue, when the Father gives His being to the Son, the Son is passive, because He is receiving and *vice versa*, when the Son communicates His essence to the Father, which is the same as the Father's essence, the Father is receptive to the Son. And when God proceeds *ad extra* to creatures and sustains them and the entire cosmic order via His Providence, then He is fulfilling the maternal aspect of the Divine nature, for He is "mothering" His world. It is in this theological insight, which we call Providence, that the Church has always acknowledged the maternal aspect of God, the receptive polarity, [22] which in this instance expresses itself as *care* and protection. Julian of Norwich greatly enlarges upon this theme of the maternal or providential aspect of God. She calls Christ "Mother Jesus", which may at first seem strange, but she does this because, like the mother who feeds and cares for her children, Our Blessed Lord feeds and cares for us unto Eternal Life. He does this of course with His Body and Blood, always caring for us. [23] And this concern for us flows from His wonderful Love.

God's Nature

Here we come to one of the central issues in the question of the Divine Mystery. When we speak of nature, we mean the act that is characteristic of God, what He is in Himself, what He is in the Persons of the Trinity and what He is in the Godhead itself.

St. Thomas says that God's nature is essentially *Esse* or the pure act of TO BE.[24] He *is* Existence, as has been mentioned above. What does this mean? Is it possible for us to understand that which is pure existence itself? Can the intellect conceive of it? To understand or conceive it would require that we understand God. We can merely refer to *aseity* as proper to God, but we cannot specify the meaning of it.

In having this insight into the Divine nature, we really only have the structure of a concept, as we do not know what it means in God's very act of being to be the pure actuality of what He is. Existence belongs to Him as the essence of His being. Whereas, we *have* existence from Him as a gift, He *is* Existence itself, for He is the One Who causes to be. He is that Divine spark in the soul that makes the soul to exist. So much is He God that He is the very act of that which makes Him to be.

St. Bonaventure, following the lead of St. Thomas, agrees that Being or Esse is the name of God, that which is characteristic of His nature. For God is *He Who Is*. And this is His primary name in relation to His Unity,[25] the "how" of His nature, how He is God. Somehow, Bonaventure must have seen that Esse just did not express for us something we could hold on to, thus, he placed the emphasis on God's essence as *Goodness*. Here he follows the Pseudo-Dionysius, who follows Christ.[26] He says that Goodness is the very name of the Trinity itself, and having this nature, it is self-diffusive to the highest degree.[27] And this is why God creates, that is, He creates in order to *share* what He has and is with His creatures, which is Himself. As a consequence, whether Bonaventure knew it or not, he was actually specifying the Esse of God as equal to the Goodness proper to Him. That is to say, Bonaventure builds on Thomas' insight. We can say that the Esse of God, His pure act *is* His Goodness; His actuality is Goodness. But now we must ask what this Goodness itself is. The answer would seem to he *hesed,* the Hebrew word for God's Holiness. God's *act of To Be*, His Esse is Goodness and His Goodness is ultimately His *hesed* or Holiness. But then what is holiness in God? Or how is God this Holiness? When we come to this question then we are right back at the beginning, because His Holiness is the profound Mystery of His Love. God's Love, His self-diffusiveness is the result of His inner being, which is Holiness. God's Holiness is the purity of His Love united to the Mystery of His Otherness, a sacred Otherness in terms of which He is this Love. It is a pure energy always sharing itself. It is God's 'indwelling', which arises as the "free spiritual personal act" among the Persons.[28] This Love or Holiness has an awesome character, which reflects its ultimate Mystery.

The Holiness of God, which is the actuality of His nature, that pure sacred love, wells up eternally as God's energies, coming forth from the Stillness of the Source, the Godhead. The Stillness is the infinite Presence of God to His Unity, flowing into the infinite act of eternally positing Himself in the place of His own Esse, His Goodness, His Holiness, His pure Love, His Stillness, a flowing ever into Himself, comprehending Himself in the *unmoving-movement* of the dialogical relations of the Trinity in which His knowledge and His holy Love are eternally established "in the threefold relative way in which God subsists".[29]

God dwells in Stillness because Stillness is the stability of His act of being. Because He already is actual, He is, thus, Still. He does not need to move or become. Stillness flowing into Stillness is yet Still, because Stillness does not move. It is the Mystery of an *unmoving-movement*. Flowing into Himself, God is being eternally Who He is. He is the Stillness of what dwells in the Stillness, which is the Presence of Himself, a Mystery that is eternally manifested in the Trinity where it is understood. In the same way, God is Silence, becuase there is nothing for Him to say that is not already said in His Son, the Word, Who expresses the Mystery and being of God, the Mystery of His Love, loving being and life into all things, as St. Ignatius says.[30]

In the Stillness flowing into itself, which is the Godhead, Unity comprehends Identity in Trinity and Trinity establishes knowledge and the possibility of creation, which is a flowing into multiplicity without being diminished. This entire dynamic happens within the compass of Divine simplicity. For God is one but in the Unity is the contrastive principle, the Trinity, which makes the Identity of God known to Himself in being the relations and essential *act* of the Trinity.

In the flowing Stillness of the Divine Abyss, Unity grasps Identity first as the Presence of Mystery, which wells up eternally as the Father, Who carries forth the act of self-comprehension in the generation of the Son and its unification in the Holy Spirit. For the Father is the Stillness stirring or flowing into the Godhead, the pure act of Unity in essence established in the Stability of a simple self-presence to itself in its act of self-posited, eternal quietude of being. The Persons, as sharing the same Unity of essence and substance, have their being in the Godhead, thus, they are Present there in a state of mystical contemplation of the Infinite Stillness of God. But they are Present just as well, and they communicate their nature to the Source. For in the Godhead, they are implicit spiritual functions; they are the eternal Presence of God's Mystery comprehending itself as they eternally arise via the Father from the Abyss into the act in which they are Trinity. The Persons, flowing into the Stillness, are directed in the Father's focus to the act of the Triune relations. The Father is the representative of the Godhead Who comes forth as its essence express- ed in His meaning in the Son or Logos and reintegrated in Unity, yet retaining distrinctions, in the Spirit. Ultimately, God is a Unity above unity or a oneness that is more than unity, because it is a dynamic Unity in which distinctions eternally arise as the necessary condition for God to be, to know Himself and to love, as we have said again and again before. For God can only be becuase He knows Himself, and He knows Himself because He is dynamic or Trinity, and He is able to love because He both is and knows what He is, which is Holy Love conscious of itself in the infinite act of being Holy Love and the Presence of Infinite Truth in the act of being Infinite Truth. And in the dialogical movement that does not move, God catches His Identity eternally in its act of being.

The Mystical Event

The absolute mystical state in which the soul receives the grace of union to the fullest extent possible in this life is an experience of *virtual* identity with God in which she perceives in and through God's act of knowledge, being and love. For God draws the soul into the Transcendent Vitality of His inner life, into His eternal Energies of Love and unites the soul with that Stream that flows into the God- head. Thus, the soul enters into the incomprehensible Stillness of the Divine Abyss and becomes a witness to its Mystery, a dark, obscure knowledge, not comprehending what is being encountered. The soul sees it from within God, not from within her usual conditions of knowledge in the corporeal situation of human nature. Here the soul is elevated to a higher form of knowing in which God does the work and the soul receives, though ill prepared to understand the content of the Impulse of God's Infinite being, Meaning and Love. As the Pseudo-Dionysius says, the soul is "led upwards to the Ray of that divine Darkness which exceedeth all existence." [31] This darkness is an excess of Light; it is God's Boundless Meaningfulness, which is a total Mystery to the human intellect. The soul knows God in a *unitive* way and possesses a *certitude* that is absolute, but she does not understand what she knows. How can it be understood? We do not have the concepts with which to organize the Reality of God's

Infinite Meaning and Love. This experience is one of pure Mystery
even in the intimacy of mystical union. God is a supreme Mystery
in Himself, and we try to articulate it but we cannot. It is beyond
our feeble capacities of conception and imagination. For God dwells
in that Superessential Darkness. He is "that One which is beyond all
things." [32] If our ideas are useless as aids to know Him or His nature,
why do we cling to them? The price for Divine Knowledge is to let
go of these our poor conceptions. We must let go of the ego, and this
includes our thoughts. We have to let go into God and allow Him
to take hold of us in our will and in our consciousness. We must
plunge into "the Darkness of Unknowing", passing beyond our awkward attempts at understanding, and, thus, giving ourselves completely to Him, we are united to Him. When our faculties are *quiet*, the
intellect is elevated into the Vision of God in His 'Darkness', in His
unlimited Mystery. In letting go of "all knowledge he (the soul) possesses a knowledge that exceeds his understanding."[RR] The soul must
enter into that secret place in the heart where God dwells. And the
Presence of God in the soul, in mystical union, is more certain than
the light of the dawn, and more lovely, as St. John of the Cross says. [34]
It is a secret knowledge that only the soul knows first hand who receives it from God. It is the intimate knowledge of the Presence of
God welling up in the soul's core, the "cave of the heart". John of
the Cross describes the ascent of the soul through darkness into the
Light of contemplation, and encourages us to persevere in the mystical
quest in his inspiring poem, "More Stanzas Applied to Spiritual Things:

> *I went out seeking love,*
> *And with unfaltering hope*
> *I flew so high, so high,*
> *That I overtook the prey.*

> 1. That I might take the prey
>   Of this adventuring in God
>   I had to fly so high
>   That I was so lost from sight,
>   And though in this adventure
>   I faltered in my flight,
>   Yet love had already flown so high
>   That I took the prey.

> 2. When I ascended higher
>   My vision was dazzled,
>   And the most difficult conquest
>   Was achieved in darkness;

But since I was seeking love
The leap I made was blind and dark
And I rose so high, so high,
That I took the prey.

3. The higher I ascended
In this so lofty seeking
The lower and more subdued
And abased I became.
I said: No one can overtake it,
And sank, ah, so low,
That I was so high, so high,
That I took the prey.

4. In a wonderful way
My one flight surpassed a thousand,
For the hope of heaven
Attains as much as it hopes for;
This seeking is my only hope
And I have not been disappointed,
Because I flew so high, so high,
That I took the prey. [35]

And in his poem entitled, "Commentary Applied to Spiritual Things",
one of two poems bearing this title, John of the Cross tells us that
God alone suffices, even in darkness and spiritual trial, because one
has heaven, has Him, the Living flame of Love:

Without support and with support,
Living without light, in darkness,
I am wholly being consumed.

1. My soul is disentangled
From every created thing
And lifted above itself
In a life of delight
Supported only in God.
So now it can be said
That I most value this:
My soul now sees itself
Without support and with support.

2. And though I suffer darkness
   In this mortal life,
   That is not so hard a thing;
   For though I have no light
   I have the life of heaven.
   For the blinder love is
   The more it gives such life,
   Holding the soul surrendered,
   Living without light, in darkness.

3. After I have known it
   Love works so in me
   That whether things go well or badly
   Love turns all to one sweetness
   Transforming the soul in itself
   And so in its delighting flame
   Which I fell within me,
   Swiftly, with nothing spared,
   I am wholly being consumed. [36]

The Infinite Love of God, being boundless, is beyond definition and even beyond cognition in the sense of grasping its plentitude. We can enter it, and it enters us, but we cannot express it in language; it cannot even be thought, although we come close in poetry, and closer still in silence. When God enters the soul by grace or when we become aware of His Presence as a result of grace, it is yet a mysterious Presence, since we do not know when God comes, goes and returns again. Again, as St. Bernard says, we cannot determine when God comes, for we are just aware of Him, [37] and do not think during the encounter in the soul's center. God touches or takes hold of the soul. He invades her being. And this union lasts but for a moment. When it does occur, as St. Teresa of Avila attests, all of the senses are suspended while the transformation into God lasts. [38] But there can be no doubt that God was there, for the mystical union confers this absolute *certitude* on the intellect and its act of understanding. [39]

In the mystical state, the soul comes into the Stillness flowing into itself. She is united to the stirring in the Abyss that is the Father eternally rising from the Divine Ground. She witnesses the act in which He concentrates His being in the Image, which is His Son. The soul participates in the absolute metaphysical *unmoving-movement* in which the Persons as functions perform eternally the *act* that establishes God in His being and is the origin of creation **ad extra**. The soul witnesses the Spirit gathering the Father and the Son into the Unity of Himself. And she is united to the Trinity in its act of mutual love, which eventually results in the creation.

The soul dwells in the unity of the Stillness where she encounters the Divine Energies that eternally arise and come forth from God and which constitute the vibrant, vital Presence of God as the Mystery of His Holy Love flowing always into itself and into the creative act of generating the universe and all creatures. There she perceives the presence of all creatures and essences. And in the Divine Unity, she comes to rest in the embrace of God's gracious Love.

In the absolute mystical state, the soul is drawn into a unity with God in which the Meaning of God is known in a *unitive* way of, as we have said, virtual identity but retaining distinction of being; the soul remains the soul and God remains God. The doing or practice of Metaphysics prepares one for a meeting with the Meaning of the Divine Principle in the absolute mystical sense of being absorbed into God's inner Life, of seeing God from within His essential act in which He is God, entering into the Secret of His being, known in the simplicity of the act making God to be a pure unity of Essence and Existence, as one dynamic Presence in the simple nature of His Unity. Thus, He *is* Existence in its underived sense of being that which is, and since He is, everything else is. Because He is, nothingness is overcome. He holds the eternal moment of To Be, that is why He is God. This makes Him to be pure Reality in His absolute rootedness in that everlasting moment of Existence in which He is forever that act, a *spot-light* on the eternal duration of Being. As a consequence, He comprehends it all in One Eternal Now, and unifies Truth in Himself.

Mystical knowledge, in which the soul gets a glimpse of God, is accessible to a few, because it is a *gift* that God gives to those He so chooses. But God grants the possibility of a relationship with Him to anyone who desires it, and seeks Him with a single-minded attention. And this is the Mystery of Christ, the Word or Meaning of God become manifest in His historical birth. Christ is the Way to this relationship with the Father in the Spirit. This is also the Mystery of the Church. The Son came to redeem us from sin but also to redeem us from that ignorance which is the chief effect of original sin. For again, there is only one true Wisdom, which is the Knowledge of God. In Christ, we have the Image of God, and God's attributes are perceived in the actions and attitudes of Christ. His human nature was the condition for revealing the Divine, and He came to lift us to the Father, not to become human Himself. He gave us a "picture" of God in His own holiness. To the Church He gave the responsibility of spreading and maintaining the faith. The Church, furthermore, is not simply the people of God, for the Church is also the Presence of God in history. And He is the foundation of her life. That is why the Church can never fail. What is given to the mystic to see in the direct relation to God, is given to each Christian in the sacramental structure of the Church, especially in the Eucharist. What the mystic perceives in the unitive relation to God, we perceive in faith. We know in faith that Christ is Present in a special way, but we only fully realize it, come to know it, in mystical elevation. Hence, mystical life is the fulfillment of the sacramental life and a forestate of Paradise.

In our journey to God, we must remember that all that the human intellect has conceived or experienced of God, in every culture, religion and age, is, in relation to the Divine itself, equivalent to an infant reaching for a spoon. Thus, the nature of God is and always remains hidden in His Mystery, awaiting our entrance into His Realm of infinite Bliss in that wonderful state called Beatitude. May we all arrive there some day.

III

THREE "SPECULATIVE" MYSTICS

THE MYSTICISM OF PLOTINUS

Plotinus (203-270 A.D.), the ascetic, "pagan monk" and master of speculative and mystical truth, sage of the spiritual life, leading from the philosophical to the contemplative realms, is the great enduring voice of Ancient Wisdom. He has had a long and steady impact on thinkers and mystics from his own time to ours. There is something very powerful, visionary and abidingly consistent in his view of reality. Hilary Armstrong, that perennial Neo-Platonist, thinks that Plotinus is quite relevant to our own troubled age, because he possesses some important knowledge of God, the Absolute or The One and our relationship to it.[1] Plotinus also has value in showing us the immanent and transcendent Presence of the Divine, and the way to unity with it, with The One. Inge puts it more forcefully when he says that Plotinus is ". . . the classical representative of mystical philosophy. No other *guide* even approaches Plotinus in power and insight and profound spiritual penetration",[2] as well as eloquence. This recognition of Plotinus as a "guide" touches upon one of the main reasons why he has contemporary relevance. He is a guide to contemplative experience and knowledge. Moreover, Inge maintains that it is not sufficient to study Plotinus as a philosopher, one must also study him ". . . as a spiritual director and a prophet."[3]

It is perhaps because of his singular metaphysical genius and his equally significant mystical knowedge (both practical and speculative) that he has had such a far-reaching influence throughout the History of much of Western Consciousness in philosophy and spiritual life. Because he is able to unite the philosophical impulse to know and understand reality with the universal desire to achieve a relationship with the Divine, the former serving the latter as the goal of life, his appeal is also universal (even reaching to India in the early centuries) and has had lasting results. Consider, for example, his striking effect on St. Augustine's life, thought and spirituality. St. Augustine is often referred to as the "Christian Plato", but it would be more accurate to call him the "Christian Plotinus", as he is much nearer the Plotinian view than that of the Platonic, and he shares with Plotinus the same desire or passion for union with the Absolute.

Plotinus heavily influenced other Fathers as well in both the Latin and Orthodox Traditions. Here his imprint is discernable in Patristic Theology and contemplative doctrine, not to mention practice. His impact on the Pseudo-Dionysius is proverbial; they could have been brothers, as both have that fluid, eloguent style that expresses their vision. Much of the Plotinian conception of The One beyond Being, the *apophatic* method, the stages (purification, illumination and union), and the notion of emanation, with noticeable adjustments, passed into the system of the Areopagite. It is also strange that neither Plotinus nor the Pseudo-Dionysius have a doctrine of grace. This is certainly another point of influence on the Areopagite. What is true of Plotinus' effect on Dionysius is equally true, but to a lesser degree, of his impact on the thought of John Scotus Eriugena, the translator of the Dionysian Corpus. Eriugena's own opus, *De Divisione Naturae*, or *Periphyseon* from the Greek title, clearly reveals the mark of Plotinus.

The chief reason, however, why Plotinus is relevant to us and the needs of our age is the influence he has had on the development of Western Mysticism, notably on such figures as St. Bonaventure via the works of the Pseudo-Dionysius, Eckhart and the other major figures of the Rhenish School, Tauler, Suso and Ruysbroek, as well as his influence on the Spanish School, St. John of the Cross, who popularized the three stages, and St. Teresa of Avila, and his impress on Fourteenth Century English Mysticism.[4] These mystics are important to us in our attempt to understand our own very rich Tradition, and as guides in the development of our spiritual lives. Because Plotinus was able to help them in their approach to God and to finally reach the unitive life of contemplation, he is also of crucial value for us, who have the same ontological need as they, the need to be *oned* with the Absolute, with God. It is precisely because Plotinus has so much to show us that we must make a serious effort to study him.

In this chapter, we will explore his contemplative method, his teachings on mystical union with The One or God, the act of union itself, the content of the experience, and the driving force of the movement in the soul to seek the Divine. There will also be an attempt to give an evaluation of his mysticism in order to determine in what sense he was a mystic. Before we turn to the major concerns of this essay, let us briefly examine the basic structure of his system so that we can better locate the place of contemplation in it, that is, how it fits into the Plotinian doctrine on reality and its ultimate purpose.

Sketch of the Plotinian System

The *One* is the Plotinian conception of God; it is similar to the Good of Plato and the One of Philo. It is probably from the latter that his doctrine of The One initially derives,[5] although Plotinus was a very brilliant and original thinker. The One is the ineffable

Source of all reality, the first *hypostasis,* [6] of which there are two others, The *Intelligence* and The *Soul*. There are only three hypostases. The One is a pure undifferentiated unity; it is devoid of form, quality and discursive or rational thought, perhaps, even of consciousness as we understand it. Plotinus says that it transcends Being, since it is the Source of Being, that it is "untouched by multiplicity", and is completely self-sufficient as the highest principle. [7] The One is also the object of contemplation. More will be said about this later.

The One generates or to use Plotinus' metaphor, *emanates* necessarily the second hypostasis, The *Intelligence* or *Nous*[8], which is eternal like the One, and in which reside the Forms, Ideas or Essences of Plato. The Ideas are in some sense conscious of themselves in The *Nous*. The Intellectual principle or The *Nous* contains all multiplicity as intelligibility of it. Multiplicity arises in *The Intelligence* as a direct result of the Ideas or essences existing in The *Nous* or *The Intelligence.* [9] This puts the doctrine of the Ideas on a firmer foundation than in Plato's theory, where the Ideas or the Forms are self-subsistent essences or concepts, existing outside the Good; they exist in themselves in the Platonic notion. The *Nous* or *Intelligence* possesses, as its very nature, the intelligibility of all things. *The Intelligence* has two immediate objects of contemplation, to which it is related by direct *intuition* or nonrational apprehension, i.e., The One and itself. When The *Intelligence* or The *Nous* turns to contemplate The One, the act itself *emanates* the third hypostasis, The Soul.

The Soul is the cosmic life force of the universe and nature. It is similar to the *demiurge* or world-soul of Plato's *Timaeus,* the semi-divine principle through which the world is brought into being from the patterns of the pre-existing Forms. The *Nous* or *Intelligence* is the contemplative object of *Soul,* [10] which is the link between the super-essential realm of The *Nous,* The *One* and the material realm. The Soul is responsible for the world or matter, which emanates from it by necessity.[11] The *Soul* has two dimensions, one directed to The *Nous* and *The One,* the other generating matter, thus, becoming the vital principle of nature. Plotinus presents a whole scheme of the Cosmic Order, the hierarchy of the human soul's ascent, which is similar to the Hindu notion.

Human souls proceed from *The Soul* but are *distinct* ontologically. At the same time, souls are united with The Soul through a bond of love. [12] Souls are bound together in the Cosmic Soul, but they are also immortal like it and have a being and nature of their own.

The lowest level in the emanative process from *The One* is the material cosmos, which comes forth from the world-soul. Matter has the least degree of actual being or reality. It is essentially a lack of what *The Soul* and *The Intelligence* possess, i.e., the intelligble and the contemplative relationship with The One. Plotinus says of matter that: " . . . it is utter destitution - of sense, of virtue, of beauty, of pattern, of Ideal principle, of quality; . . . by its alienism in regard to the beauty and good of Existence, matter is therefore a non-exist-ent." [13] So much for Plotinian Metaphysics.

We are able to see in the procession or emanation of all things from The One a glimpse of our own purpose, which is to *return* to the Source. Plotinus' entire system is directed to that end. It is essentially a speculative or mystical philosophy that is oriented to *beatitude.* Our happiness is to be found in contemplation, which involves a movement back through the hierarchy of Being to The One beyond Being and unity with It. Plotinus exhorts us to this purpose with the words: "Let us flee then to the beloved Fatherland . . . The Fatherland to us is There whence we have come, and There is the Father", [14] i.e., The One. This represents the Good for the soul to which she is ordered by nature. The soul has a natural love and longing for God and a desire to be united with Him. [15] This is the end and purpose of exist-ence, but getting back to God, in the unitive life, requires a certain *method*, having three basic stages. Let us now turn to the Plotinian Mystical doctrine proper and consider the method of ascent, the mys-tical union with The One, with God, the act itself, the content of the act, and the dynamism of our movement toward God as well as the higher reaches of the Spiritual Life.

Plotinian Mysticism

In the method of the soul's long journey to The One, she must pass through a *moral* purification, which is the life of virute; she must become like God, "the Supreme Exemplar", [16] from Whom pure Goodness emanates. In the second stage, the soul has to *participate* in the intelligibility of The *Nous,* of The Intelligence and must exercise her faculty for contemplating the essences in the Divine Mind or in The Nous. This is part of the process that leads to mystical union. It is also of course the stage that Plato made the highest and called it *dialectic*, true philosophy or Wisdom. The West has never recovered from this emphasis, which was reinforced during the Enlightenment, and remains to this day, far too rational in all aspects of public knowl-edge. The third stage is the most important and is the one most recog-nizable to Christians who practice the life of contemplative prayer. This is the point at which true *purification* occurs. This purgative process is, according to Plotinus, one of *simplification*, and simplification means becoming like The One. Now, we become similar to The One by being inwardly *one* ourselves, and not scattered here and there among sense images and throught. This is the significance of simplification, a transformation into a single-minded attention. It is a withdrawal from all multiplicity, the multiplicity of the material world, that is, of sense experience and the multiplicity of all thought-content. We can see here the same method that is found in Christian mystics, and the mystics of many other traditions as well. This method is a process of "cutting away" all that the soul has acquired in her descent into a body. The soul *must* turn within and, by the inner path, make her way to that primal absolute simplcity that is akin to God's Unity. Plotinus tells us that this goal of inner simplification is achieved by this cutting away of everything. [17] It is an *apophatic* approach but in an *existential* sense, not simply as a theological method governing predication to the Divine nature. It really has little to do with theological methodology, since it is rather an approach to the experience of The One in contemplative union. Plotinus was the first to develop it in the West, although it was implicit in some of Plato's later speculation on the Good. The moment we hold that God is ultimately beyond Being, then we must adopt the spophatic way. Since contemplation aims at this One beyond Being and since discursive reason is totally useless in this task, John Rist offers the opinion that the Plotinain use of the *via negativa* is the only method of reaching that which is beyond all things. [18] And this is why Plotinus introduced it. Plotinus describes this form of the via negativa as a process of *divesting* all things in the ascent, a "laying aside of the garments worn before, and the entry into nakedness". [19] It is a journey above all form, whether sensible or intelligible, to a realm that is uncharted by man's feeble explorations. And this is the real nature of the via negativa, a method of contemplation itself not of reason.

Finally, the method of purification, the inward path to God, is a self-forgetting, a firm *renunciation* of self, of the ego and its ways. It is a total overcoming of oneself; one even forgets one's name, individuality and all preoccupation with oneself. This leads to an awareness of God and an elevated existence in Him. [20] Perhaps this is what Christ meant in His sober exhortation that we must lose ourselves in order to find ourselves. When the soul has gone through this progressive purification and has simplified her life to the point of becoming like The One, then the mystical experience dawns in its fullness. The very self-abnegation or self-forgetting is also the first fruit of mystical life, for in God, we achieve true *liberation*, which takes us beyond the range of our limited identity as an ego. This is also a common theme in the Asian religions.

Union with The One leads to an *enhanced* identity, an awareness of being united to the Supreme Unity and Identity, that which has given being to all things. The consummation of contemplation, which is of course union, comes quite suddenly. It is a "leap" into the pure illuminating life of The One.[21] Although the soul can prepare for it, she cannot force the mystical event to happen, just as one cannot force a flower to bloom; it must happen naturally. Plotinus says that she must " . . . wait tranquilly for its appearance, as the eye waits on the rising of the sun . . . "[22] And when God comes or when the soul is carried away into the Divine, she possesses *vision* of The One or *Theoria*.[23] It is more accurate to say that the experience of the soul is one of *afee* or of *Contact* with God or *touch (sunafee)*,[24] a touching that is a merging or mingling with the Divine Unity.[25]

God is also a kind of Presence, and the soul achieves a *communion* with this Presence, but, again, it is essentially unknowable. When the soul has been granted the vision of God, of The One, she is in a manner "grafted unto" God's being. In the midst of this intense communion with the Divine, distinction is transcended in the consciousness of the state. Plotinus expresses it in this was: "Soul must see in its own way; this is by *coalescence, haplosis,* or *unification;* but in seeking thus to know the Unity it is prevented by that very unification from recognizing that it has found (it). It cannot distinguish itself from the object of this intuition."[26] This experience can also be called *ecstast (ecstasis)*, since, as Elmer O'Brien says:" . . . the mystic 'stands outside' himself."[27] Plotinus, however, is not fond of this term and uses it only on rare occasions. What the term suggests is that the soul *participates* in the Divine life[28] by "going out" of herself, that is, by transcending her normal mode of consciousness as a discursive intellect.

Now, the *act* by which the soul "sees" in the mystical state is a self-transcending power of "seeing" what is above or beyond. The soul is united in her act to The One, becomes "immanent" to it, and it becomes "immanent" to her. It does not involve thought in any form; it is a higher way of "seeing". It is a different kind of vision, if indeed it can be called vision.[29] This act is "flooded" with the Divine in such a way that the soul is carreid out of herself by love. She has become "intoxicated" with The One, which is totally formless. It is an act of the soul which has merged with God's act, and which has swept away the awareness of one's own identity in the moment of the mystical transformation. The soul's act is a passive surrendering to The One, an *invasion* of her being, a quieting of the faculties and an identification with the Divine essence in its act of self-possessed unity. In that unity, the soul rests[30] or reposes. For the soul's act *seems* to have become God's act.

What then is the *content* of this precious mystical knowledge that the soul acquires? or rather, what is the *content* of the experience itself? The soul is illuminated by the splendor and glory of the Divine Light. It is not an apprehension of an object distinct from the Light or revealed by it; it is the Light itself and the Source of the Light; she sees at once both the seen and that by which she sees, the pure Light of the Divine self-illumination. The soul then "becomes very vision itself".[31] She is brought into this experience of the Divine by her preparation in the intelligible realm, in the contemplation of the essences in The Nous. There comes a point, however, when knowledge is superseded by the dissolution of all multiplicity and the soul passes into The One, into God, which is really the later notion of reposing in the Godhead that both the Pseudo-Dionysius and Meister Eckhart elaborate. Plotinus says:

> Here we put aside all learning; disciplined to
> this pitch, established in beauty, the quester
> holds knowledge still of the ground he rests
> on, but, suddenly swept beyond it all by the
> very crest of the wave of Intellect (Nous)
> surging beneath, he is lifted and sees, never
> knowing how; the vision floods the eyes with
> light, but it is not a light showing some other
> object, the light is itself the Vision.[32]

There is a merging together of the soul and The One. Somehow, the soul perceives The One in the light in which The One subsists. There *seems* to arise a *consciousness* of a single indentity, which is the Divine itself. This would also seem to imply monism or even a form of pantheism. This, however, does not appear to be Plotinus' position. When we have arrived at the point of evaluating his mystical doctrine, then it will be shown why Plotinus is neither a monist nor a pantheist. To continue, Plotinus tells us that in the union with The One, difference is "overcome". He says: "In this state of absorbed contemplation there is no longer a question of holding an object: the vision is continuous so that seeing and seen are one thing; object and act of vision have become identical; of all that until then filled the eyes no memory remains."[33]   And in another place, Plotinus mentions virtually the same thing, that we are unable to reason or to remember what we experience or "to make any affirmation", because of this character of *apparent* identity. He says that we only reflect upon the nature of the experience subsequent to it, not during it. This is also a common motif in many mystics, as has been said above. All we know is that we have been filled with the Divine Light and this in the midst of the experience.[34]   In the mystical state, our attention is fused with the Light, and we are just aware of the state itself.

The *content* of the mystical state, again, is ineffable. It is also true that the content of this experience is the *same* as the act in which the soul knows the object of her contemplation. For because the soul has been raised to unity with The One, a state in which distinction is transcended, and the soul "becomes" The One, sees in and through The One, this being pure Light and unity, this content, which is the consciousness of it, is *also* the act in which she is aware of it. The soul is aware that "seeing and seen are one thing", and that "the object and the act of vision have become identical", which means that there is no *apparent* distinction between them. It must be re-membered though that it is precisely the soul "seeing" in this state of the experience in mystical oneness with God, and, thus, there has to be some actual ontological difference, even though there is a consciousness of unity, and a *unity of consciousness* between them. This is not the same as an identity of being. Hence, they are one in God's consciousness , but they are not one in the actuality of their separate natures. We will have more to say on this later. The content of the mystical state is, as a consequence, *identical* with the act in which the soul is conscious of this content, since distinction has been layed aside in the larger consciousness of their *apparent* identity. It would seem that in the mystical state, the soul somehow comes into a transcendent knowledge of The One, of God from the experience of being united with Him. What the reality of God is in this act, in which the soul participates, is not possible to reveal in language, for language does not correspond to the fullness of the experience. The One is infinite, and this quite assuredly cannot be grasped or expressed, as we have indicated before, since it is this infinite in one moment, all at once in its very eternality. In this respect, language is like a leaking cup trying desperately to contain the ocean. For language cannot capture the infinite in its boundless context of being the Unlimited Truth holding all truths within itself.

Now, what directs the soul to its proper act in The One, that which is, for Plotinus, the very dynamism animating this act of seeking The Absolute and of union with it, is *Eros*, which is an intense love originating in The One. It is God Who gives it to the soul, implanting it in her nature. The soul is stirred by the Divine energy or outflow of love from The One, and she is "seized with a Bacchic passion", which is this Eros, a desire or longing for God. Plotinus says that when the Divine Eros comes into the soul, she ". . . gathers strength, awakens, spreads true wings . . . (and) its very nature bears her upwards, lifted by the giver of that love."[35]   It is a desire for The One that drives the soul to seek it within by withdrawal and contemplation.

Rist suggests that the Plotinian notion of Eros is that special quality in the soul's nature that makes her most akin to The One. It is the inherent, compelling energy of her movement toward God. He also sees in Eros a *bond*, which links together the positive and negative methods of approaching The One,[36] for both approaches stem from the same profoundly real concern of the soul.

Eros propels the soul on through the various levels of purification; it is the power of an innate relationship with the Source. It is the inner dynamism of the soul's nature and purpose. When finally the soul has attained to the mystical union, Eros is transformed into adoration of The One, into awe, worship and heroic self-surrender. Plotinus conceives of the change in this way:

> And one that shall know this vision -- with what passion of love shall he not be seized, with what pang of desire, what longing to be molten into one with This, what wondering delight! If he that has never seen this Being must hunger for It as for all his welfare, he that has known (It) must *love* and *reverence* It as the very Beauty; he will be flooded with *awe* and *gladness*, stricken by a salutary terror.[37]

Eros, the innate power of longing love for God that prompted the soul to renunciation and inner simplification through a process of purification and contemplation, the spiritual force that drove the soul to the Divine unity, the inner guide leading to the mystical heights, and once achieving this, the goal of existence, is changed into the living relationship itself, orientating the soul's attention and will to God as her final end. This impulse of Divine love in the soul is the bond that holds together all of the elements of her ascent to The One. It is the very energy of the spiritual life, leading through purification, illumination by the Divine Light to *union* with The One. As we have observed above, these themes are picked up later in the development of Western Mysticism and attest to the abiding relevance of Plotinus' insights. This brings us to the juncture of considering and assessing Plotinian spirituality.

Evaluation of Plotinian Mysticism

It is interesting to note how some scholars, notably Elmer O'Brien, deny that Plotinus was even a mystic. He is of the opinion that the mystical states described by Plotinus are more psychological than spiritual, resulting from intense concentration. O'Brien says that Plotinus desperately wanted to be a mystic, but was not. He theorizes that the supposed mystical experiences of Plotinus are either 1) residues "of symbolic imagery or of conceptual thought", which remain unrecognized after purification, or 2) the result of concentration in which the soul enters into "a state of momentary unconsciousness." [38] O'Brien reduces Plotinian mysticism and metaphysics to what he calls Plotinus' "Psychology of introspection." [39] This is of course an extreme position, one which this author does not share.

Hegel is also another thinker who has a questionable interpretation of Plotinian mysticism. What Hegel does is to read into Plotinus his own principle of Reason. It is a classic example of "isogesis", i.e., reading into the text what is not there. Hegel had a propensity to do this with every other major thinker in the History of Western Thought. We should recall that Plotinus emphatically holds that mystical union is *beyond* thought or reason in any form. He says this again and again. In Hegel's interpretation, however, we get a distortion of Plotinus' position, which serves the purposes of Hegel's system. Here is an example of Hegel's blatant misreading of Plotinus on mystical life:

> Ecstasy is not a mere rapturous condition of the senses and fancy, but rather a passing beyond the content of sensuous consciousness; it is pure thought that is at home with itself, and is its own object . . . The Idea of the Philosophy of Plotinus is thus an intellectualism or a higher idealism, which indeed from the side of the Notion is not yet a perfect idealism; that of which Plotinus becomes conscious in

his ecstasy is, however, philosophic thought, speculative notions and Ideas.[40]

This is typical of Hegel's historical method; he seems to fit the facts to his own systematic demands. In his interpretation of Plotinus, he is only half right. The earlier stages of the ascent involve contemplation of intelligible objects, essences, ideas, etc., but these are left behind in the mystical stage, that of *ecstasy*, where even thought and the subject-object dichotomy are overcome for the duration of the unitive experience. We can expect this kind of distortion from Hegel, who did not appreciate Mysticism, since he had no understanding of it. In the same lectures in which he makes the above comment on Plotinus' notion of contemplative union, when he considers the Medieval Period, he gives exactly a half page to St. Thomas, which reads like something his grandmother told him third-hand as hearsay.

The evidence that Plotinus is indeed a mystic would seem to be indisputable from the texts themselves and historical evidence. Of the former, we have given numberous indications, and of the latter, we can present the judgement of his devoted disciple, Porphyry, who addressing himself to this very question, says that in the six years that he was a follower of Plotinus, he is certain that his master had had the ecstatic union with The One or God at least four times.[41] Porphyry himself claims to have had the same experience once. In further considertion of the historical evidence, witness also the great impact he had on St. Ambose and St. Augustine, to mention only two, in terms of their spiritual development, two contemplatives who were aware of Plotinus' spiritual insights and had high regard for him as a contemplative as well. They also regarded him as a giant among metaphysicians.

Also, A.B. Sharpe has no doubt that Plotinus is a true mystic. He feels that the Plotinian doctrine has all the marks of a genuine supernatural form of Mysticism, especially close to the Christian variety. For there are many elements that his experience has in common with that of Christian mystics,[42] such as St. Teresa of Avila and the Pseudo-Dionysius, to mention two very prominent ones. We will briefly enumerate some of the important common elements further on.

Paul Henry, who wrote the introduction to the Mackenna translation of *The Enneads,* agrees with Sharpe's conviction, along with many other writers, that Plotinus was indeed a mystic. He assumes this fact to be incontrovertible. Where he does take issue with Sharpe, and with others who emphasize the similarities between Plotinian and Christian Mysticism, is on the more difficult question of what *kind* of mystic Plotinus was. Henry suggests that there is a considerable difference between the two forms, although he does not hold that Plotinus was a monist or a pantheist. He thinks that the two profoundest disparities between Plotinian and Christian Mysticism, other than in the area of language or terminology, are the two doctrines of *prayer* and the *dark night* or mystical 'darkness', which have no place in Plotinus' view,[43] but which are central to the Christian Tradition. We have also mentioned above the lack of a doctrine of grace in Plotinian theology.

Given the differences, what kind of mystic is Plotinus (if we may safely make this assumption)? This is a challenging question because of Plotinus' gift for metaphysical subtlety evident throughout his writings. Is he a monist, a pantheist or a theist? We have alluded to this issue earlier. Armstrong would seem to hold that Plotinus is a theist, since he defends him on this score, but a theist who has worked out the intimate details of immanence and transcendence in such a way that there is a *continuity* between God and the world, and between God and the soul. The way in which Plotinus has accomplished this feat evokes a sense of identity and, thus, also of monism, and yet this is not Plotinus' position, as Armstrong understands it. Armstrong himself would probably accept the *theistic* interpretation of Plotinian mysticism.[44]

Plato Mamo, writing in the same anthology on Neo-Platonism, calls Plotinus a "qualified monist".[45] The reason for employing this interesting term is because he thinks that Plotinus is not fully a theist, which he holds to be clear from his many utterances that are seemingly monistic, for instance, the notion of mystical union as a "converging of centers" (Enn. VI. 9. 10).[46] The One of course is the "Center of centers" (Enn. VI. 9. 8, 11-12). Souls are little centers, and they converge with the Center of centers, "becoming" it. Mamo though is probably following Dodds' interpretation, who views Plotinian mysticism as similar to that of some Indian mystics of the monistic kind.[47] Although Mamo is inclined to the monistic interpretation, he does not go all the way with it, since he feels that the text indicates the extreme reluctance of Plotinus to assert absolute identity, that such terms are lacking in Plotinus, and where used, are often done so with qualification[48] or ambiguity. It is perhaps this ambiguous quality that lends itself to misunderstanding.

Arnou is convinced that Plotinus is a theistic mystic, because the way in which he speaks of the human soul and The One indicates that they are definitely separate substances.[49]   Furthermore, he says that the qualifying expressions Plotinus uses, demonstrate that the mystical union is not one of identity between the soul and The One, but of a unity that preserves the ontological distinction between them.[50]   This would appear to be the most accurate assessment of the Plotinian doctrine.

Even when Plotinus seems to imply identity, and hence a monistic orientation, this is not his intention. He appears to be struggling with the inadequacy of language whenever he attempts to describe mystical experience in its highest state. It would seem that what he actually wants to say is that mystical union results in an identity of *consciousness* with The One, with God, but not an *ontological* identity, that is, an identity of being, which would obliterate the distinction between them. If we view mystical experience in this way, and if this is the correct interpretation of its nature, then we have come a long way in clearing up the problem of monism and pantheism as they have haunted the question of mysticism's nature and its meaning. For then we will have shown them to be misinterpretations of what is essentially a unique experience with its own conditions of knowing. It is because of its uniqueness, that it *is* a penetration into the Divine Consciousness and unity with this Consciousness, as well as its totally alien character in relation to the ordinary modes of experience, that it has often been described inaccurately in terms of identity by some mystics and their followers.

The most significant reason, however, for maintaining the theistic nature of Plotinian mysticism comes not from a hermeneutical consideration, but from Plotinus himself. And this is a metaphysical and theological point. It is precisely Plotinus' oft repeated statement that the Divine Principle, The One is absolutely *transcendent*. This removes it at once from the monistic and pantheistic categories, and places Plotinus' metaphysics and mysticism on a solid *theistic* foundation, which arises from his own intellectual and contemplative experience.

If this is an accurate interpretation, that Plotinus is a theistic mystic, then his influence on Western Mysticism in general becomes more crucial, since it means that he has many very important insights into the nature of contemplation, which are just as relevant today as they were in the time of St. Augustine and in the ages subsequent to his. Certainly, Plotinus' contemplative method, with the emphasis on the stages of purification, illumination and union has made an enormous contribution to our Tradition, especially in the systems of the Pseudo-Dionysius and St. John of the Cross, although the stages have been stressed by various other mystics in the Christian Tradition with some differences of formulation. Furthermore, what Plotinus has to say concerning God's utter transcendence and the necessity for an *apophatic* approach are essential and enduring lessons for Theology and Contemplation. Plotinus is, thus, *relevant* to every age, since he has *genuine* knowledge of God, of which every age has need. This is particularly true of our own, which is seeking to find the Source of life in the quiet of a renewed prayer life.

10

THE MYSTICAL PHILOSOPHY OF THE PSEUDO-DIONYSIUS

This essay has as its chief concern the exploration of the 'Divine Philosophy' of Dionysius, the Pseudo-Areopagite. This seminal mind has woven together a lofty metaphysics with an even more sublime mystical doctrine. We have referred to this mystical teaching in preceding chapters. Now, we will take a closer look at both Dionysian metaphysics and mysticism, attempting to gain an insight into their relationship, and ultimately, a clarification of his mystical vision. We hold the view that his metaphysics is primarily constituted by his mysticism, and that actually, his metaphysics *is* his mysticism expressed in the conceptual terms of Late Neo-Platonism. It is thus important to consider their relationship. For his entire ontology seems to be an elaborate inference from his mystical glimpses. Given the reality of his experience, he seems to have understood what kind of metaphysical doctrine flows from the Vision of God, the *Thearchy**. Such a relationship between mysticism and metaphysics is very subtle but we may find that it has generated many systems in the History of Consciousness. In the case of the Pseudo-Denys, his metaphysics is a form of *anagogy*, which we may call the mysticism of intelligibility; it is indeed a speculative mystical doctrine, which is metaphysically commited to an intuition of intelligibility or *absolute meaning*, as the central Impulse of the Divine nature, but which is totally ineffable to the human intellect. This emphasis on intelligibility is very Greek, but Pseudo-Dionysius gives it a much higher connotation than rationality, for it connotes the very being of God. The doctrine of Dionysius is quite unique; it provides for the soul's journey to the celestial heights and to *henosis* or union with the Godhead.

There is little doubt about the importance of the Areopagite and of his profound influence on Western Philosophy, Theology and Mysticism. In the long period of the Middle Ages, he was an *auctoritas*, an authority to whom thinkers turned in reverence, citing him and orienting their works in relation to his. He provided the 'data', which on many questions, helped to form Theology.[1] His works were thus highly privileged. So influential were they that St. Thomas cites them no less than 1700 times, more than he quotes any other authority.[2]

---

*Thearchy is the term that Dionysius uses to signify the Godhead, the Immovable Source.

Thomas was greatly interested in the question of the role of the Angels in the Divine government, and the Pseudo-Dionysius was the first acknowledged authority on this issue of how the angelic intelligences participate in God's government.[3]

The writings of the Pseudo-Dionysius had a universally recognized appeal in all of Christendom from the time of the Latern Council in 649 A.D. until the Fifteenth Century. [4] During this Council, St. Maximus, a contemplative theologian who understood their extraordinary value, tried to explain obscurities in Dionysian doctrine by his glosses (P.G. IV). His explanations, which facilitated the universal acknowledgement of Dionysius in the Middle Ages, cast doubtful points into an orthodox light. This rendered his insights accessible to the Church.[5] The *corpus* of Dionysian works first surfaced during the raging controversy of the Monophysite question.[6] It was at the Latern Council (649) that the Pseudo-Dionysius was quoted as an important witness against the heresy of Monothelism.[7] Scotus Eriugena's translation of the Areopagite's writings (about 858), furthermore, helped to enhance his recognition by making his works more available to the Latin West. From then on, not only were they considered of great worth, but they were also regarded as sacred. And one has only to notice his profound influence on other mystics, especially on St. Bonaventure, Eckhart, Tauler, Suso, Ruysbroeck, the author of *The Cloud of Unknowing* and countless others, to realize how far-reaching was his effect. [8]

In terms of his philosophical and theological efforts, he was able to achieve a theological synthesis in which he reconciled Christian and Neo-Platonic doctrines, which formed the intellectural climate of his day.[9] He tried to "baptize" Neo-Platonic Idealism and Mysticism,[10] and to make them palpable to Christian sensibilities. Any trace of pantheism, which his opponents may think they perceive in his doctrine, mediated through the inadequacy of his utterances, is an "optical illusion,"[11] born of a superficial acquaintance with his position. It is easy to make a thinker or mystic sound controversial if his statements are read out of their proper context.

As to the Pseudo-Areopagite's over-all influence and value in the formation of Theology in the Middle Ages, Gilson says that the Dionysian view "provided Christian thinkers with a general framework within which their interpretation of the world could easily take place." [12] Consequently, Dionysius the 'auctoritas' has had a wide influence on Medieval Theology in general, and on the formulation of structures in speculative mysticism in particular, although the content of mystical insights remains the unique experience of each mystic.

Of the Pseudo-Dionysius' works, four are extant. They are: *De Caelesti Hierarchia* or *The Heavenly Hierarchy,* in which he deals with the question of the Divine government and how the Angels participate in God's Life and order; *De Ecclesiastica Hierarchia* or *The Ecclesiastical Hierarchy*, which treats of the Divine Impulse hidden in the symbols and rites of the Church; *De Divinis Nominibus* or *The Divine Names,* which considers his metaphysical doctrine concerning God and His relationship to the world; *De Mystica* Theologia or *The Mystical Theology* in which the Dionysian contemplative doctrine and method are presented. This is the shortest of his works, being about ten pages long. There are also eleven Epistles, dealing with various topics occasioned by his above works and essentially elucidating his insights. The last letter is thought to be spurious.[13]

THE GENERAL STRUCTURE OF HIS SYSTEM

In all of his works, Dionysius is discussing his theologico-mystico vision of reality. It is a mystical knowledge that also expresses itself in metaphysical intuitions. The former gives rise to the latter. Dionysius is following a systematic "science of God." [14] Even though he develops a metaphysical doctrine in *The Divine Names*, still we feel certain he is always conscious of the mystical meaning that he has glimpsed and its essential inexpressibility. He interjects this awareness into all of his works. For he says, in *The Divine Names*, in which he is considering the manifested dimension of the Godhead, that is, God as the Trinity, in its attributes reflected in the things He causes that: ". . . I pray God grant me worthily to declare the beneficent and manifold Names of the Unutterable and Nameless Godhead. . ." [15] With this prayer and its paradoxical statement 'Unutterable and Nameless Godhead,' Dionysius is returning to his ultimate theme, which is the mystical union, the *henosis* with the Divine Source. It is in this oft repeated truth, this unvarying Principle of his system, that we can reasonably discern the direction his thought pursues, and that is to treat the mysical reality metaphysically, to show its relationship to the rest of creation, and to determine what we can know about God from this relationship. In the long run, however, the rational, metaphysical approach is negated for the realization of this union with God in the Divine Darkness, a darkness more luminous than the dawn. The metaphysical consideration is a stage in the ascent. Furthermore, in *The Heavenly* or *Celestial Hierarchy* he says: "We rightly describe its (the Godhead's) non-relationship to things created, but we do not know

its superessential, and inconceivable, as well as unutterable indefinability. . ."[16] In other words, in the areas of philosophical and theological activity, we do not touch God's essence. We do not even approach
His indefinability, for we cannot in any way define Him, and , because
we cannot, we do not know how or why He is indefinable. As a consequence, we must cross over into mystical consciousness, and there,
plunging into "the Darkness of Unknowing." we come to know God in
His essence by this 'Unknowing;' we reject all rational knowledge and
become content with the experience of God's Presence, which is "a
Knowledge that exceeds all understanding."[17] *The Mystical Theology*
speaks for itself on this point of Dionsysius' ultimate theme. Again,
also in *The Ecclesiastical Hierarchy,* Dionysius announces the essential
purpose of the work to be the facilitation of *deification,* by
which he means "the assimiliation to, and union with God. . ."[18]
Thus, the mystical principle is clearly stated in each of his works as the
central point of his profound doctrine; it is the absolute theme of all
his speculation, which is based on his own mystical encounters with
the Source. Indeed, in the same *Ecclesiastical Hierarchy,* from the very
beginning, he says that all of his thought on hierarchy (and this applies
to his entire system) is based on "the inspired and Divine, Deifying
Science." [19] Even his Epistles bear the same task of clarifying the
Divine Philosphy, the mystical doctrine, in some of its aspects, whether
they be in the philosophical, theological or purely mystical sections of
his system. For instance, in the First Letter to Caius, the monk, the
Pseudo-Dionysius is talking about the Darkness or the *Agnosia,* the
unknowing-knowing through which God is known. Dionysius says of it:
"And the all-perfect *Agnosia,* in its superior sense (as opposed to its
common usage), is a knowledge of Him, Who is above all known
things." [20] Hence, we see the core emphasis of his thought.

If we take all of his works together, which we know are few, we can
determine that there are basically three levels to his philosophy. Before
we mention these levels, we should keep in mind the general framework;
it is Divine Philosophy, a reflection, based on experience, on the nature
of the ultimate Principle from which all reality flows forth. The title
'Divine Philosophy' is not a polite designation reminiscent of the Greek
idealizations of philosophy as a way of life, but represents the notion of
his "science of God," which includes Mysticism and Theology as well.
Within this general framework, there is an ontology or metaphysics,
which is the rational, intelligible unfolding of his primary insight
concerning the Divine nature, i.e., the Godhead and its relation
to creation. There is also the profound mystical doctrine proper, the

very substance of his position, And then there is a practical *method* of ascent, a method of contemplation, the following of which leads to *henosis* or union, the deifying union with the Divine Life.

There are also three paths to the Knowledge of God in the Dionysian vision, which, being closely related to the levels of his system, are also methods of Theology. They are the *via affirmativa*, the *via symbolica* and the *via negativa.* These are the names for three very different approaches to the Absolute, the *Thearchy,* who is the Immovable, inaccessible, dynamic Deity.[21]

The *via affirmativa* or the Cataphatic Theology, also called the descending Theology, since it begins with predications of God taken from Scripture, God's descent into History and the human situation, is the method followed in *The Divine Names.* It is a positive Theology or knowledge of God, because it makes positive assertions about His nature. It considers God as *proodos,* as proceeding from Himself to creation and to the Angelic Orders. In this way or method, God is being discussed in His role as "the Efficient Cause of the Forms," which are the attributes ascribed to Him[22] or to His Knowledge. It is in this theological discourse that the proper domain of Dionysian metaphysics operates. The ascription of attributes to God draws heavily on the Platonic, Neo-Platonic and Biblical Traditions. This positive Theology also deals with the question of how the world comes forth from God and how it is sustained by Him. Consequently, the Cataphatic Theology is a philosophical method, or, more precisely, a theological method corresponding to the requirements of metaphysics.

The *via symbolica* or the Symbolic Theology is concerned with God as Final Cause. In this approach, God is known through the process of *conversion,* the turning back to the Source. This movement back to the Final Cause, the Thearchy, is also called the *epistrophe,* the conversion back or return to God. This method seeks God "through sensible and intelligible symbols." Dionysius refers to his *Symbolic Theology,* but the work is not extant. This method and its use, facilitating the conversion or *epistrophe,* is operative in *The Celestial* and *Ecclesiastical Hierarchies* and in *Epistle IX.*[23] The symbolic method attempts to make contact with the Divine Impulse, God's intelligibility, the secret of His nature, which passes through and illumines the Orders of Angels, descending into *The Ecclesiastical Hierarchy,* as *symbol* and *rite* and *sacrament,* but which is essentially hidden. The point is to penetrate through the symbols and liturgical rites to the Life-giving Impulse, and thus to make the ascent back, the conversion or *epistrophe,* the return to God.

The *via negativa* or Apophatic Theology, also called the ascending theology, because it endeavors to pass beyond form and concept to what God is in His essence and is thus an *ascent* of the intellect to God by a progressive purification or negating of attributes predicated of the Divine nature, approaches God as *mone,* who is immutable and "inaccessible to sense experience and intellect." This is the domain of Mystical Theology, and it is pursued in the work bearing that title. Again, the Apophatic Theology moves towards God by denying the affirmations of His attributes made in the Cataphatic Theology, which predicated these of Him as Cause. The apophatic Theology proceeds by way of negation, because it holds that such affirmations made of the Divine nature really only apply to God as Efficient Cause of all things and not to Him as the transcendent, unknowable, unmanifested Godhead.[24] The soul can only reach God as transcendent essence by way of *Agnosia* or Unknowing, since the intellect cannot grasp the boundless Meaning of the Absolute; it can know this Meaning by experience, as we have said before, but it cannot understand it. The way of *Agnosia* brings the soul to *henosis,* to union with the Divine Life.

In all three theological methods there is a triadic structure. The Cataphatic Theology deals with God as the Good, Being and Wisdom; this is the metaphysics of God as self-diffusive. The Symbolic Theology follows the triad of *Legal, Ecclesiastical and Celestial Hierarchies.* And the Mystical Theology presents a course that passes through the three celebrated stages of purification, illumination and union, which, as we saw above, originated in Plotinus and were later popularized by St. John of the Cross. In the last stage, the soul is united to God.[25]

The Divine Impulse of God's intelligible essence that emanates through the Orders of Angelic Intelligences and returns through *The Ecclesiastical Hierarchy* up into *The Celestial Hierarchy* and back into God's being is the Impulse of Divine Love or Eros, the energy of conversion or driving force of *epistrophe.* This has some similarity to the Plotinian notion of Eros. It is, again,the moving force behind emanation and conversion.[26] This *proodos* or proceeding, this emanation from the immovable Godhead, the *mone,* and conversion, the *epistrophe* or ascent, which is the return of the soul through the intelligible gradations of *The Ecclesiastical Hierarchy* as the soul grasps the meaning of the symbols, passing through these into *The Celestial Hierarchy*, in which the soul traverses the varying degrees of the Divine illuminations, the Impulse contemplated by the Angels, *is* this Divine Eros, this 'yearning' that carries the soul on its crest back to the Godhead and to *henosis* or Divine union. It is only in the Mystical Theology that the soul begins to make real progress on the Way to Knowledge of God. In the Affirmative Theology, the soul is beginning to get a sense of God and of His Mystery; in the Symbolic Theology, she is beginning to see the intelligible Meaning or significance of the symbols, which transcends in its brilliance the significance of philosophical and theological conceptions, as well as the intellect's capacity to receive the meaning and organize it in the understanding. This penetration of the symbolical order in the sacramental life of the Church forms the living link with *The Celestial Hierarchy,* because what the intellect perceives of the significance of the Divine symbols *is* the weakest illumination descending from the most subordinate order of the Angelic Intelligences.

In the Mystical Theology, the soul comes at long last to union, in which she "tastes" the Divine vitality in a direct way. This is the *telos* of the whole doctrine that Dionysius so painfully elaborated. From this vantage point, the metaphysical aspect of his doctrine seems almost incidental, because it is ordered to the final, mystical realization, to which purpose all the other elements of his system are organized.

INFLUENCES ON THE PSEUDO–DIONYSIUS

Before we begin a more detailed consideration of his metaphysical and mystical doctrines as well as their interrelation, let us look briefly at the sources that have aided the Pseudo-Areopagite as he formulated his position. This is a bit difficult because we are not able to be too precise. We cannot be certain of the full extent of the influences, but we can at least have some understanding of those elements that must have contributed to his system, having an impact on his thought.

To begin, we know that he was quite familiar with the Plotinian and Proclian systems. This was, as has been mentioned above, the intellectual climate of the Fifth Century. He was also intimately acquainted with the Biblical Tradition, both the *Old and New Testaments.* He had also read the works of many Fathers, and was versed in the writings of the Alexandrian School, especially those of Cyril.[27] It is probably from the Alexandrines that he learned the concept of hierarchy.[28]

In the expression of his vision, Dionysius also uses many of Plato's concepts. For the Dionysian scheme so closely resembles the Platonic, in its primary points, in Plato's essential intuition, that some hold that

Dionysius completes or fulfills this Platonic insight, which is concerned with the intelligibility of Being.[29] Many of the names or attributes predicated of God in *The Divine Names,* which are not biblical but philosophical, bear a close likeness to the Platonic list of attributes that are ascribed to the One, the Platonic God, in *The Parmenides.*[30] In the Dionysian insight that God is the absolute Good,[31] and that it is characteristic of His nature to share and to create, he comes very near the Platonic notion of the Good elaborated by Plato in *The Republic* (VI, 509).[32] There is also evidence of Plato's influence in the Areopagite's doctrine of the Ideas or Forms. Indeed, it is unmistakable that the Dionysian idea of God as Super-Essential Beauty has a direct relation to the Platonic and Neo-Platonic positions.

The intelligible universe in which the Angelic agencies act is certainly Plotinian in its triadic structure. This triadic element in the Pseudo-Dionysius corresponds to the three hypostases in Plotinian metaphysics, of The One, The Intelligence and The Soul. In Iamblichus and Proclus, the three hypostases are conceived as Being, Life and Intelligence, and each of these generates its own terms. Iamblichus' *Book of Mysteries* and Proclus' *Elements of Theology,* both of which are Plotinian in inspiration, resemble somewhat the Angelic Hierarchy of Dionysius insofar as they both reveal a preference for gradations of intelligibility that become more and more intense as we near the summit. For the same structure is present. The superior orders of Angels help the subordinate ones to receive the Divine Impulse of intelligibility.[33]

The Christian sources of his angelology include Gregory of Nazianzen, John the Eunuch, Cyril of Jerusalem, St. John Chrysostom and *The Apostolic Constitutions.* In all of these thinkers and in *The Apostolic Constitutions,* there is a hierarchical order of Angelic Intelligences set forth. Although the names of the Angelic orders and their places within the nine-fold scheme may differ, still we can see that these sources have contributed to Dionysius' effort to reveal the structure of *The Heavenly Hierarchy.*[34]

In his mystical doctrine, which is an expression of the uniqueness of his own experience, he has probably borrowed certain structural aspects from St. Gregory of Nyssa, that incomparable mystical theologian of the Early Church, especially the latter's anagogy of the mystical ascent. Also, in his stages of purification, illumination and perfection or union, which transcend sense and intellect in the soul's movement towards God in *Agnosia,* Dionysius might have taken these from Plotinus or at least was familiar with them, perhaps, using them in his own interpretation[35] of the stages in the mystical ascent to God. Also, in his notion of evil as non-being and his distinction between the *via affirmativa* and the *via negativa,* Dionysius is perhaps indebted to Proclus,[36] even though he interprets these methods in his own way, in conformity with his own insights into the nature of the Divine Life in the transcendent stream of eternity. He also inherits from Plotinus and Proclus their notion of the absolute, undifferentiated unity of The One. He seems to conceive the Trinity as the manifested "side" of the Divine nature, and the Godhead as such, beyond the plane of manifestation, as the primary dimension of the Divine Reality. For him, as for Plotinus, God is ultimately the super-essential Unity, and since Proclus follows Plotinus in most things, it is also true of his position. Dionysius, furthermore, seems to have borrowed the notions of emanation and return from them. This is apparent in the development of his principles of *proodos* and *epistrophe.*[37]

Pseudo-Dionysius made an attempt to reconcile his Christianity with his Neo-Platonic philosophical understanding. This was a difficult task, as Augustine later realized. For there are inherent weaknesses in the Neo-Platonic system of principles, which, when adapted to Christian Revelation, obscures the nature of the Trinity and the Incarnation. Insofar as the Trinity is concerned, the Neo-Platonic emphasis on the undifferentiated unity of The One makes it troublesome to conceive how the Unity can admit of the dynamic reality of the Persons. Given the immutable nature of The One and its extreme abstractness, the Incarnation presents a problem as far as the formulation of the doctrine is concerned. Dionysius had to deal with these basic issues that haunt any Christian who adopts Neo-Platonism,[38] in part or in whole. But being a mystic, and having flirted with the Gnostics,[39] he had an even more difficult task of discussing that which by definition is impossible to express in its actual reality. Still, he made the attempt, and we will see how well he succeeded.

I
DIONYSIAN METAPHYSICS

The metaphysics of Dionysius rests on an essentialistic doctrine. The emphasis is on intelligibility, the meaning of God (that He possesses in Himself) and on creation as dependent upon God. Whether it be the Divine Impulse in itself, or passing through the orders of the Angels, in the liturgy of the Church or in the Divine Ideas, it is all a question of an intelligible content that bears an ontological meaning in relation to the Divine Mystery. All the levels of the metaphysical order possess something of the inexpressible nature of God, and yet He transcends everything. God is the center of Unity in terms of which all things are unified, including the hierarchies and creation, as well as all intellectual beings. It is held together in being through Him. For it all serves His inscrutable purpose. The Impulse of His nature, communicating light, illumination or a noetic content about His mystery, flows throughout the entire cosmic cycle, which is propelled by the Divine Eros, the 'yearning', proceeding (proodos) from God, the Thearchy, the absolute *arche* or Principle, the Necessary One, through the nine orders of Angelic Intelligences, progressively growing weaker with each rank of the three triads, into the Hierarchy of the Church, in her sacraments, liturgy, rites and ministerial structure where its profound significance is veiled behind symbols that only the faithful or devout can grasp and penetrate. From here, the cycle begins to return (epistrophe) to God by way of the mystical ascent, which begins in *The Ecclesiastical Hierarchy* when the soul makes this penetration of the symbols. This seems to be primarily an intuitive process. When the soul does this, she is put into contact with the inner, transcendent significance, the Divine intelligibility and Meaning, which is carried on by the Divine Eros up into the 'Darkness' in which the soul grasps God in Unknowing, not comprehending the mystical Meaning but experiencing it. This is the great cosmic cycle of Dionysian metaphysics. Now we must go back and examine the details of the system in their ontological aspect. Here we are concerned with his metaphysical Principle, the Godhead as *mone* or immutable One and as dynamic, the Trinity. We are also interested in His attributes, the Forms, *logoi* and with creation, as well as with the Divine emanation and conversion.

II
THE GODHEAD

From the outset of his treatise on *The Divine Names* or attributes of God, in which he presents his metaphysics, the Pseudo-Dionysius states with great clarity that the attributes ascribed to God are *symbolic,* because God in His Godhead, in His ultimate essence, is the Nameless One.[40] His being is Nameless because the human intellect cannot grasp the infinite and ultimate Meaning of His nature. The Divine Names symbolically refer to God's "beneficent Emanations".[41] Thus, God is named through His causality. The rule for the predication of attributes, applied to the Godhead, requires that the Names be taken from Scripture.[42] But scriptural meanings are only true as far as they go. Their ultimate meaning is not apparent from the text. In this sense, they are symbolic.

The only way in which we can make meaningful predications of the Divine Reality concerning its being, which still remain vague, is to make affirmations about God, deny them and then reaffirm them of Him in a super-eminent or transcendent way.[43] In this way, attributes have an absolute significance that refers only to the Divine nature and not to creatures. Dionysius signifies this unique status of the Divine attributes by affixing the prefix 'hyper', 'super' or the adverb 'very'. Thus, God is referred to as very Being, super-Goodness, hyper-Meaningfulness, very Life, super-Wisdom etc.[44]

Now, when making these predications of God's nature, we have to keep in mind the crucial distinction which Dionysius makes between the unmanifested and manifested dimensions of the Divine nature. Moreover, this is the distinction between the undifferentiated and the differentiated Godhead. Strictly speaking, as undifferentiated, beyond distinction, form or concept, God is the Godhead, but as differentiated or manifested, conceived etc., God is the Trinity, the dimension turned toward creation, the dynamic aspect of the Divine nature. The Godhead is the Divine nature in its essence as *mone,* the unmovable stability of absolute, established self-dwelling and self-sufficiency, whereas, the Trinity is the Divine nature as *Eros,* spreading itself (proodos) without being diminished. The Trinity is the self-diffusive aspect of the Godhead. As the ultimate 'Form', it is beyond all apprehension. It is incommunicable and totally ungraspable. The unmanifested side of God is the immutable Ground where everything dwells in its essential implicitness. All essences are hidden in the Essence, the Godhead in its Solitude. From the undifferentiated Godhead, the differentiated God as Trinity eternally comes forth. What the attributes are in the Divine Ground, in the Godhead is an "ineffable and unknowable" Mystery that is hidden from us. In the Godhead, they are "incommunicable Ultimates", but in the differentiated Trinity, the revealed aspect of the Godhead, the attributes are called "Emanations and Manifestations."[45] The Godhead, as the "Transcendent Cause of all things"[46] cannot be approached by the rational mode of intellection. It has to be approached through the intuitive faculty, which takes the soul into the mystical Darkness and through this into the Divine Light.

Now again, the Trinity seems to be the Godhead's eternal act of comprehending its intelligibility through the contrast of the Persons, which allows the absolute Meaning of the Divine nature to shine forth from the dynamic interaction of the Persons. Somehow, the Trinity is the metaphysical and mystical Absolute of the Godhead-nature, which eternally accounts for God's self-knowledge. We have spoken of this before. It is the Divine Eros comprehending its essential meaningfulness and then over-flowing in a free, creative act, sharing its loving being, the intelligible Impulse, which is a communication of its inner Reality, passing it into creation and into individual intelligences, both angelic and human.

The only absolute predication we can make of the Divine being is that of its Unity. Hence, we can call it The One. To the whole Godhead this name of One is applicable.[47] Although we apply the terms of 'Trinity' and 'Unity' in our efforts to talk about God, these terms are inadequate to the Reality of the Godhead[48] when we speak in the absolute sense. Even the attribute of Unity does not tell us what this Unity as such means. And these terms actually are only meaningful when they refer to the differentiated aspect of the Divine nature.

Dionysius divides the Divine attributes into Undifferentiated Names and differentiated ones. He says that the "Undifferentiated Names belong to the entire Godhead", and these are the predications which are made super-eminently. Thus, the entire Godhead is "Super-Excellent, Super-Divine, Super-Essential, Super-Vital and Super-Sapient", etc.[49] The differentiated names, however, apply to the manifested side of God and, hence, belong to the Persons of the Trinity.[50]

When the Pseudo-Dionysius extols the absolute transcendence of the Godhead, its characteristic of being incomprehensible to the human mind, he is surely maintaining the Plotinian doctrine.[51] And this is emphasized by most Western theologians and metaphysicians, especially in the Christian, Jewish and Islamic Traditions. But the distinction between the transcendence of God as Godhead and His manifestation in the Trinity, which Dionysius belabors, is picked up by Eckhart[52] as we shall see in chapter twelve. It is also the theme of countless other mystics. It is a distinction, however, that is little noticed in the Christian philosophical and theological Tradition, especially from the Middle Ages on. This distinction, nonetheless, becomes more and more important as Christianity inevitable approaches, in dialogue, the religions and philosophical systems of Asia, especially Hinduism and Buddhism.

After the name of One or Unity, the intelligible idea which most applies to the Thearchy is the Good. This is the Platonic influence again. For the Good is the absolute value toward which all is moving. Predicated of God in a super-eseential manner, goodness is Goodness itself, sharing Himself, as this Goodness, with all of creation.[53] From the Source, the Divine Goodness, the Eros of Love, flows forth and shares its illumination with every intelligence. All things proceed from the Goodness of God. For all things "are grounded" and maintained in this Goodness.[54] This Goodness is communicated to the Angels, who relect it back to its Source. And they "manifest the Secret Goodness in themselves, and so to be (as it were) the angelic Evangelists of the Divine Silence and to stand forth as shining lights revealing Him . . ."[55]

The Good is the Absolute Standard that grounds the order of the universe. Not only giving its Impulse to the Angels, it also gives life and being to created entities. The Good is also Light, because Light is an archetype of the Good, of God; it extends to all things, as God, in His Goodness, offers Himself to all creatures (intelligences), who are open to receiving the Divine energy.[56] This Light, as the Divine Goodness, also communicates Spiritual Truth; it is a revelation of the Divine, a theophany.[57]

Goodness is also the Source of Unity, drawing all things to it. For "the Godhead . . . (is) the Supreme Fount and Producer of Unity . . ." [58] It is the Cause that unifies all of creation. All things seek the Good by the necessity of their respective natures.[59]

The Good is also Absolute Beauty. It is "the Super-Essential Beauty because of that quality which it imparts to all things severally according to their nature, and because it is the Cause of the harmony and splendour in all things . . . " It shares with all, according to the capacity of each, "the beautifying communications of Its originating ray . . ."[60] It is because of Divine Beauty that all things exist and have a harmonious relationship to others, in sympathy and more intensely, in community.[61]

The Good is also Love or 'yearning'. It is the Source of all love and the end, for every creature seeks this Love that, in its actuality, leads to the ecstatic union with God.[62] This Divine Eros runs through all things, ordering them to their Origin.

God is also Being, Life and Wisdom. He is Being insofar as He causes to be, bringing everyting into existence. It is Being that is His "primary gift" to all things. For all things exist because they first of all participate in Being, which flows forth from the Divine nature. Insofar as God is very Being, which He is in the manifested dimension of his Godhead, He is the absolute Cause of every existent.[63] All the principles, Ideas and essences of things derive from their participation in very Being; this is where they have always been present. From very Being, existence arises, as well as the order binding all things together. [64]

Existence is the primary participation in the Divine being, in the differentiated aspect of the Godhead. The Godhead, again, in its ultimate essence, is even beyond Being. For Being is the notion binding all manifestation. It governs multiplicity, order and the preservation of all things in existence. Being is thus not an absolute category in the Dionysian perspective, as it is in that of Aristotle and others. Being is usually the principal notion defining metaphysics, but in the case of Dionysius, it is the Super-Essential Godhead as transcendent Ground, beyond Being, that defines metaphysics, although he elaborates it in its manifested function as Efficient Cause.

Being, in God, is the intelligible principle that gives existence, which is, again, God's first and free gift to creatures. It *is* the primary participation in His manifested being, because He is necessary in Himself, and all things must first *be* participants of His existence insofar as they are contingent beings. For they "lean"on His Absolute Existence in order that they may themselves be. Dionysius says of God's being that: "From It and in It are very Being and the Principles of the world, and the world (itself) which springs from them and all things that in any way continue in existence."[65] All things exist implicitly in God, though He is none of them. The principles, exemplars or Divine Ideas exist in Him as Being, as well as the world and the universe or the notion of them.

God Himself, as Godhead, though His Impulse is expressed in all of His atrributes arising in His differentiated nature, yet transcends these Names. He resides "in a Secret Place beyond all Goodness, Godhead, Being, Wisdom and Life . . . " etc.[66] We can only 'celebrate' Him as the Giver of Being, Life and Wisdom to us,[67] but we cannot as such 'name' Him in His ultimate essence. Here as always, the mystical Dionysius speaks. His meatphysics, as a rational science of God, is chiefly characterized by the constraining limits of *qualification* and his constant appeal to the utility of Negative Theology as the proper approach to the ultimate Knowledge of God.

From God as Being, as First Cause and the Universal Source of all, come forth the Angelic Intelligences and also the human ones. He is the Source of our existence and that order which sustains us. He upholds the universal "natural laws" that govern the cosmos and souls.[68] We exist, as well as the Angels and all creatures, and we and they have our 'blessedness', because we exist and are happy in Him. In the Hierarchy of the Angels, He has bestowed a higher degree of being in some, those nearest to Him, than in others. All receive their being from His. His being, however, is only one of His attributes; it does not contain Him, but He contains it. He is the absolute "Measure of Existence," being anterior to Essence and essential Existence and Eternity, because He is the Creative Beginning, Middle, and End of all things."[69] Insofar as He is the Cause of all things and the upholder of their existence, He *is* all things. And insofar as He is transcendent to all things, He is not any of them, being totally beyond. "Hence all attributes may be affirmed of Him, and yet He is No Thing."[70] God is above all limitations, however they may be conceived. As his metaphysical doctrine unfolds, we see how beautifully his mystical vision is interwoven with it. It is actually a mystical metaphysics, since mystical consciousness probably produced it, for surely, Dionysius' own ineffable glimpses into the nature of the Godhead have greatly influenced his ontology. They are its eyes. Indeed, we will try to show that his mystical intuition most likely generated this ontology. As we have said above, he is constantly referring to the heights of the contemplative Vision of the Godhead beyond God. This is also one of Eckhart's themes, as we shall see.

Insofar as God is anterior to essence and essential existence, He is an absolute Unity. He is this Unity before He is essence and existence, since His Unity is ontologically prior to His essence or existence. This means, furthermore, that He precedes His intelligibility and even His essence as the essential Ground in its eternal quietude. For as the Godhead, He is infinite, immutable Stillness comprehending the simplicity of its Unity as a dwelling within its boundless Presence, which is formless, an absolute Identity resting in its ultimate, uncomplicated attention to its mysterious nature. The Trinity, as we have said before, is the Godhead's essential act of eternally grasping its nature, which is the comprehension of its Identity in its Meaning. The Trinity is what makes the Godhead to know itself. It is the TO BE of the Godhead. And the soul can see this and "be" this in God, in the Trinity.

III
EMANATION AND CONVERSION

God emanates (proodos) His "Absolute Essence into the universe of things."[71] This is essentially how He is related to creation and to His creatures. The Divine essence, as Trinity, overflows from its Love into creation; it shares itself with its creatures. This is an act that proceeds from God's freedom. It is not a consequence of ontological necessity, as it is in the view of Plotinus and others. Rather, God creates and gives Himself because of His Love and His Goodness. For He is self-diffusive, which is the nature of Goodness, that is, to share itself. He has a 'yearning' to do so, but this proceeds from His Will; it is freely given as a gift of His Goodness.[72]

The Divine *Proodos,* the emanating of God's Impulse, expressing the intelligibility, Meaning and inward essence of His nature, and the conversion of gazing back to Him, the return or *epistrophe,* mounting up through the Divine Darkness into the luminous orders of Angels, is "a perpetual *circle* for the Good, from the Good, in the Good, and to the Good, with unerring revolution, never varying its centre or direction, perpetually advancing and remaining and returning to Itself."[73] The motive behind His emanation, again, is precisely His Love or the Divine Eros, which passes through the cosmic circle and is its very being. This is how the Divine Purpose advances, for it proceeds through the sublime power of the Divine erotic, God's Love, which is a communication of His nature. Dionysius says of the Divine Eros that:

> . . . they call Him Yearning and Love as being a Motive-Power leading all things to Himself, Who is the only Ultimate Beautiful and Good (Reality) - yea, as being His own Self-Revelation and the Bounteous Emanation of His own Transcendent Unity, a Motion of Yearning simple, self-moved, self-acting, pre-existent in the Good and overflowing from the Good into creation, and once again returning to the Good.[74]

It is this simple desire of God to share His Secret, His absolute and infinite Meaning, so luminous and perfecting, with all intelligences, that accounts for His movement into the creative act, which brings forth the cosmos and all intellectual substances. Love follows a higher law, that although it appears as necessary to us, is yet *free,* because it arises from an absolute affirmation of its Goodness and the free desire to communicate itself to others.

The conversion, ascension or return to God, the *epistrophe* begins in the visible structures of *The Ecclesiastical Hierarchy* (as has been indicated above), which is the link with *The Celestial Hierarchy,*[75] in the 'mysteries' or sacraments of the Church, which symbolically contain, hidden within them, a *mystical content* conducive to the mystic ascent of the soul to the Source. For when the intellect understands these symbols and makes contact with the *logoi,* the intelligible content, then the soul begins the ascent. She makes contact with

The Celestial Hierarchy, which is reflected in *The Ecclesiastical Hierarchy* in whole and in the elements of its structure.[76] The soul, through Unknowing or *Agnosia,* passes among the orders of Angels and, in degrees, comes to the all-luminous Source of existence. We will discuss the mystical doctrine further on in this chapter and the next. Before doing this, however, let us consider how God creates the universe, the Angels, souls, and how He sustains them all, according to the Pseudo-Dionysius.

IV
THE DIVINE IDEAS OR EXEMPLARS

God, as the transcendent Cause of all things, as self-established essence, contains within Himself the eternal essences or exemplars of all things, and through these, He creates the cosmos, creatures and the Angels. Whereas in Plato, there is the semi-divine Demiurge[77] (demiourgos), the divine artisan, who takes the Forms or Ideas as models and creates the world in the Cosmic Receptacle, in the Pseudo-Dionysius' view, it is God Himself Who creates through His Eternal Ideas, which give Him the form for all things. There is here, in the Dionysian perspective, a slight equivocation between the Plotinian notion of strict emanation, which is monistic, and the Christian understanding of creation, which is dualistic. In the Christian view of creation there is a dualistic emphasis, since it procliams an absolute distinction between God and creatures. Reality is not reduced to one principle that plays the part of everything else (Monism). Reality, in the Christian view, includes the ontological integrity of individual substances, who are distinct in being from God. Dionysius seems to be torn between both of these powerful influences, but the Christian appears to predominate.

The Divine Ideas or Exemplars are for God the essences and patterns of things and also the laws which dtermine necessarily that essences will have fixed natures, thus, allowing for their realization or actualization, avoiding confusion. From these, He creates or emanates them into Being, into actualization. They were always present in the Divine Mind. The Exemplars are archetypal Ideas. Dionysius calls them the "preordinations and the beneficent Volitions."[78] These are the Platonic Forms, the Eternal essences of things. The Exemplars pre-existed in the super-essential Divine Unity. These Ideas, Forms, Exemplars or *logoi* are the essences that are *concreteable.* They can be actualized in existence. They were differentiated from the Divine Unity by a

Divine procession (proodos) from the unutterable essence of the God-head.[79] The Exemplars, as Divine Laws, distinguished the essences of all things from the undifferentiated Unity of the Godhead in which they were in a state of essential implicitness. The Exemplars were able to do this through the Divine Will, as a consequence of his action. The Exemplars, as Laws, are spoken of as "Preordinations or Divine and beneficent Volitions, Laws which ordain (direct) things and create them, laws whereby the Super-Essential pre-ordained and brought into being the whole universe"[80] These Divine Ideas also have a life of their own, even through they are guided by the Divine Will.[81] For as 'Pre-ordinations' and 'beneficient volitions', they are expressions of God's Purpose, and so, exist as intelligible Forms, essences etc., bearing the nature and structure of things, but they are also distinct from the Divine nature in which they participate, and yet which no idea, no matter how sublime and angelic can reveal.

Through the Forms, the Thearchy communicates knowledge about itself to the hierarchies. These Forms are the 'Divine Volitions', which contain God's purpose, and they proceed from Him into the realms of sense experience and the intelligible. They become immanent in the sensible and the intelligible as *logoi*. Through the *logoi*, God draws intelligences back to Himself.[82] From the *logoi* and from the Divine order itself, the intellect receives "certain images and semblances of His Divine Exemplars," which permit the soul to ascend through the Divine Darkness, the infinite, incomprehensible Meaning, to the Godhead beyond conception, form and all things.[83] And so, the soul returns to the transcendent Source, Who is the "Beginning and End of all things: the Beginning as their Cause, and the End as their Final Purpose."[84]

Dionysian metaphysics is a simple circle, a Divine circle, which begins with the absolute, dynamic aspect, the Cause of the universe and of all beings, and through the instrumentality of the Divine Eros, expressing itself through the intelligibility of the Ideas, communicates to *The Celestial* and *Ecclesiastical Hierarchies* and to creation, as well as to souls, something of its mysterious Meaning. The Divine Eros passes through these and inspires souls, who ascend by way of *Agnosia* (Unknowing), through the Angelic orders back to the Source. In God, they experience *henosis* or union, which results in *Theosis* or 'deifica-tion', in which the soul becomes God-like. It is easy to understand that the metaphysical doctrine of Dionysius is through and through impreg-nated with mystical insights. We will take up this point further on. Let us now turn to his mystical doctrine.

THE MYSTICAL INTUITION

Vanneste, in his brilliant work, *Le Mystere De Dieu,* [85] says that on the ontological level, the transcendence and causality of God are opposed. [86] The transcendence here represents the more ultimate, unmanifested dimension of the Divine nature. It is the sphere of the *via negativa.* Vanneste's point seems to be that in order to have a metaphysics, Dionysius has to accept a contradiction, albeit one that is resolved in God Himself. For how can we have metaphysics if God is so transcendent that we can say nothing about Him? Insofar as we can speak of Him in metaphysical terms, and thus have metaphysics, we must refer to Him as Cause. This approach, however, gives us no positive knowledge of His actual essence other than symbolic representations.

It is this Divine essence that concerns the mystical doctrine of the Pseudo-Dionysius. For this is the Omega Point toward which his entire system moves. Furthermore, Vanneste says that the mystical doctrine depends totally upon the category of transcendence. [87] Dionysius expresses this absolute transcendence in his simple but classical term 'beyond all', [88] which means that all that the intellect may conceive or know does not in any way come near to an actual revelation of God's being in His act in which He is the One Who Is. The way we may approach Him and be united to Him is not the way of rational knowledge. It is rather the way of inner Vision, and this is a path that is obscure to the normal expectation of reason. The supreme value of Dionysius' works is that, as Sharpe says, they "appeal to that perception of the inner Truth of things, which is alike in all ages and all countries, and which probably no man is altogether without." [89]

To explore the inner Vision that leads to the contemplation of God's essence, becoming aware of its absolute Meaning, but uncomprehending, being united with its Divine Impulse of Love, requires that the soul become *quiet* and it demands that she withdraw her attention from sense experience and intellection. [90] This is a universal requirement found in all systems of Mysticism. Moreover, it requires that after the understanding is "laid to rest", the analytical faculty being in abeyance, and in purity, the soul being freed from her passions, that she move "towards a union with Him whom neither being nor understanding can contain" [91] nor conceive. When the soul has reached this point of renunciation of understanding, sensible form and the realm of the earthly erotic, she is "led upwards to the Ray of that divine Darkness which exceedeth all existence." [92] This is the *Docta Ignorantia,* which leads to union or *henosis*. It is "the Super-Essential Ray of Divine Darkness",[93] which leads the soul into the Divine essence, and penetrates all ignorance, replacing it with Celestial Knowledge. The intellect cannot form a concept of God's Meaning when exposed to the Divine Light. We can be aware of God in a direct intuition or experience of Him, but this knowledge is *incommunicable,* because God is for us who have glimpsed Him or hope to, "incomprehensible."[94] And our poor words are worthless insofar as they cannot convey the Reality of God, for they can at best only evoke an *inkling* of Him.

The soul must pass beyond all standards of this world, beyond all spiritual experiences, if they are of the more primitive variety, such as visions and voices. She then enters "into the Darkness where truly dwells, as saith the Scripture, the One Which is beyond all things."[95] God is beyond all form. He is known in the Darkness of Unknowing, in uncomprehending, which does not depend on form, even the most refined, such as light and trumpets, the things which greeted Moses as he approached the dwelling place of God on Mount Sinai, things which only represented the Presence of God, but were not themselves God.[96]

When the soul, in Stillness, is united to God, she transcends all normal understanding, and becomes so *one* with Him that she can only behold the Divine Meaning directly, gazing upon Him. The soul then perceives the Form of God, Who is Himself formless, in the usual sense of form. She is united "to Him that is Wholly Unknowable, of whom thus by a rejection of all knowledge, she possesses a knowledge that exceeds her understanding."[97] God is unknowable because the intellect cannot organize His Meaning in human thought or language. The soul is blinded by the sheer intensity and scope of the Divine Impulse. She can only behold it and know it, but she cannot understand it. She knows it, but does not have the concepts to express what she knows. That is why God is 'Unknowable'. This Divine Darkness "is above the intellect". As the soul moves towards *henosis* or union with God, her words and concepts become suspended; she becomes "totally dumb, being at last wholly united with Him Whom words cannot describe."[98] In the ascent, we are practicing the *via negativa*, because we are disengaging our ideas in relation to God. But we must also transcend this practice and *rest* in God's Unity, the goal having been attained.

God, as Cause, transcends the sensible[99] and intelligible[100] realms. Dionysius goes on to say that the Godhead, the Divine Unity, is beyond "all affirmation by being the Perfect and unique Cause of all things, and transcends all negation by the pre-eminence of Its simple and absolute nature-free from every limitation and beyond them all."[101] Because it is "the Perfect and unique Cause of all things", it eludes description. It is perfect, and we have no actual idea that realizes this kind of perfection, that is, the Divine extent of perfection. He transcends the range of the category of negation, since He is so unique that we cannot conceive a negateable content. His existence is so transcendent that negation is not possible. For He is ontologically *prior* to both affirmation and negation. His nature, as a consequence of His metaphysical uniqueness, is free from all limitation. God's being cannot be captured in a concept. What the Godhead is, trascending affirmation and negation, is wholly unknowable to us.

In the First Epistle to the monk Caius, Dionysius says that the intellect, in its normal state of consciousness, addicted as it is to created lights, cannot reach the mystical Knowledge. Thinking only makes us blind to God's Presence, which is a Knowledge that makes all else pale in comparison. The mind can only know God. And this Knowledge comes "by a supernatural operation, which transcends its natural functions."[102] God is above the human intellect and even existence itself. In the manner in which He exists, He cannot be known (by concepts), and it is, to the intellect, as if He were non-existent, since the intellect cannot get a hold of what *is* there. For He exists in Himself, transcending existence or life as we know it. He is known in a special way, different from our normal operations. Because this Knowledge is incomprehensible and incommunicable, it seems like ignorance ,[103] to those who do not know. The Knowledge of God is a solitary venture, because it cannot be communicated to another in the same way in which it is first known. For what is spoken or written or even thought does not convey the absolute Reality of the mystic Vision of Truth.

Once the soul reaches the Divine Darkness and is knowing God to some degree, she can make contact with *The Celestial Hierarchy*, having passed through *The Ecclesiastical* one, and she knows "the simple sublimities of *The Heavenly Hierarchy.*"[104] The hierarchies are so arranged that they communicate knowledge of God's nature. They are directed to the facilitation of 'deification', the process of becoming God-like, which occurs in this mystical ascent. The Impulse that God communicates to the Angelic Intelligences gives them Light according to their capacity to receive it.[105] The soul probably is drawn into the Divine Stream of the Angelic orders and is purified, illuminated and perfected before entering into the Divine Presence in its fullness. In steps, the gradations of the Angelic Intellects, the soul moves towards God. The Angels lead her to Him, revealing more of His nature through

the Impulse of the Divine intelligibility and Light which they possess.
[106] Consider, for example, the Angelic ordering in Dante's *Paradiso,*
[107] which bears the mark of Dionysian influence. It portrays this important function of the Angels of leading souls to God and of imitating
the God-nature in themselves as far as their ability permits. For they
are Reflectors of His Rays.

When the soul arrives into the Divine Presence in itself, then she
has reached the Fount of Pure Unity in Stillness, which is infinite
Meaning resting in itself, established as eternal, Necessary Existence,
where God dwells in the absolute, ultimate intelligibility or Meaning
that He possesses as His very being. Here in God, the soul awakens and
beholds the mysterious act of the Godhead in which it is the dynamic
Trinity. The soul achieves *henosis* or union, which is, again, a *theosis*
or a 'deification', in which the subject-object polarity is superseded
and the soul experiences a union beyond words and thoughts. She is
overcome in the intense, luminous Presence of God's boundless, majes-
tic *Significance.* This great ecstasy is an adumbration of ultimate Beatitude. We will explore this 'deification' further in the following essay.

It is thus that the Dark, obscure Knowledge, the object of *The
Mystical Theology,* the ascending or Apophatic method, is probably the
Angelic Knowledge of the Divine Source, the *divinizing* Knowledge,
which is the highest level of mystical understanding. In this Knowledge, the soul attains a direct *awareness* of God's Presence insofar as
she knows God from within His own awareness of Himself, but only to
the degree that He permits and of which she is capable.

THE RELATIONSHIP OF MYSTICISM AND METAPHYSICS

To return now to our original assumption, that Dionysian metaphysics flows from Dionysian mysticism, we can observe three points
that support this contention. For we find that Dionysius is indeed a
mystic, that he possesses a mystical doctrine, and that he announces the
utter importance he attaches to his mystical intutition within the very
workings of his metaphysical treatise, *The Divine Names.*

That the Pseudo-Dionysius was himself a mystic would seem indisputable. Hence there is no point in estalishing this further. His writings
are a solid proof of his own mystical insights. Also, no one can deny
the second point, i.e., that he has a mystical doctrine, since we are all
aware that he in fact does. This is too obvious to pursue any further as
well. Now, the third point, that of his announcements of his mystical
intuition and their importance, announcements which occur within

the body of the treatise on *The Divine Names,* is more subtle, even though his declarations are clearly stated. They are cryptic asides, pronouncements of principle of utmost significance, and they occur all throughout his treatise and his other works. We will consider three of them.

In the very beginning of his work on the Divine attributes, when he is discoursing on the approach to Divine Knowledge, he refers to that ". . . Union which exceeds our faculty, and exercise of discursive and intuitive reason", which is an obvious reference to *henosis* or the ecstatic elevation of the intellect. He says, furthermore, that the Super-Essential Godhead is known super-essentially by "unknowing, which (is found) in the Super-Essence."[108] This 'Unknowning' is *Agnosia,* the 'Unknowing' found in the Divine Darkness, the characteristic of incomprehensibility that the soul encounters as she makes the ascent to God. *Agnosia* is the soul's inability to grasp the Divine nature. There will be more on this in the next chapter. Further on in the treatise, Dionysius comes right out and says that he has had mystical experiences.[109] The way in which he does this supports the thesis of a direct relationship existing between his mystical Vision and his metaphysics, for his metaphysical doctrine attempts to approximate rationally the structure of Reality flowing from God, but *known* in Him. When Dionysius comes to clarify the distinction between the Cataphatic and Apophatic approaches to the Divine Mystery, he says:

> And yet . . . the Divinest knowledge of God, the which is received through Unknowing, is obtained in that Communion which transcends the mind, when the mind, turning away from all things and then leaving itself behind, is united to the Dazzling Rays, being from them and in them, illumined by the unsearchable depth of Wisdom.[110]

Rolt, in a note commenting on the above, says that here Dionysius is not being theoretical, but is presenting his own mystical intuition, which is based on his own actual experience.[111] This sublime realm is God's Place; it is beyond the deomain of the rational and the human. It is even beyond the soul's own subjectivity, because in mystical union, she enters God's Subjectivity and adopts His conditions of knowing, which infinitely surpass our conditions and concepts. For he perceives the unlimited range of each essence and of Essence itself. Most of all, He is aware of Himself as the Infinite Essence, for He is that Meaning Himself.

Thus, the entire movement of Dionysian thought, his ontology and his mysticism, finds its fulfillment not in metaphysical speculation, but in the *attainment* of union with the Godhead. Ultimately, we learn far more about God in "suffering" the Divine Rays of the Sacred Source,[112] than we do from speculative theology or even from Scripture, both of which are secondary instruments of Divine Truth. In leading others to the mystical heights, Dionysius is, as St. Bonaventure remarks: "the prince of mystics."[113] For Dionysius succeeds in awakening our consciousness of God in order that we too may be led up to and, in God's time, which is Eternity, allowed to enter:

> . . .*in (to) the dazzling obscurity of the secret Silence, outshining all brilliance with the intensity of their darkness (the Unchangeable Mysteries of Heavenly Truth), and surcharging our blinded intellects with the utterly impalpable and invisible fairness of glories which exceed all beauty.*[114]

This is the Dionysian experience expressed in a prayer. May it also be ours, as we pass from his 'Divine Philosophy,' his mystical metaphysics into the Living Reality of God's immense, luminous and incomprehensible Presence, but always remembering that we cannot grasp God's essence, and thus to know that we cannot understand Him, *is* the ignorance that is yet wisdom. His Meaning, beyond existence as we know it, is the Stream that carries the soul into His Dwelling, a place beyond time and the Universe. The soul is brought into His Supreme Intellect, resting in His simple Meaning that is complete, Living Truth in Himself grasping all other meanings in His absolute Essence.

In the following chapter, we will enter further into the Apophatic Theology, the *method* of mystical ascent. The emphasis will be on the contemplative realization of union with the Divine.

II
THE RELIGIOUS EXPERIENCE OF THE PSEUDO—DIONYSIUS

Dionysius is quite relevant to our times just as he was in the Middle Ages, which revered him so. For he is a *link* or bridge between Catholicism and Eastern Orthodoxy, a celebrated mystical theologian, who provides common ground for the ecumenical dialogue in terms of a shared spirituality. Not only is he a bridge between Eastern and Latin Christianity, however, but also between Western and Asian Thought, particularly on the level of Theology and Mysticism. His theme of the essential unknowability of God, in the discursive mode of intellection, is also found in the great Vedic Tradition, especially as it is elaborated in its commentaries, *The Upanisads*. Since it is principally with Hinduism and Buddhism in Asia that Christianity must dialogue, the contribution that the Pseudo-Dionysius can make is truly enormous. He is relevant to all ages and traditions. For he is the noble teacher who hands on not a speculative structure, but a *mystical* doctrine and a method for reaching Wisdom, as we have seen above. This Wisdom is not a dry theological system, but a living, intimate knowledge of God based on an *experiential* approach. It comes from a realtionship with Him, taking place beyond the bounds of sense perception ad reason.

Such a method of Theology is very important, and especially so in our time when so much of Western Theology lacks this experiential foundation. The Pseudo-Dionysius has something valuable to teach us about the nature of genuine Theology, which is *always* centered on God. For again, the Areopagite's doctrine is first and foremost a "science of God".[1] Like all authentic knowledge, it has a direct relation to experience, in this case, to his religious or mystical experience. It is thus existential in the profoundest sense.

In this chapter, we will discuss the mystical experience of the Pseudo-Dionysius on the level of his contemplative methodology, the Apophatic way or the *via negativa*. Of course this does not attain to his own intimate consciousness of God's ineffable Essence which cannot be captured in language, as we have observed so many times above, but it does suggest the way to discover this knowledge and thus also a way for Theology to speak more adequately of God.

THE DIVINE 'DARKNESS'

The Pseudo-Areopagite's religious insights are absolutely central to his thought. For, as we have seen, even his metaphysics is a product of his mysticism. This is true because it is generated by his keen awareness of the Divine nature. Again, his metaphysics, is, in a sense, incidental to his mystical doctrine. He shows that God is the Good[2] because He is the Beginning and the Destiny of all souls. All things exist as a result of the Good. He is also Being, since He causes all things to be and thus is the life-giving Source. All creatures must participate in His being in order to be at all.[3] In the same way, God is also called Life, because He is the Source of Angelic and human immortality as well as our very existence. For He is very Life Himself,[4] This is how Dionysius emphasizes the absolute uniqueness of God's kind of existence. He is the Essence of Life but He trascends our life.[5] He is also the Living Wisdom, the very Reality of Truth, the Truth which is known in ecstatic union. He is Wisdom because He knows Himself and in knowing Himself, He is able to know all things as well.[6] He is also the Truth, the actuality of Perfect Meaning and intelligibility.

We can predicate all of these attributes of God, but this knowledge which is on the metaphysical level does not reach to the Divine Essence itself. It cannot express the content of God's Essence, for God's essential nature is bound up with His eternal act of being Who He is. And this act is unlimited in all senses, being indescribable in its dynamic Reality. It is only in treading the path of negation, the *via negativa* being drawn into God's infinite actual Meaning, beyond positive statements of attribution to the Divine nature, that we come to the absolute Knowledge of God. Again, Dionysius says of it:

> . . . *The Divinest Knowledge of God, the which is received through Unknowing, is obtained in that communion which transcends the mind, when the mind, turning away from all things and then leaving even itself behind, is united to the Dazzling Rays, being from them and in them, illumined by the unsearchable depth of Wisdom.*[7]

The soul arrives into the Divine nature and knows it in an unknowing manner; she is made aware of the Divine Impulse, being united to it. She is unable to grasp the Meaning, the Living Wisdom of God's Essence in the pure actuality of being Infinite Truth, possessing total Reality in Himself. Again, we can know it, but we cannot understand it with our limited capacities and categories. We can know God in His Way and through Him in His 'dazzling' Light, and this is the only way in which we are able to know Him. So, we must give up any attempt to grasp God with the speculative reason. We should rather apprehend

Him in His own self-luminosity, which trascends our metaphysical power to contain in thought or language. We must enter into God's Dwelling with Himself which is beyond Being and beyond our attempts to name him.[8] Only the Apophatic method suffices to give us some intimation of God's uncircumscribable nature, but this does not grant us a positive content that the intellect can hold on to in a clear fashion.

He cannot be named because the mind cannot convey the boundless *Significance* of His nature. Again, all that the soul can do before God is to receive an awareness of His Presence in the process of Vision. She cannot understand what is being known. For God's being exceeds the limits of our ideas. Concepts are tools through which we extend our understanding, but these tools are fragile, finite instruments. We cannot know God with them. At best we can see Him faintly reflected in them. We can and must receive God in and through Himself, in and through His Supreme Concept of Himself which is His Meaning and in His love.

To acquire this Meaning, which is the end toward which "mystic contemplation" leads, demands that the soul pass beyond sense experience and the operations of the intellect. The understanding has to be suspended[9] in order for the Divine Ray of Wisdom to enter the soul's rest and communicate itself to the intellect and the will in an inenarrable way. By going beyond the impressions of the senses, images, forms, thoughts and concepts of the mind, the soul is "led upwards to the Ray of that divine Darkness which exceedeth all existence."[10] But this 'darkness' is an excess of Light; it is God's infinite meaningfulness, which is a total Mystery to the human mind. God is a supreme Mystery in Himself Who will not be known through reason. For He dwells in this Super-Essential Darkness that is too bright or intense for the soul to handle. He is, in His Darkness, "that One Who is beyond all things."[11] We have to let go of our ideas (all reasoning), especially about God,and allow Him to teach us about Himself in the 'darkness' of this 'Unknowing', an 'Unknowing' that gives us a knowledge that is more certain than our own existence. So we must plunge into "the Darkness of Unknowing", passing beyond our awkward and feeble attempts at understanding, and thus giving ourselves completely to Him, we are united with Him. When our faculties are suspended, the intellect's capacity is expanded to embrace the Vision of God in His 'Darkness', in His boundless and unutterable Mystery. By letting go of "all knowledge he (the soul) possesses a knowledge that exceeds his understanding."[12] Between this world of the senses and the super-essential Realm of the Godhead there is this 'darkness',

THE VIA NEGATIVA AND 'UNKNOWING'

Again, this knowledge of the Divine Essence can be known but not understood. The soul has it from unitive Vision but lacks God's self-understanding, His comprehension of Himself. How God knows Himself is too overpowering for the soul. The infinite intelligibility and simplicity of God's inner truth appear as darkness to the intellect. The intellect cannot make sense of His Essence, especially is this true in the rational mode of knowing. The soul can know the Divine Essence but not in the sense of a precise understanding as one can know a finite object. The soul knows more in the way of an experience whose meaning is intuited without clearly defining it. One can know God through this 'Unknowing', that is, by *experiencing* the Divine Reality in a direct way but without understanding this ungraspable Reality.

Mystical experience or contemplation, the direct unitive Vision of the Godhead, the Trinity, the absolute in the soul and in itself, that is, in the consciousness of the creature which is an elevation into God's being, is an experience vastly different from every other situation of human life. For it is not human consciousness in the ordinary sense, whether bodily or speculative. Insofar as contemplation constitutes the meaning of being human in its highest sense, it is thus the most important activity. It is a transcendent level of Truth. It is not reached by any of our usual ways of knowing, such as sensation, imagination or conceptualization in the discursive mode of thought. The mystical life attains a degree of understanding, of direct Vision of the Absolute, in a way of consciousness that belongs wholly to God. The soul is progressively brought into God's Stream of Transcendence, the pure Luminosity of God's way of being which is 'darkness' to her intellect, because it is above the range of the soul's conception, capacity and other acts of understanding. To "understand" God the soul would have to be God. The way "to be" God is to become united to His inner Truth which is Himself. And the way to this state of consciousness, the highest, is through a rejection of sense perception, form, imagination, thought, sin all together, and pass into the 'Darkness' of the Divine, which is more luminous than all of the stars combined. It is thus as darkness to the soul in the act of "Unknowing', the obscure knowing of that which is indeed being known.

This darkness, the non-comprehension of what is being experienced, is a condition in which the soul has absolute knowledge or Wisdom from a straightforward exposure to the Divine Source but not an understanding of what is encountered in this state. Thus, to know God is not to know what is in fact known, a perfect paradox. Indeed, it is one of the profoundest paradoxes of the Spiritual Life which is true in any of the world religious traditions. There is no real contradiction in this situation, since one does *know* God. It is just that one does not grasp His intelligibility, nor can one adequately explain the content of mystical experience to another. It is similar to someone who perceives an event take place without knowning its context, and hence not understanding its significance.

We must make the *ascent* to God through the medium of the *via negativa,* because God can only be known in His own way and through conditions that are proper to Him. The *Via negativa* finds its way ineluctably into the *via mystica,* and is itself this mystical way. No experience or notion in any way approximates the absolute Reality of God as He is in Himself. That is why one best begins the mystical journey to God by way of the Apophatic method. This method is a kind of *purification* of the intellect and the will as well as the soul's consciousness, for one is then centered on God, the very destiny toward which one moves. The person has said *yes* to God's invitation and to His design. The soul is seeking the Source, and this is an important decision of the will. In fact, it is the most essential decision that one can make in life. The Apophatic way thus purifies the soul's faculties and rightly orders them, preparing one for the Vision of God. Through the *via negativa,* the soul is led into that 'Unknowing' in which the Divine Darkness, God's brilliance and glory, are beheld,[13] which are beyond the range of all experience that is bounded by the temporal conditions of earthly life. The Apophatic way is not really a theological method in the conventional sense. It is rather an exercise in stopping the mind's ceaseless "chatter" in order to transcend thought and become attuned to the Divine Silence and activity. And this practice leads to that 'Unknowning', as a result of God's grace, as a river finds the sea. This 'Unknowning' is like the situation of a child who is open to experience but uncomprehending what is unintelligible to him, since he has not yet acquired sufficient experience of life. Of course, the only difference between this child and the mystic is that the mystic never comprehends God, while the child learns to understand something in his range of experience.

Again, the emphasis in the Dionysian method of contemplation is on this process of Unknowning or *nescience,* as Elmer O'Brien calls it,[14] following J. Vanneste. O'Brien says that this *nescience* or un-knowing is not ignorance. It is the way God is known and the only way.[15] It results in a unitive Vision of the Divine, but one is silent before that which defies description. What propels the soul to the mys-tical heights is this dynamic *nescience*[16] or knowing by not knowing, knowing but not comprehending. Thus, according to Dionysius, it is not love that unites us to God, as it is for St. Augustine, St. Bernard, the author of *The Cloud,* St. John of the Cross and countless others. Mystical union with the Source is a passive act of attention, the intel-lect being devoid of its own content. 'Unknowing', *nescience* or the *via negativa* is an exercise in freeing the intellect from all finite con-ceptions and objects in order that the soul may be prepared to receive the Divine Impulse of God's being which eternally proceeds forth from Him as 'darkness' and then returns to Him. The Impulse coming from the Divine Source is too great for the intellect to perceive un-aided. Only grace permits us to have an awareness of it. As the Areo-pagite says: "We must be transported wholly out of ourselves and given unto God."[17]

The nearer we get to the Source in His eternal and inaccessible Light, the more circumscribed our language and conceptions become in re-lation to Him. Our thoughts and ideas are too discursive and purely intellectual to be of any value in this Realm above the mind. This is true of the state of most of our knowledge. But the closer the soul comes to God, the more sparing become her utterances, until at last she is struck dumb before the eternal glory of God.[18] The higher we go in the ascent, the greater becomes our inability to express our thoughts and feelings concerning what we are perceiving of God. Our Vision of Truth becomes progressively more unified. We no longer see things simply in their multiplicity but in their *unity* in the Divine Mind, in the Source.

As the soul continues her climb to God, she is still aware of distinc-tion, of the subject-object relation. But when she arrives at the point where thought itself is left behind then the soul reaches pure Unity in which she knows herself for the first time, for she perceives herself as she is in God, in His Unity. She knows herself in and through His in-expressible Oneness. And as Dionysius says, the soul is "at last wholly united with Him Whom words cannot describe."[19] The mind is liber-ated from the constraining limits of mortality and knows the embrace of eternal Bliss, the promise of Immortality in the blessedness of Heaven. The soul thus has a foretaste of Beatitude.

To reach the heights of contemplative Vision we must lose ourselves in God. We must give up ourselves and renounce our thoughts, for thoughts are what drag us down and bind us to this veil of tears.[20] This is what Our Blessed Lord was trying to teach His Apostles. We are victims of our different moods that pass before the screen of consciousness, but we should learn to ignore them, as they are as ephemeral and volatile as the individual waves of the ocean. We must rather let them go and seek the blissful and ineffable Presence of God, Who is *always* there waiting to lead us into His infinite, unitive domain of being. What Dionysius is exhorting us to is a simple method of freeing ourselves from the slavery of all thought, imagaination and ordinary experience. The one "object" that we may concentrate on is the Divine Darkness above the mind, the Source in His luminous, blinding Presence, in His Unity of inconceivable Essence.

Again, God as He eternally is in Himself *is* beyond our affirmations and negations. Dionysius says that God transcends every affirmation because He is the underived Cause of all that is or can be, and that He is beyond every negation because of His utter simplicity. We have mentioned this before. He is totally unlimited and is above even the possibility of limitation, affirmation and negation.[21] He *is* or exists in such a way that neither affirmation nor negation can reach His domain of existence. We do not exist in comparison to the absolute way in which He does. God's boundlessness prevents us from capturing His Mystery in any sense or in any system, for our descriptive definitions are wholly inadequate as a consequence of their finitude. He is in His own right in a total way.

The method of the Pseudo-Dionysius leads us through the 'unknowing' of the intellect in mystical Vision, an experience in which the soul perceives the Divine Essence, the Darkness of the Godhead's awesome brilliance and enters the dynamic Presence of God in His Mystery. There, we find Him in His eternal Now and ourselves; this is His everlasting relation to Himself in the Persons of the Trinity, the eternal act of the Divine being in which He grasps His Identity and is able to love. The soul sees all of this in a unitive relationship with God, a relationship that proceeds at the initiative of His grace, but which is encouraged by her response to His invitation. It is God's comprehension of Himself which happens eternally that the soul meets and in which she participates in a direct act of her attention, having been elevated by Divine grace into the unitive Vision of Truth.

There are many ways or methods to come to the *experiential* knowledge of God. Several of these have been practiced for countelss centuries in India and from the earliest times in the Church, especially in the great tradition of the Desert Fathers and having developed in the Middle Ages within the context of a thriving monastic culture. Even though this is true, the mystical Vision, culminating in the unitive life with the Source, a permanent state of God-centered realization, the awareness of His Presence, is yet a grace given to whomsoever God chooses to give it. Methods prepare us; they are a seeking of God, a knocking and God responds by elevating our consciousness to a penetration of His Mystery in "the dazzling obscurity of the Secret Silence, outshining all brilliance with the intensity of (its) darkness. . ."[22]

'DEIFICATION'

The Pseudo-Dionysius shows us that Theology must ultimately be grounded on relaization of God's inner Light, an intimate union with Him, a near identification with His eternal way of existence. This is what Dionysius means by 'deification' which is a common term used in all of his works or is at least what he is attempting to communicate. This is his notion of *theosis* which we have mentioned in the preceding chapter. This notion is integral to the Spirituality of the Orthodox Church, although it is equally attested to in the Latin Church and expressed in the theme of the mystical marriage, which many mystics discuss in great detail. This is especially true of Spanish Mysticism. 'Deification' is the ultimate situation of being one with God's essential Consciousness and Truth. It is the state of being God-like. Theology, in its rational mode, is addicted to discursiveness, an overabundance of reasoning from premise to conclusion, as if Wisdom could be attained simply by this approach. Furthermore, the attributes that man conceives God of having, which are taken from Scripture, His effects in history, such as Being, Goodness, Mercy and many others are derived from the way in which God has acted toward us. These positive attributes, however, do not touch, reveal or contain the Divine Essence, the Truth of God. The Divine Essence is the Truth of God Himself, as He is in Himself. To reach God as he is in Himself, the soul must realize first that God alone holds the key which unlocks the Secret of His Reality. We are not only dependent upon Him for our life but also for our eternal Happiness.

One cannot extort this knowledge of the living Truth, of God in

Himself, the Source in His sourceness. This is the knowledge of His essential whatness, His Secret act of being Who He Is. To acquire this knowledge one must be united to Him in that divinizing elevation of the intellect to the celestial heights of God in the super-dazzling Presence of His ultimate Reality. Again, this absolute knowledge, which is Wisdom from an experiential awareness of His being, must arise from the purification of the understanding in the Divine Darkness of God's ever-lasting, luminous comprehension of Himself.

'Deification' means that the soul has become like unto the Divine or has been 'deified' insofar as the intellect, will and consciousness are so totally one with God that the soul shares the Impulse of God's eternal inner Life. One is thus 'deified' through direct *participation* in what God is in Himself, that which is always hidden from creation. 'Deification' in no way means that the actual, metaphysical distinction between God and creature is overcome. Such is not the case and can never be so. Many mystics in several traditions caution that we guard against making this claim of actually being God. There is always the unbridgeable ontological gap between God and the soul. God in His great mercy extends His invitation to us to share His unending life, but not to take His place. We have our Beatitude from Him and in Him. It is a terrible conceit or vanity to claim that one is God. Not only does such a statement lack humility, it also lacks truth. The Areopagite's doctrine does not suggest that direction.

The mystical state itself, which is a permanent acquisition, perhaps, once seen in terms of the insight gained, holds the *key* to Truth. God in His Trinity is the content of the Divine TO BE, how He is in Himself and how we can particpate or 'be' this with Him. We can and must have this unitive life with God, that which reveals the celestial strings of the Divine Harp, the angelic music of God's everlasting Reality. This is our vocation as human beings.

The mystical state, furthermore, is like the all-encompassing wind in the forest which surrounds one on every side, revealing a Presence that speaks in just being present. To be in God as a candle is one with the sun in being held up to it, to be 'deified' is to be completely absorbed (while retaining one's own identity, a distinct substance) into God's inner Truth, being united to Him and seeing everything in His unitary Vision, in His understanding, but limited by our lack of capacity to receive too much of the Divine Light, the absolute Reality of Who God is. 'Deification' or *theosis* is a *transformation* of the one who faces God in prayer, the contemplative life beyond the reason. It is like being in the presence of a great Light that again surrounds one, and then slowly grows stronger and brighter while permitting one to become accustomed to it. All of a sudden, the Light increases its brilliance to an unlimited degree and one is penetrated on every side and through and through with the radiance of God's unutterable glory. This is something of what the Pseudo-Dionysius means when he speaks of this deification or divinization. It is the Divine Light itself that transforms a soul into a 'deified' being, for such a one becomes like unto God Himself. It is a knowledge and a way of higher existence that is open to every person. And it is the chief need of our age as of every other. For every epoch of history is like every other in the basic structure of reality and life which never change regardless of technological progress. 'Deification', as the goal of contemplation and the Christian Life, is what is most befitting the Church's supernatural dignity, and it is what she is entrusted to teach. It is also what Theology has for too long neglected until comparatively recent times. Theology must regain its contact with mystical Wisdom, with contemplation, else it assumes the quality of being a parasite. It must become what it was for Dionysius, i.e., 'a science of God', and this has a practical end, nothing less than helping souls to discover the Presence of God in themselves and in everything else. This is the true nature of Theology.

12
ECKHART'S MYSTICAL DOCTRINE OF THE GODHEAD

Meister Eckhart (1260-1328), the "mystic's mystic", although he is perhaps one of the least understood of the great spiritaul masters, still, few have had as much influence in history as he has had. His well known disciples, Tauler, Suso and Ruysbroeck are proof of this, and there is also considerable contemporary interest in him. His impact on Western Thought and Mysticism generally, as well as his influence on German Philosophy in particular, cannot be over-emphasized. In a sense, the Germans have been intoxicated with elements of his fruitful vision. His impact on Fichte and Hegel is proverbial. Even Heidegger, in his later years, was somewhat inspired by his unique insights. There has always been confusion, however, as to Eckhart's meaning when he speaks about the Godhead. Thus, we turn to the task of elucidating this central idea of his mystical experience. We have touched upon the Godhead above but not in sufficient depth. Here we will try to go a bit further.

In this essay, we would like to consider Eckhart's notion of the Godhead in its various dimensions, i.e., God, the Trinity and the Ground or Essence, which is the Godhead itself, in order that we may form a tentative view of what precisely the Godhead is, that is, what God is in His essential nature. We will also deal with the question of the soul's relationship to God. We attempt this consideration of the Divine Mystery only insofar as this is possible in language.

Eckhart uses many terms to express the inexpressible Reality of God's ultimate essence. Some of these terms are metaphors, while others are more technical. For he calls the Godhead the Superessential Unity, the Ground, the bottomless sea of the Godhead, the Stillness, the flowing fountain, the Abyss of the Godhead, the river and fount of the Godhead, unnamed being, nameless essence, Divine loneliness, the Solitude, the Desert and Wilderness of the Godhead, unnatured nature, and countless other expressions.

In the development of the formal structure of his doctrine - the content being his own experience of the Divine - Eckhart was influenced by Plotinus, Proclus, St. Augustine and the Pseudo-Dionysius,[1] to mention the important figures who helped in the formation of his speculative structure. For surely, there can be little doubt that Dionysius' idea of the Godhead looms large in Eckhart's reflections and formulations. The fact of his influence should become apparent as we unfold his doctrine. Moreover, Eckhart's Absolute, the Unknowable, the Wilderness of the Godhead, the *Wüste Gottheit* is The One beyond knowledge and Being of Plotinus and the Pseudo-Dionysius.[2] This *Wüste Gottheit* or wilderness of the Godhead is God's essence or *Wesen.* This is His very being. It is also the Source and being of the world.[3]

For Eckhart, God qua God is not absolute. God as such is the manifested "side" of the Godhead. He is the Absolute turned toward creation, the active dimension of the Divine nature. Eckhart says of this relationship between God and the Godhead that: "God reigns (forever) in distinction of Persons, but His reign in the beyond is in unity of nature. There God is the Kingdom of Himself, being superessential."[4] Here we see the clear influence of Plotinus and Dionysius. God creates and guides events, but the Godhead, as the Superessential Unity above distinction is idle or Still, being at rest. As absolute Unity, God is "free from all activity."[5] It is this Superessential Unity, the Godhead, that is the Kingdom of God.[6] Eckhart thus places the emphasis upon Unity as Essence. It also (his position) assumes that the active or dynamic aspect is inferior to the *quiescent* aspect. Of course such a notion is unacceptable for a Christian, although perfectly intelligible for a Buddhist.

THE TRINITY

It is more precise to say that it is the Trinity which is the manifested side of the Godhead rather than God Himself, because when Eckhart says God, he means either the Godhead or the Trinity; thus, God is the term referring to the entire Mystery of the Divine Life. In Sermon LVIII, entitled "Divine Understanding", Eckhart portrays the Trinity as a game or a *play* which the Divine Persons eternally enact. We have alluded to this above. This is a very beautiful and profound insight into God's nature, and is probably the product of a more common experience in the heights of contemplation. Eckhart says:

> *What is this play? It is His eternal Son. There has always been this play going on in the Father-nature. Play and audience are the same. The Father's view of His own nature is His Son. The Father embraces His own nature in the quiet darkness of His eternal essence which is known to none except Himself. The glance returned by His own nature is His eternal Son. So the Son embraces the Father*

> *in His nature, for He is the same as His Father, in His nature. Thus, from the Father's embrace of His own nature there comes this eternal playing of the Son. This play was played eternally before all creatures . . . The Son has eternally been playing before the Father as the Father has before His Son. The playing of the twain is the Holy Spirit in Whom they both disport themselves and He disports Himself in (them) both. Sport and players are the same. Their nature (is) proceeding in itself. 'God is a fountain flowing into itself', as St. Dionysius says.* [7]

Eckhart is not being merely poetic here. What he is trying to express is the inner *dynamic* of the Divine nature, which is based on God's contemplation of Himself in which He knows Himself as other in His Son. In this play, God is grasping His very meaning, His intelligibility which is revealed to Him as the Son Who manifests to Him eternally the infinite range of His Meaning, Truth and Being. It is a game or play because the script is known before hand. It has always been happening. Many mystics are attuned to this dimension of Divine Life, and most would see it as the expression of the essential nature of God. This is certainly the case with numerous mystics in the Christian Tradition. For this seems to be where Ruysbroeck would place the emphasis of his experience. Thus, from this glimpse, we can see something of the Divine simplicity revealing itself in an essential act of play, which is actually the very dynamic of God's self-identity.

But this dynamic act of self-identity is also one of love. Again, the profoundity of it all is that God is this 'simple' *unmoving-movement* within the Trinity which accounts for God's self-knowledge and also for His perfect Love. For it is His Love which inspires the play in the "theatre" of His own being; it is the energy of this Divine "drama". This very dynamic of intelligibility, in terms of which He eternally knows Himself in His Image, the Son, and which is confirmed and unified in the Holy Spirit, is a pure self-offering of Love. That is the motive force intrinsic to the trinitarian interaction of the Persons. Love desires to know, but in God, the act of knowing or self-identity, expressed in the play, is in itself the very act of Love. It is the Divine fecundity. It is also a pure contemplation occurring within the Life of the Persons.

Eckhart says that creatures arise out of this contemplation in which the Father beholds the Son. All creatures receive their form in the Son.[8] For He is the Absolute Exemplar and the ground of their being and intelligibility. The Son is God's conception of Himself. And this conception is the Father's knowledge of His own eternal Meaning through the reflection of the Son. As Eckhart says: ". . .God spoke one Word . . . and that Word was His Son."[9]

The Father passively wells up in the Godhead. It is an aspect of the Godhead's nature that the Father stir in the Divine Ground. He is the beginning of the Godhead insofar as self-knowledge is concerned. The Father eternally begets the Meaning of the essence, the Godhead, but the Father stirs as its dynamic Center. The Father is being in the Godhead according to Paternity, His function in the Divine Life, and not according to essence. For the Godhead is the Essence, but needs the Father, as the Father is the Essence eternally actualized. The Father's power is active when He has welled up from the Divine Ground. The impulse He passes to the Son, in which the Son receives His divinity, is passive in the Son. Now the Divine Persons, although they proceed from the Divine Essence, also constitute it, but they themselves are constituted by their properties or notions. As the Father's formal notion is Paternity, and the Son's is Filiation, so that of the Holy Spirit is Unity, the property of unifying the Love. The Holy Spirit is a unifying Love. These properties or formal notions signify the inner relations of the Persons. Insofar as the Godhead is concerned, these properties are accidental, since they depend upon the Divine Ground of Unity which is the Essence of the Godhead and thus the Essence of the Trinity as well.

The Son is eternally born in the Father. As the Word, He remains within, as the Word is the Essence intelligibly grasped, but as the dynamic Second Person, He goes forth. He proceeds as Person. The Father observes or contemplates the Essence as expressed in the Word, but He is contemplating Himself and this gives Him another property, ie., that of being observed. The Son is the "object" observed by the Father, and as inexpressible Essence or Secret of the Divine nature, He remains within the Divine Unity, but He proceeds as Person, as Word of the Father. Eckhart says in this respect that: "Corresponding with the divided nature of this act, the Son is born and proceeds out of the paternal heart."[10] The Father contemplating the Essence as Word is the first aspect of the act, and the Son, as the Word and "object" observed, which is the self-comprehension of the Father's being, the Father realizing this property of being observed, observing Himself, is the second aspect of the Father's act. From the two aspects, the Son is eternally born and proceeds as Person. For the Father in contemplating His being, the Word, Who reflects back to Him His nature, realizes that this other is Himself, and also a unique member in the Trinity, the absolute Community from which all things arise. He contemplates His nature, but then discovers that His nature, expressed as the Word, is also contemplating Him. And this is the eternal Mystery of the Son. Eckhart says, furthermore that: " . . . the Son emanates from the Father as an intelligible Word proceeding from the act of the exuberant nature of the Father . . . For the Son is the image of the Father from Whom He emanates naturally."[11]

The Father and the Son, from a common spiration, a result of their Love, give rise eternally to the Holy Spirit Who is the mutual outpouring of their Love. This is the formal notion which distinguishes the Holy Spirit from the Father and the Son. He proceeds from the two as from one active Origin, the common spiration of the dialogical act of the Father and the Son. This spiration is the consequence of their inner freedom.

Now the Godhead is the nature that grounds the Trinity. In the Unity of their nature which is their common Essence, the Persons of the Trinity *are* the Godhead. As Eckhart puts it: "The three Persons, as Person and essence, flow with their essence into the essence wherein they are Godhead."[12] In other words, it is all the *same* Essence. The Essence flowing into itself *is* the Trinity resolving itself into the Unity of the Godhead, Essence comprehending Essence, for only Essence can know itself. Essence comprehending itself in itself is established on secure *Stillness*. The flowing in the Trinity and the Godhead is their Unity, a flowing that knows their Oneness. Eckhart says:

> In this same flux, the Father flows into the Son and the Son again into the Father . . . The Father utters His Son and in His Son tells forth Himself to creatures as a whole, all in this flow. And the Father returning to Himself speaks Himself to Himself: 'The fountain flows into itself', as St. Dionysius says. This proceeding in the Godhead is a speaking without words and without sound; a hearing without ears; a seeing without eyes. In this proceeding, each Person wordlessly utters Himself in the others. It is a flow where nothing flows.[13]

Somehow the Identity of the Persons is even expressed in the vast Wilderness of the Godhead. They realize their Unity and yet the metaphysical reality of the Persons exists even in the midst of the flowing Stillness of the Divine Ground, which is pure undifferentiated Unity.

The Trinity, the active dimension of God's being, simultaneous with the Divine Desert or Solitude, the unmoving, unknowable Godhead, flows into the Quiet dimension of the Divine nature. The Trinity is thus carried into its primordial Unity, but still the Persons are always aware of their functions, their properties in the absolute Essence. This suggests that the Persons are not just secondary elements but rather abiding Presences in the Divine Ground and nature. There, they whisper themselves to each other in their Essence, which is pure Unity grounded on an unspeakable Mystery. Even in the Unity of the Godhead the Trinity is performing its characteristic play, and this helps to constitute the eternal actualization of the Godhead's nature. The Trinity is far more than a mere projection of the Source, for it is its very inner Life.

THE GODHEAD

Eckhart speaks of the Godhead as *unnatured nature*. This means that it is wholly undetermined as to form and above activity. It does not nature itself; it is not confined to any formal or intelligible meaning in such a way that one could grasp the Godhead. It is totally beyond conceptualization. The Father, however, *natures* the Son. He gives the Son His active power, His impulse or energy. This impulse or energy is passive in the Son, as it was passive in the Father as the Father welled up in the Godhead, and it became active when the Father realized His being. The Father *mediates* between the *unnatured nature* and the natured nature, the two sides of the Divine being. He is both. He is also the bridge between the two aspects, i.e., the Godhead and the Trinity. As *unnatured,* He is the beginning of the Godhead, because He constitutes the hidden Presence welling up in the Divine Ground, and He is *identical* with the Essence that the Godhead is. He is also the means through which the Godhead realizes itself. Through the Father, the Godhead is unspoken word or underived Essence, which comprehends itself in and through the dynamic interaction of the Trinity. As *natured nature,* the Father is established in His function of Paternity, the Source of the Son's function; this is His determined property given to Him by the necessity of the self-comprehending aspect of the Divine being. The Father must be the Father in order for God to know Himself. The same is true of the Son. The Father and the Son together *nature* the Holy Spirit, constituting Him through the mutuality of *spiration.* The Holy Spirit does not *nature.* In *unnatured nature* they are a unity, but they are distinguished in the *natured nature.* The Persons of the Trinity are eternal in both their *unnatured nature* and in their *natured nature.*[14] This is true because both the *unnatured nature* and the *natured nature* are necessary in the absolute Reality of the Divine Life. There is a complementary relationship between these aspects that mutually ground each other and hence make possible the creative activity of bringing forth the cosmic order and the vast assortment of creatures. This creativity comes through the mediation of the Word through Whom all things arise and have their being.

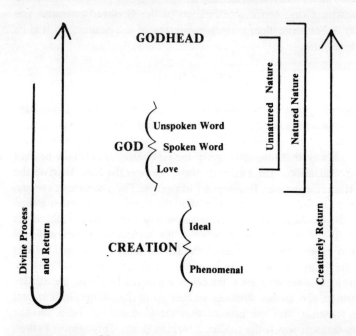

In this scheme, [15] the Father is the Unspoken Word, the Son, the Spoken Word and the Holy Spirit is Love. The Father's being partakes of the incomprehensible nature of the Godhead. He is thus the unexpressed Essence. The Son, since He is the upholder of meaning and Identity, the conveyor of the intrinsic intelligibility of God's Essence is thus the Spoken Word. The Word is the expressed nature proceeding through the Father from the Ground. He is the result of the Father's eternal welling up, the *unnatured nature* inclining itself towards *natured* manifestation in the Trinity. The Holy Spirit comprehends it all as *unifying* Love.

The Godhead is the Divine Essence; it is free of all activity. It is self-possessed and self-sufficient. It is also the inaccessible Light. The Godhead contemplates itself alone; it is unconcerned with what is outside of itself. It is nameless. All that matters is that the soul "drown in the bottomless sea of the Godhead."[16] Eckhart's description of the Godhead's total transcendence has the echo of Aristotle's conception of God or even that of Deism. Of course, this is not the origin of his notion. The Godhead as Essence "subsists in permanent, immanent stillness . . . it is a mode of its own in that same absolute stillness. There the distinctions of Persons are subsumed to this simple modeless now."[17] In the Godhead, God has a fundamental or elemental character. We can say nothing of it except that, in relation to the human intellect, it is as if it were not, because we cannot understand it. Here God is spiritual substance, ungraspable and inconceivable.[18] Spiritual substance is the Unspoken Word, the nameless Essence. But Bliss or happiness is the "nature and substance of the Godhead."[19] This corresponds to the Hindu notion of Brahman as Absolute Bliss, one of the attributes of His nature. For Brahman is Bliss as well as Knowledge and Being. The Godhead is also absolute simplicity. This is the way that God conceives Himself in the Desert of the Divine Unity.[20] This Desert or Wilderness of the Godhead is a "place" where 'no one' is at home. It is a simple stillness without movement, and yet everything comes forth from it,[21] because it implicitly contains the very foundation of all things in itself. It is "abiding potentiality, containing in itself distinctions as yet undeveloped . . . It is Darkness and Formlessness."[22] The Godhead is a great 'treasure house' of possibility for the Father to carry into the manifested or active dimension of the Divine being. The Godhead as pure Essence, undifferentiated Unity, does not beget or create.[23] It is essentially Stillness comprehending Stillness. This is the very nature of the Godhead. Again, Eckhart says of it:

> *The Godhead in itself is motionless Unity and balanced stillness and is the Source of all emanations. Hence, I assume a passive welling-up. We call this first utterance being, for the most intrinsic utterance, the first formal assumption in the Godhead is being: being as essential Word. God is being, but being is not God.* [24]

This 'essential Word' is the intrinsic 'yearning' of the Godhead for self-knowledge. It is a 'passive welling-up', an attempt to grasp the essential Reality, the absolute Meaning of the Godhead's Identity. That is why it is 'essential Word', being an absolute Meaning.

'NOTHING' IN THE GODHEAD

This is a very critical aspect of Eckhart's doctrine. Many have misunderstood it. They think that when he says "nothing", he means complete negation of existence proper to the Godhead and reality - pure nothingness. The notion of pure nothingness would appear to be contradictory. This is Suzuki's misguided interpretation of Eckhart's meaning. For Suzuki clearly asserts that Eckhart holds the Godhead to be "absolute nothingness".[25] Suzuki's interpretation seems to be quite erroneous, since it is certain that this was not Eckhart's position. Blakney says that this 'nothing' (Nihte) does not literally signify nothing, but that it is more akin to what Eckhart means when he speaks of *poverty*.[26] By poverty, Eckhart is trying to convey a state of "conditionless being, which is above God and above distinction."[27] This is quite different from absolute nothingness. Eckhart maintains that "He (the Godhead) has it (Reality) of His (own) proper nature, which in itself is truly aught though naught to the intelligence of creatures."[28] Thus, the Godhead's nature is beyond the capacity of the intellect to conceive, and so much so is this the case that it is as if it were 'naught' to the mind. This is the point that Suzuki neglects to mention, but which would significantly modify his interpretation. Eckhart is always careful to qualify his statements, but he does not always do so within the same Sermon or Tractate. That is why it is imperative to read several of his works. Doing so, we get the larger picture of his doctrine. Eckhart has more to say about this 'nothingness':

> As the worthy Dionysius says: 'Lord lead me to where Thou are a nothingness,' meaning: lead me, Lord, to where Thou transcendest every created intellect; for as St. Paul declares: 'God dwells in a Light that no man can approach unto'; that is: God is not to be discerned in any created light whatever . . . So that by saying 'God is nothing', Dionysius signifies that there is NO–THING in His Presence. It follows that the Spirit must advance beyond things and thingliness, shape and shapeness, existence and existences: then will dawn in it the actuality of happiness which is the essential possession of the actual intellect.[29]

Here is an instance (one of many) where Eckhart says God but means the Godhead. This is plain from his attribution of no-thing to God Himself. Furthermore, Royce says that this 'nothing' is really "unborn reality or nameless nothingness." It is a kind of potentiality. This refers to the Godhead Who is above distinction.[30]   Again, what Royce is suggesting is that since our feeble intellects cannot grasp the Essence of God, which is a pure undifferentiated Unity, it is thus for us a 'nameless nothingness'. It is 'nameless' because we cannot comprehend it, and it is 'nothingness' because it is actually "no-thingness", of which we have no adequate sense.

The Godhead is above Being, since Being refers to multiplicity; it is the one all-embracing category that renders the universe existent and intelligible. The Godhead, however, is pure Unity. Being is inappropriate for it, because its Unity is the negation of Being (for itself) insofar as its nature is one and above the category of the many. Being bounds the manifested realm of the external world, but God is boundless. Thus, Being can have no direct, determining relation to His nature. In this sense and only in this sense is God non-being, because He is so transcendent that He is even beyond Being, that which all His creatures are grounded by and from which they receive their existential definition. The Godhead presents a paradox for the intellect. For it is at once emptiness (the Buddhist conception) and fullness.[31] Absolute Reality resides in the 'non-being' of the Godhead. We in the West, since the time of Plato, have associated reality with Being and unreality with non-being or 'nothingness'. But this prevents us from seeing the more important point that God in His Godhead is beyond our categories and is free of our limits which our concepts impose.

THE SOUL AND THE GODHEAD

Eckhart's conception of the soul, in its ultimate reality, that which is united to the Godhead is what he means by the term Divine Spark or the *Funkelin*. It bears some similarity to the Atman doctrine of Hindu Mysticism. The soul, in her essence, *is* the Divine Spark which is eternal, having always existed in the Godhead, and immortal, because it can never die.[32]   It is a permanent tendency towards God. This core or Spark of the soul is pure *silence;* it is receptive only to God. In this aspect, it is like the Indian metaphor "cave of the heart". It is here in the Spark or core that God utters His Eternal Word, the Secret of the Godhead's nature.[33]   Eckhart says of it: "The Spark in the soul (is) being drawn up in this Light and in the Holy Spirit (is) borne aloft to its first Source."[34]   The Spark has one purpose, to be absorbed into God.[35] For the Godhead is the soul's destiny.

In order to attain God or union with the Godhead, the soul must tread the path of self-negation, which requires freedom from self-will. The person must become "as he was when he was not, "[36] which is precisely the state of this Divine Spark. Before we were phenomenal identities (egos), we were each an eternal self in the Godhead, for the Godhead houses the essential implicitness of all things. Primarily, however, this 'naughting' or negating refers to attachments and the growth in spiritual freedom. The soul has to be *liberated* from all attachments. For God only enters a *free* soul. In this way, the soul slips out of her created nature and discovers her uncreated nature in the Godhead,[37] which is the Divine Spark. She also discovers her uncreated prototype.

The soul flows out of normal, everyday consciousness and flows into the Divine Consciousness. She passes through the Trinity into the Abyss or Wilderness of the Godhead. For, according to Eckhart:

> *The Trinity is the heart of divine and human nature, and human nature flows into the Trinity in a steady stream of love. Supposing the soul crosses over, then she sinks down in the ABYSM of the Godhead nor ever finds a footing unless it be that she has taken with her some temporal thing; resting in temporal things brings her back into the Trinity.*[38]

When the soul comes to this Union with the Divine Essence, then she has followed "God into the desert of His Godhead."[39] The soul is carried out of herself in ecstasy and flows into the 'unnamed being' or the 'Nameless essence' of the Godhead, the Source. In this way, she achieves the highest perfection possible to her. In the Godhead, she is absorbed into the unspeakable Light that envelops her and transforms her into God.[40] When the soul arrives into the Godhead, she delves deeper still until she discovers God "in His solitude; she finds Him in His desert, in His actual ground . . . When the soul, being kissed by God, is in absolute perfection and bliss, then at last she knows the embrace of unity." She is transformed into her eternal form in the Godhead and becomes "as noble as God is Himself."[41] In this state, she knows the Godhead as it is, an undifferentiated Unity and unutterable Bliss. For this is the Wilderness, the immense Divine Stillness, where difference is finally transcended.[42]

In this mystical state of Unity, the soul is completely at home; she has found her natural dwelling in that "innocence" of being. She rests in the secret place of the Godhead, in the Wilderness of His being at the end of the journey, the goal having been achieved. When the soul is united to the Godhead, to the Ground, 'in the bottom', 'in the river and Fount of the Godhead', she is beyond all creatures. She has returned to the primordial condition. People only question us in life. Here, they talk about God. But in the Godhead, there is no one to ask. Everything is as it should be. As Eckhart says: "When I go back into the ground, into the depths, into the well-spring of the Godhead, no one will ask me whence I came or whither I went. No one missed me: God passes away."[43] God passes away because the soul is then in the Godhead, the *quiescent* dimension of the Divinity, beyond the active side, the Trinity. There at last the soul rests in the Divine Stillness that is the ever rising Vitality of Divine Bliss. The soul knows God in and through Him; she sees Him in His inaccessible Light. For she is illumined in this ineffable Light of the Divine Reality. Coming to know God because of His Presence within her, the soul also comes to know herself. From thence, she comes to know the Divine Essence, God's 'Isness', but again, in and through Him.[44] In this way, the soul enters into the Divine Solitude, into God's Dwelling.

And this Solitude, this Abyss, this Desert or Wilderness of the Godhead, the unending and unbeginning Mystery of His Silence as He dwells in the undifferentiated Oneness of Essence, *is* the pure, attributeless Unity in Contemplation of Himself, the Stillness of His nature in which Absolute Necessity flows forth from the eternal Stability of the Established Divine Foundation. This is the grounded Ground, grounded in its own Necessity which is this Blissful Stillness comprehending its Essence as pure Luminosity of Divine Existence. And it must be what it is because the weight of Truth, of the Divine 'TO BE' is upon it, resting in its Necessity. The Stillness, as this Blissful Ground, harbers the Unspoken Word, the Father, the Divine Stirring within the Unity of the Godhead. In the Eternal Now, the Father, Who is the Divine Vitality, wells up and utters the Word, the Son, the very Meaning of the Godhead's Mystery. But this Meaning *is* the Father Who sees Himself in His Son, and the Son in turn seems Himself in His Father. The intensity of that realization is so profound that neither can contain it, and so it overflows into them, Who together eternally generate the Holy Spirit, Who then enternally grounds that realization in Himself, for He is that realization become Conscious. The Holy Spirit is thus the Third Person. He confirms the Reality of the dynamism between the Father and the Son. He upholds it in His function. For He is the Beholder of the Divine Unity. He *is* the Divine Unity. The Holy Spirit is also the basis for all proceeding into Creation. The Godhead is the primordial Home of the Trinity, but the Trinity is the Living Spirit of the Divine

Ground realizing itself, proceeding from the Father's Mysterious power To Be and to rise up eternally from the Wilderness of the Godhead. The Father is probably more fundamental and ontologically important than the Godhead as such, since the Father is the very Life of the Godhead. He is the metaphysical bridge spanning the gap between the Unmanifested Ground and the Manifested Trinity, the two imperishable aspects of the Divine Mystery. Perhaps this is what Christ meant when He said that "The Father is greater than I."

Eckhart's doctrine is born of a very subtle form of Mysticism bearing some similarity to Oriental forms. At times, he seems to make outrageous statements, but he is just like any other mystic who attempts to express that union with the Divine that defies reason, language and conceptualization. A mystic always has to "stretch" language in order to achieve a higher modulation of meaning that frees language from its ordinary usage. This is done in order to convey his experience of God. Despite all the talk of monism[45] and pantheism, of which some are wont to accuse him, Eckhart remains essentially a theist. This is demonstrated by his emphasis upon grace, love, devotion, personalism, fellowhsip etc.[46] He will always be the "mystic's mystic", and he will continue to exert an important influence on Mankind's quest for Truth and Transcendence.

SUMMING UP

What we have tried to do in these essays is to give some indication, a feeling if you will, for the absolute *reality* of mystical experience and the knowledge consequent upon it. This has taken the form of a dialectical relationship between experience of God, the contemplative interiority of the mystics and reflection, which is the fruit of speculation about the nature and content of the experience. The purpose of this approach is twofold: first, to show that Mysticism has very significant implications and consequences for Knowledge. For it is, in a sense, the final answer. And this takes the form of a living Metaphysics that approximates the contemplative insights as far as this is possible to do in language. Secondly, we have taken this avenue in order to advance the supreme *value* of contemplation, mystical life, Spirituality, interiority, meditation, whatever you like. It is all the same, however it may be called.

It should be abundantly evident at this point that mystical life is *experiential;* it cannot be learned from books, which can help. Books can give guidance; teach techniques; share experience and confirm one's own, but they are not a substitute for the actual work of contemplation. Each person must make the journey alone, for we are all hermits in that ultimate experience on the frontier of consciousness. The most important thing to learn, however, is an attitude of interior *silence,* which is the Divine language, what the Desert Fathers taught, the practice of *heyschasm (Hesychia,* "quiet"), of inner freedom from thoughts. This is how we come to dwell in "the cave of the heart" where the soul meets God. Mysticism is *practical* in the highest sense as a *way* leading to union with the Divine Life. It is the most precious knowledge that one may acquire, for it is the purpose of life itself.

NOTES

I. SYMBOLS OF THE MYSTICAL

Chapter 1
1. Raimundo Panikkar in a recent public lecture. Dr. Panikkar is a prolific writer, and holds doctorates in chemistry, philosophy and theoology.
2. William James, *The Varieties of Religious Experience* (London: Collier-Macmillan Ltd., 1961), p. 336.

Chapter 2
1. Bede Griffiths, *Return To The Centre* (London: Collins, 1976).
2. But the ancient wisdom of the Vedas also speaks of the Transcendence of God, of Brahman, the One beyond name and form.
3. Aldous Huxley, "Visionary Experience," in *The Highest State of Consciousness*, ed. John White (New York: Anchor Books, 1972), cf. pp. 34-57.

Chapter 3
1. Cf. James Plastaras, C. M., *The God of Exodus: The Theology of The Exodus Narratives* (Milwaukee: The Bruce Pub. Co., 1966), pp. 86-100.
2. *Ibid.*, p. 87.
3. Edmond Jacob, *The Theology of The Old Testament*, trans., Arthur W. Heathcote and Philip J. Allcock (New York: Harper, 1958), p. 49.
4. *Ibid.*, p. 48.
5. *Op. Cit., The God of Exodus,* pp. 88-89.
6. *Ibid.*, pp. 89-90.
7. Bernard W. Anderson, *Understanding The Old Testament* (Englewood Cliffs: Prentice-Hall, 1957), p. 36.
8. *Op. Cit., The God of Exodus,* pp. 90-91.
9. *Ibid.,* pp. 92-93.
10. *Ibid.,* p. 94.
11. *Ibid.*
12. *Ibid.*
13. *Ibid.,* p. 95.
14. Brevard S. Childs, *The Book of Exodus* in *The Old Testament Library* (Philadelphia: Westminster Press, 1974), p. 69.

15. Op. Cit., p. 51.

16. *Op. Cit., The God of Exodus*, p. 97.

17. *Ibid.*, p. 98.

18. *Ibid.*

19. Foxwell Albright, *From The Stone Age To Christianity* (Garden City: Doubleday, 1957), p. 261.

20. *Op. Cit., The God of Exodus*, p. 98.

21. *Ibid.*, pp. 98-99.

22. *Op. Cit., Theology of the Old Testament*, p. 51.

23. *Ibid.*, pp. 51-52.

24. *Ibid.*

25. Cf. Pseudo-Dionysius, *The Divine Names and The Mystical Theology,* trans., C. E. Rolt (London: SPCK, 1923).

26. Moses Maimonides, *The Guide For The Perplexed,* trans., M. Friedlander, Ph.D. (New York: Dover, 1956), p. 90.

27. Cf. Meister Eckhart, In Librum Exodi, LW II, p. 131, n. 146, (Latin Text).

28. Master Eckhart, *Parisian Questions and Prologues,* trans., Armand A. Maurer, C.S.B. (Toronto: Pontifical Institute of Medieval Studies, 1974), cf. Appendix "Eckhart's Exegesis of the Divine Name 'I Am Who Am'" in his *Commentary On The Book of Exodus*, p. 108.

Chapter 4

1. Georges Habra, *La Transfiguration Selon les Pere Grecs* (Paris: Editions S.O.S., 1973), p. 47.

2. Matthew 17:1-8.

3. Mark 9:2-8.

4. Luke 9:28-36.

5. Thomas Keating, O.C.S.O., "Historical Insights into Contemplation" (Spencer, Massachusetts: St. Joseph's Abbey, 1976), side 1.

6. 1 Timothy 6:16.

7. 1 John 1:5.

8. James 1:5.

9. Cf. *Republic,* Bk. 7.

10. Petro B.T. Bilaniuk, "A Theological Meditation On The Mystery of Transfiguration," *Diakonia,* vol. 8, number 4, 1973, pp. 318-319.

11. *Ibid.*, pp. 319-320.

12. 2 Cor. 4:6.

II. EXPERIENTIAL KNOWLEDGE OF GOD

Chapter 5

1. *Op. Cit.,* "Historical Insights Into Contemplation." This beautiful talk gives a history of contemplative prayer from its origins in the Patristic Period up until the present. It also contains a valuable discussion of what contemplation is in the act of its highest mystical state, which is in the tradition of St. Gregory the Great.

2. *The Cloud of Unknowing and The Book of Privy Counselling,* ed. William Johnston, S.J. (Garden City, New York: Image Books, 1973), ch. 6, p. 54.

3. *The Divine Names and The Mystical Theology,* ed. C. E. Rolt (London: SPCK Press, 1923). The Pseudo-Dionysius speaks of this knowing as an unknowing, since, although the soul is intimately conscious of God and knows Him in a direct manner, she yet cannot understand what she knows. Cf. *Mystical Theology,* ch. 1-2.

4. *Op. Cit., The Cloud,* p. 55.

5. *Ibid.*

6. *Op. Cit.,* "Historical Insights" etc., side 1.

7. Psalm 46:11.

8. William Johnston, S.J., *The Inner Eye of Love: Mysticism and Religion* (San Francisco: Harper & Row, 1978), pp. 34-35.

9. George Maloney, S.J., *Invaded by God: Mysticism and The Indwelling Trinity* (Denville, N.J.: Dimension Books, 1979), pp. 121-122.

10. Mark 1:15.

11. When Buddism, Hinduism and the Platonic Tradition speak of the world as an "illusion," they are not saying that it does not exist, but that *reality* is more subtle, and in the Christian Tradition this means that it is the Divine notion, the Purpose of existence that has its Source in the Eternal. Of course, this is not evident in immediate sense perception. What *is* an illusion is the worldly attitude, which is a world that does not exist, as it is contrary to Truth.

Chapter 6

1. Rene Latourelle, S.J., *Theology of Revelation* (Staten Island, New York: Alba House, 1966), p. 12.

2. *Ibid.,* p. 15.

3. St. Thomas Aquinas, *Summa Contra Gentiles,* Bk. IV, ch. 1, 5.

4. Bede Griffiths, *Return To The Centre* (London: Collins, 1976), cf. pp. 16-33.

5. *Ibid.,* p. 71.

6. Ewert Cousins, "Bonaventure And World Religions," *Philosophica,* III, 1974, p. 698.

7. *Ibid.,* p. 699.

8. S. Bonaventura, *Hexaem.,* coll. 1, n. 12-17 (V, 331-332; and *Questiones Disputatae de Mysterio Trinitatis,* q. 8, ad. 7 (V, 115); and *De Reductio Artium Ad Theologiam,* n. 12 (V, 322-323, of *Opera Omnia*).

9. *Op. Cit.,* Cousins, Bonaventure, p. 699.

10. *Op. Cit., de Mysterio Trinitatis,* q. 1. a 2, concl., *Opera Omnia* (V, 54).

11. *Ibid.,* (V, 55).

12. *Op. Cit., Varieties,* p. 336.

13. Exodus 3:14.

14. St. Bernard of Clairvaux, *On Loving God,* Cistercian Fathers Series, *Treatise II, Bernard of Clairvaux,* vol. V, trans., Robert Walton, O.S.B. (Washington, D. C.: Cistercian Publications, 1974), ch. x, 27.

15. Luke 14:26; Mt. 16:24.

16. *Op. Cit., On Loving God,* ch. x.

17. *Ibid.*

18. *Cantica Canticorum, Opera S. Bernardi,* ed. Jean Leclercq, H. M. Rochais, C. H. Talbot (Romae: Editiones Cistercienses, 1958), vol. II, Sermon 52.5, pp. 92-93.

19. *Ibid.,* Sermon 74, 5-6, pp. 242-243.

20. *St. Francis of Assisi: Writings and Early Biographies. English Omnibus of the Sources For The Life of St. Francis,* ed. Marion Habig, O.F.M. (Chicago: Franciscan Herald Press, 1972, *Thomas of Celano's Life of St. Francis,* ch. XI, p. 250.

21. Johannes Jorgensen, *St. Francis of Assisi* (Garden City, New York: Image Books, 1955), p. 245.

22. *Op. Cit., Bonaventure's Legenda Maior,* ch. 13, pp. 729-736. *Omnibus sources.*

23. St. John of the Cross, *The Collected Works of St. John of the Cross,* trans., Kieran Kavanaugh, O.D.C. and Otilio Rodriguez, O.C.D. (Washington, D. C.: I.C.S. Publications, 1973), pp. 711-712.

24. *Ibid.,* pp. 717-718.

25. *Ibid.,* pp. 718-719.

26. *Op. Cit., Mystical Theology,* ch. I, p. 191. Rolt.
27. *Ibid.,* pp. 191-192.
28. *Ibid.*
29. *Ibid.,* p. 193.
30. *Ibid.,* p. 194.
31. Wayne Teasdale, October, 1979.

Chapter 7

1. TB II, 2, 9, 1-2., Raimundo Panikkar, *The Vedic Experience, Mantramanjari: An Anthology of the Vedas for Modern Man and Contemporary Celebration* (London: Darton, Longman & Todd, 1977), p. 49.
2. *Ibid.,* p. 56.
3. *Ibid.*
4. G. W. F. Hegel, *The Logic of Hegel, from The Encyclopaedia of The Philosophical Sciences,* trans., William Wallace (London: Oxford University Press, 1873), pp. 162-163.
5. *Op. Cit.,* p. 57, cf. "Nasadiya Sukta," Rg Veda, X. 129.
6. *Ibid.,* p. 55.
7. *Op. Cit., Divine Names,* ch. 2, 10, Rolt, pp. 77-78.
8. *Ibid.,* cf. DN, ch. 2.
9. Meister Eckhart, *Meister Eckhart,* ed. Franz Pfeiffer, 2 vols. Trans., C. De B. Evans (London: Watkins, 1947), Sermon LVIII, "Divine Understanding," vol. I, p. 148.
10. *Ibid.,* Tractate, *The Kingdom of God,* p. 267.
11. *Ibid.,* Tractate, XIX, *The Beatific Vision,* p. 412.
12. *Op. Cit.,* pp. 51-52.
13. *Ibid.,* p. 53.
14. *Ibid.,* p. 57.
15. Cf. Raimundo Panikkar, *The Trinity and The Religious Experience of Man* (New York: Orbis, 1973).
16. *Op. Cit.,* VE, p. 98.
17. *Ibid.,* p. 89.
18. *Ibid.,* p. 100.
19. *Ibid.,* p. 91.
20. *Op. Cit.,* "Historical Insights," side 2.
21. *Ibid.*

Chapter 8

1. *Op. Cit.,* Inner Eye, p. 38.

2. St. Thomas Aquinas, *Summa Theologiae,* Q. 2, a 3, *Prima Pars* (Madrid: Biblioteca De Autores Cristianos, 1955).

3. *Op. Cit., Divine Names,* Rolt, DN II. 4, p. 69.

4. *Ibid.,* DN. II. 3-7, pp. 68-74.

5. *Op. Cit.,* I, q. 2, a. 3.

6. *Op. Cit., Eckhart,* Pfeiffer, Tractate XV, *The Three Creations,* p. 385.

7. *Ibid.,* Tractate, *The Kingdom of God,* p. 267.

8. *Ibid.,* Tractate XIX, *The Beatific Vision,* p. 412.

9. *Ibid.,* Tractate XI, p. 355.

10. *Ibid.,* Sermon LXXXIII, St. Germanus' Day, p. 209.

11. In all likelihood, the Godhead and the Trinity mutually inhere in each other. Neither dimension is dominant, for they need each other.

12. *Op. Cit.,* The Trinity, p. 59.

13. St. Augustine, *The Trinity,* trans., Stephen McKenna, C.SS.R., *The Fathers of the Church Series,* vol. 45 (Washington, D. C.: Catholic Univ. Press, 1963), Bk. V, ch. 5, pp. 179-180.

14. *Ibid.,* Bk. V, ch. 11, p. 189.

15. *Ibid.,* Bk. VII, ch. 4, p. 229.

16. Karl Rahner, S.J., *Theological Investigations,* "Remarks On The Dogmatic Treatise 'De Trinitate,'" vol. IV, *More Recent Writings* (Baltimore: Darton, Longman & Todd, 1966), p. 91.

17. St. Hillary of Poitiers, *The Trinity,* trans., Stephen McKenna, C.SS.R., *The Fathers of The Church Series,* vol. 25 (Washington, D. C.: Catholic Univ. Press, 1954), Bk. 2. 6, p. 39.

18. *Ibid.,* Bk. 2.6, p. 41.

19. *Op. Cit.,* Sermon LVIII, Divine Understanding, p. 148.

20. For the Trinity is the eternal situation in which the Giver, the Receiver and the Given are the same.

21. *Op. Cit.,* p. 42.

22. Jean Leclercq, Preface, *Julian of Norwich: Showings,* in *Classics of Western Spirituality* (New York: Paulist Press, 1978), p. 9.

23. *Ibid.,* Long Text, p. 298, ch. 60.

24. *Op. Cit.,* S.T. I, Q. 2, a. 3.

25. St. Bonaventura, *The Mind's Road to God,* trans., George Boas (Indianapolis: Bobbs-Merrill, 1953), ch. V, p. 34.

26. *Ibid.,* ch. V, p. 35.

27. *Ibid.,* ch. VI, p. 39.

28. *Op. Cit.,* Rahner, p. 95.

29. *Ibid.,* p. 96.

30. St. Ignatius, cf. "Contemplatio ad Amorem" in *The Spiritual Exercises of St. Ignatius,* trans., Anthony Mottola (New York: Image, 1964), pp. 103-104.

31. *Op. Cit.,* MT, ch. 1, p. 192.

32. *Ibid.,* MT, ch. 1, p. 193.

33. *Ibid.,* MT, ch. 1, p. 194.

34. *Op. Cit.,* Collected Works, p. 711.

35. *Ibid.,* pp. 721-722.

36. *Ibid.,* pp. 734-735.

37. *Op. Cit.,* Cantica, vol. II, Sermon 74, 5-6, pp. 242-243.

38. St. Teresa of Avila, *The Autobiography of St. Teresa of Avila,* trans., Allison Peers (New York: Image, 1960), ch. XX, p. 197.

39. St. Teresa of Avila, *Interior Castle,* trans., Allison Peers (New York: Image, 1961), VII Mansion, ch. XI, p. 214.

III. THREE "SPECULATIVE" MYSTICS

Chapter 9

1. Hilary Armstrong, "The Apprehension of Divinity in the Self and Cosmos in Plotinus," from *The Significance of Neo-Platonism,* ed. R. Baine Harris (Norfolk: Old Dominion Univ., 1976), pp. 187-197.

2. William Ralph Inge, *The Philosophy of Plotinus.* The Gifford Lectures at St. Andrews (1917-1918), 2 Vols. (London: Longmans, Green and Co., 1923), p. 7.

3. *Ibid.*

4. Plotinus also shaped somewhat the development of Jewish and Islamic Mysticism, especially *The Kabbalah,* though this has Gnostic elements as well, and the doctrines of Al Gazali, one of the primary figures in Sufic Mysticism and Islamic Philosophy.

5. Emile Brehier, *Les idees philosophiques et religieuses de Philon d'Alexandrie,* 2 ed. (Paris: Vrin, 1925), pp. 78-79.

6. Hypostasis is a term for substance but also signifies in Plotinus a transcendent source of Being and reality.

7. *The Enneads,* trans., Stephen Mackenna (London: Faber & Faber, 1962), Enn. V. 4. 1.

8. *Ibid.,* Enn V. 9ff.

9. *Ibid.,* Enn V. 9. 9.

10. *Ibid.,* Enn. III. 9. 5.

11. *Ibid.,* Enn. VI. 3. 5-6.

12. *Ibid.*, Enn. III. 5. 4.

13. *Ibid.*, Enn. II. 4. 16.

14. *Ibid.*, Enn. I. 6. 8.

15. *Ibid.*, Enn. VI. 9. 9.

16. *Ibid.*, Enn. I. 2. 7.

17. *Ibid.*, Enn. I. 6. 9.

18. John Rist, *Eros and Psyche: Studies In Plato, Plotinus and Origen* (Toronto: Univ. of Toronto Press, 1964), Phoenix Series, vol. VI, pp. 88-89.

19. *Op. Cit.*, Enn. I. 6. 7.

20. *Ibid.*, Enn. V. 8. 11 and V. 5. 8.

21. *Ibid.*, Enn. V. 5. 4.

22. *Ibid.*, Enn. V. 5. 8.

23. *Ibid.*, Enn. V. 5. 7.

24. *Ibid.*, Enn. VI. 9. 5.

25. *Ibid.*, Enn. VI. 9. 11.

26. *Ibid.*, Enn. VI. 9. 3.

27. Elmer O'Brien, S.J., "The Mystical Doctrine of Plotinus," *Thought*, Vol. XXXIX, Number 152, Spring, 1964, p. 68.

28. *Op. Cit.*, Enn. VI. 9. 9.

29. *Ibid.*, Enn., VI. 9. 11.

30. *Ibid.*

31. *Ibid.*, Enn. V. 3. 17; V. 5. 7-8; V. 8. 10; I. 6. 9.

32. *Ibid.*, Enn. VI. 7. 36.

33. *Ibid.*, Enn. VI. 7. 35.

34. *Ibid.*, Enn. V. 3. 17.

35. *Ibid.*, Enn. VI. 7. 21-22.

36. *Op. Cit.*, Eros and Psyche, p. 96.

37. *Op. Cit.*, Enn. I. 6. 7.

38. Elmer O'Brien, S.J., *Varieties of Mystic Experience* (New York: Mentor-Omega, 1965), pp. 23-24.

39. *Op. Cit.*, "Mystical Doctrine of Plotinus," p. 73.

40. *Hegel's Lectures On The History of Philosophy*, trans., E. S. Haldane and Frances H. Simson (London: Routledge & Kegan Paul, 1968), (reprint), 3 vols., Vol. II, p. 412.

41. Porphyry, *Plotini Vita*, 23, 138.

42. A. B. Sharpe, *Mysticism: Its Nature and True Value* (London: Sands & Co., 1910), cf. pp. 154-158.

43. *Op. Cit.*, *Enneads*, introduction, cf. pp. Ixiv-Ixx.

44. Cf. *Op. Cit.*, "Apprehension of Divinity" etc., pp. 187-197.

45. Plato Mamo, "Is Plotinian Mysticism Monistic?," from *The Significance of Neo-Platonism, ed. R. Baine Harris (Norfolk: Old Dominion Univ., 1976), p. 206.*

46. *Ibid.,* pp. 207-208.

47. E. R. Dodds, *Pagan and Christian in an Age of Anxiety* (Cambridge: The Univ. Press, 1965), p. 88. Quite frankly, Dodds' interpretation of Plotinus and of Indian Mysticism strikes me as misconceived.

48. *Op. Cit.,* p. 209.

49. R. Arnou, *Le Desir de Dieu dans la Philosophie de Plotin* (Paris: 1921), p. 246.

50. *Ibid.,* pp. 246-248.

Chapter 10

1. St. Thomas Aquinas, *Summa Theologiae,* vol. 14, "Divine Government" (Ia 2ae. Qs. 103-9), Trans., T. C. O'Brien, cf. Appendix 3: 'The Dionysian Corpus' (New York: McGraw-Hill, 1974), p. 182.

2. *Ibid.,* p. 183.

3. *Ibid.,* p. 189.

4. Joseph Stiglmayr, "Dionysius the Pseudo-Areopagite," *The Catholic Encyclopedia,* vol. V, ed. Charles G. Herbiman, et al. (New York: Universal Knowledge Foundation, 1909), p. 15.

5. *Ibid.,* pp. 16-17.

6. *Ibid.,* p. 17.

7. *Ibid.*

8. *Ibid.*

9. P. Godet, "Denys L'Areopagite (le Pseudo-)," *Dictionnaire De Theologie Catholique* (Paris: 1911), vol. IV, p. 433.

10. *Ibid.*

11. *Ibid.,* p. 434, III.

12. Etienne Gilson, *The History of Christian Philosophy in the Middle Ages* (New York: Random House, 1955), p. 85.

13. J. P. Migne, *Patrologiae Cursus Completus, Series Graeca,* vol. 3 (Parisiis apud Carnier et Migne, 1886). It contains all of them: *De Caelesti Hierarchia* 119-370; *De Ecclesiastica Hierarchia* 369-584; *De Divinis Nominibus* 585-996; *De Mystica Theologia ad Timotheum* 997-1064; Epistolae XI, 1065-1122.

14. *Op. Cit.,* DN I. 8; II .1; III .1, pp. 63-65; 65-67; 81-83, Rolt.

15. *Ibid.,* DN I. 8, p. 64.

16. Rev. John Parker, M.A., *The Works of Dionysius The Areop-*

agite. Part II, *The Heavenly Hierarchy* (Merrick, New York: Rich-wood Pub. Co., 1976, Reprint), Ch. II, sec. iii, pp. 7-8.

17. *Op. Cit.,* MT I, p. 194, Rolt.

18. *Op. Cit.,* Parker, Ecclesiastical Hierarchy, Ch. I, sec. iii, p. 71.

19. *Ibid.,* Ch. I, sec. i, p. 67.

20. *Ibid.,* Letter I, p. 141.

21. "The Pseudo-Dionysius," *The Cambridge History of Later Greek and Early Medieval Philosophy,* ed. A. H. Armstrong (Cambridge: The Univ. Press, 1967), p. 460.

22. *Ibid.*

23. *Ibid.*

24. *Ibid.*

25. *Ibid.*

26. *Op. Cit.,* DN IV. 14, pp. 106-107, Rolt.

27. *Op. Cit.,* Catholic Encyclopedia, vol. V, p. 13.

28. *Op. Cit.,* "Dionysian Corpus," O'Brien, S. T., Vol. 14.

29. Dom Denys Rutledge, *Cosmic Theology: The Ecclesiastical Hierarchy of Pseudo-Dionysius. An Introduction* (London: Routledge & Kegan Paul, 1964), p. 10.

30. E. Von. Ivanka, "Der Aufbau der Schrift "Die Divinis Nominibus" des Ps.-Dionysius," *Scholastik,* XV (1940), cf. pp. 389-399.

31. *Op. Cit., The Divine Names,* IV, p. 86ff., Rolt. Hereafter, DN.

32. *Op. Cit.,* Gilson, History, p. 82.

33. Pseudo-Dionysius, La Hierarchie Celeste, Traduction et Notes par M de Gandillac, Etude et texte critiques par G. Heil, cf. Introduction de Denys L'Areopagite par R. Roques, Collection Sources Chretiennes, vol. 58 (Paris, 1958), pp. LXIV-LXVI.

34. *Ibid.,* cf. pp. LVII-LIX.

35. *Op. Cit.,* Cambridge History, Armstrong, p. 468.

36. Frederick Copleston, S.J., *A History of Philosophy,* vol. 2, Part I, *Augustine To Bonaventure* (Garden City, N.Y.: Image-Doubleday, 1962), p. 110.

37. *Ibid.,* pp. 111-112.

38. *Ibid.,* p. 115.

39. *Op. Cit.,* Rogues, *La Hierarchie Celeste,* p. XXXII. Also cf. Guntram G. Bischoff, "Dionysius The Pseudo-Areopagite: The Gnostic Myth," *The Spirituality of Western Christendom,* ed. Rozanne Elder (Kalamazoo, Michigan: Cistercian Pub., 1976). This article is not too sympathetic to the Pseudo-Dionysius, but it has some good points on the Gnostic element. Bischoff wants to suggest that the Dionysian doctrine is Gnostic. But then, the whole Tradition of

Christian Mysticism and Mysticism generally is gnostic in the good sense.

40. *Op. Cit.,* DN (Table of Contents), p. 50, Rolt.
41. *Ibid.,* DN I. 4, p. 56.
42. *Ibid.,* DN I. 1, p. 51.
43. *Op. Cit.,* Gilson, History, p. 84.
44. *Op. Cit.,* DN V. 5, p. 136.
45. *Ibid.,* DN II. 3-7, pp. 68-74.
46. *Ibid.,* DN II. 7, p. 74.
47. *Ibid.,* DN XIII. 3, p. 187.
48. *Ibid.,* DN XIII. 3, p. 188.
49. *Ibid.,* DN II. 3, p. 68.
50. *Ibid.*
51. Cf. *Op. Cit.,* Enneads V. 4. 1.
52. Cf. *Op. Cit.,* Eckhart, Pfeiffer, The Kingdom of God, p. 27ff, vol. I.
53. *Op. Cit.,* DN IV. 1, pp. 86-87.
54. *Ibid.,* DN IV. 1, p. 87.
55. *Ibid.,* DN IV. 2, p. 88.
56. *Ibid.,* DN IV. 4, p. 91.
57. *Ibid.,* DN IV. 4, pp. 90-94.
58. *Ibid.,* DN IV. 4, p. 92.
59. *Ibid.,* DN IV. 4, p. 93.
60. *Ibid.,* DN IV. 7, p. 95.
61. *Ibid.,* DN IV. 7, p. 96.
62. *Ibid.,* DN IV. 12, 13, pp. 104-106.
63. *Ibid.,* DN V. 5, p. 136.
64. *Ibid.,* DN V. 5, p. 137.
65. *Ibid.,* DN V. 6, p. 137.
66. *Ibid.,* DN V. 2, p. 132.
67. *Ibid.*
68. *Ibid.,* DN V. 7, p. 138.
69. *Ibid.,* DN V. 8, pp. 138-139.
70. *Ibid.,* DN V. 8, pp. 139-140.
71. *Ibid.,* DN V. 1, 131.
72. *Ibid.,* DN IV. 10, pp. 99-102.
73. *Ibid.,* DN IV. 14, p. 107.
74. *Ibid.*
75. *Op. Cit.,* Cosmic Theology, Rutledge, pp. 3, 26.
76. *Ibid.,* p. 12.
77. Cf. *Timaeus,* 42a-49a.

78. *Op. Cit.*, DN V. 8, pp. 140-141.

79. *Ibid.*, DN V. 8, p. 140.

80. *Ibid.*, DN V. 8, p. 141.

81. *Ibid.*, DN V. 6, pp. 137-138.

82. *Op. Cit.*, Cambridge History, Armstrong, pp. 462-463; also cf. DN V. 9-10.

83. *Op. Cit.*, DN VII. 3, pp. 151-152.

84. *Ibid.*, DN V. 10, p. 142.

85. J. Vanneste, S.J., *La Mystere de Dieu* (Malines: Desclee De Brouwer, 1959)

86. *Ibid.*, p. 147.

87. *Ibid.*, p. 148.

88. *Ibid.*, p. 149.

89. *Op. Cit.*, Sharpe, Mysticism, pp. 202-203.

90. *Op. Cit.*, MT I. 1, p. 191, Rolt.

91. *Ibid.*, MT I, pp. 191-192.

92. *Ibid.*, MT I, p. 192.

93. *Ibid.*, n. 1.

94. *Ibid.*, n. 3.

95. *Ibid.*, MT I, p. 193.

96. *Ibid.*, MT I, pp. 193-194.

97. *Ibid.*

98. *Ibid.*, MT III, p. 198.

99. *Ibid.*, MT IV, p. 199.

100. *Ibid.*, MT V, p. 200.

101. *Ibid.*, MT V, p. 201.

102. *Op. Cit.*, Sharpe, Mysticism, Epistle I, pp. 224-225.

103. *Ibid.*

104. *Op. Cit.*, CH, ch. I, sec. iii, pp. 3-4, Parker.

105. *Ibid.*, CH, ch. III, sec. i, p. 13.

106. *Ibid.*, CH, ch. III, sec. iii, p. 16.

107. Dante Alighieri, cf. *Paradise,* Trans., Dorothy L. Sayers and Barbara Reynolds (Baltimore: Penguin, 1962).

108. *Op. Cit.*, DN I. 1, pp. 51-52.

109. *Ibid.*, DN III. 3, p. 85.

110. *Ibid.*, DN VII. 3, p. 152.

111. *Ibid.*, n. 3.

112. *Ibid.*, DN II. 9, pp. 75-77.

113. *De Reductione Artium Ad Theologiam,* 5.

114. *Op. Cit.*, MT I, p. 191.

Chapter 11

1. *Op. Cit.,* Divine Names I. 8, pp. 61-63; II. 1, pp. 65-67; III. 1, pp. 81-83, hereafter DN and MT as in preceding chapters.

2. *Ibid.,* DN IV. 1, pp. 86-87.

3. *Ibid.,* DN V. 5, p. 136.

4. *Ibid.,* DN VI. 1-3, pp. 144-145.

5. *Ibid.,* p. 146.

6. *Ibid.,* DN VII. 1-2, pp. 146-151.

7. *Ibid.,* DN VII. 3, p. 152.

8. *Ibid.,* DN XIII. 3, p. 188.

9. *Ibid.,* MT I, p. 191.

10. *Ibid.,* MT I, p. 192.

11. *Ibid.,* MT I, p. 193.

12. *Ibid.,* MT I, p. 194.

13. *Ibid.,* MT II, pp. 195-196.

14. *Op. Cit.,* Varieties, p. 68.

15. *Ibid.*

16. *Ibid.*

17. *Op. Cit.,* DN VII. 1, p. 147.

18. *Ibid.,* MT III, p. 198.

19. Ibid.

20. We are not suggesting a program of escapism, nor is the Pseudo-Dionysius. What we are trying to show along with him is the *way* to God in the contemplative realm. Rather than an escape, this is a path of great service in the act of witnessing to the most essential value, that which is conducive to our Salvation.

21. *Op. Cit.,* MT V, p. 201.

22. *Ibid.,* MT I, p. 191.

Chapter 12

1. *Op. Cit.,* O'Brien, Varieties, p. 123.

2. Josiah Royce, *Studies of Good and Evil* (New York: Appelton, 1910), p. 270.

3. *Ibid.,* p. 275.

4. *Op. Cit.,* Pfeiffer, Eckhart, *The Kingdom of God,* p. 270, vol. I.

5. *Ibid.*

6. *Ibid.*

7. *Ibid.,* Sermon LVIII, "Divine Understanding," p. 148.

8. *Ibid.,* Tractate XIX, *The Beatific Vision,* p. 411.

9. *Ibid.,* Sermon LVIII, p. 146.

10. *Ibid.,* Tractate, *The Kingdom of God,* pp. 268-269.

11. *Ibid.,* p. 269.

12. *Ibid.,* Tractate II, *The Nobility of the Soul,* p. 283.

13. *Ibid.*

14. *Ibid.,* Tractate XV, *The Three Creations,* p. 385.

15. *Op. Cit.,* O'Brien, Varieties, p. 125.

16. *Op. Cit.,* Eckhart, Tractate, *The Kingdom of God,* pp. 276-277.

17. *Ibid., Liber Positionum,* p. 468.

18. *Ibid.,* Tractate XI, p. 354.

19. *Ibid.,* Tractate XIX, *The Beatific Vision,* p. 412.

20. *Ibid.*

21. *Op. Cit.,* Royce, Studies, p. 282.

22. F. C. Happold, *Mysticism: A Study and an Anthology* (Baltimore: Penguin, 1963), p. 270.

23. *Op. Cit.,* Sermon LVIII, "Divine Understanding," p. 148.

24. *Ibid.,* Tractate, *The Kingdom of God,* p. 267.

25. D. T. Suzuki, *Mysticism: Christian and Buddhist* (New York: Perennial Library, Harper & Row, 1971), p. 17.

26. Meister Eckhart, *Meister Eckhart,* trans., Raymond B. Blakney (New York: Harper & Row, 1941), p. xi.

27. *Op. Cit.,* Sermon LXXXVII, "The Poor In Spirit," p. 220.

28. *Ibid.,* Sermon, XXXIV, p. 95.

29. *Ibid.,* Tractate XIX, *The Beatific Vision,* p. 412.

30. *Op. Cit.,* Studies, p. 291.

31. *Op. Cit.,* Eckhart, Blakney, Sermon XX, "Ego Elegi Vos De Mundo," Purity of Heart, p. 190. In the context of speaking about the nature of true purity, Eckhart says that purity is of the essence of the Godhead, that it is an emptiness and yet a fullness, from which the Father eternally draws His being and His creativity.

32. *Op. Cit.,* Royce, Studies, pp. 288-289.

33. *Op. Cit.,* Eckhart, Blakney, Sermon I, "Dum Medium Silentium Tenarent Omnia Et Nox In Suo Cursu Medium Iter Haberet," p. 97.

34. *Op. Cit.,* Eckhart, Pfeiffer, Sermon XXXII, "The Soul Spark," p. 87.

35. *Ibid.,* p. 88.

36. *Ibid.,* Tractate, *The Kingdom of God,* p. 272.

37. *Ibid.,* pp. 274-275.

38. *Ibid.,* Tractate XI, p. 355.

39. *Ibid.,* Sermon LVII, "Such is The Nature of God," p. 145.

40. *Ibid.,* Tractate II, *The Nobility of the Soul,* pp. 281-282.

41. *Ibid.,* Sermon LXXXIII, "St. Germanus' Day," p. 209.

42. *Op. Cit.,* Royce, Studies, p. 286.

43. *Op. Cit.,* Sermon LVI, "The Emanation and Return," p. 143.

44. *Op. Cit.,* Eckhart, Blakney, "Intravit Jesu In Templum Dei," p. 160.

45. Although Eckhart speaks as if he were a monist, in some of his Sermons and Tractates, it is fairly certain that he is not. What Eckhart is attempting to utter in these passages that appear to assert absolute identity is the profoundity of the union, the knowing in and through God. There is no language to express such a unity, thus, he uses the language of identity to convey a unity of consciousness or of communication, not a unity of substance.

46. Rudolf Otto, *Mysticism East and West* (New York: Macmillan, 1970), p. 153.

SELECT BIBLIOGRAPHY

The following titles are not meant to be exhaustive, but to give the reader some furthr help in the study of Mysticism. That is why this is called a "select bibliography."

Alighierei, Dante. *The Divine Comedy*. vol. 3, *Paradise*. Trans. Dorothy L. Sayers. Penguin Books: Baltimore, 1962.

Aquinatis, S. Thomae. *In Librum Beati Dionysii De Divinis Nominisub. Expositio.* Marieti: Romae, 1950.

Augustine, St. *The Confessions*. Trans. Rex Warner. Mentor: New York, 1963.

Bernard of Clairvaux, St. *On Loving God. Cistercian Fathers Series,* vol. 5. Trans. Robert Walton, O.S.B. Cistercian Pub.: Washington, D.C., 1974.

_____. *Opera S. Bernardi.* ed. Jean Leclercq, O.S.B. et al. Editiones Cistercienses: Romae, 1958.

Bonaventura, St. *The Mind's Road To God*. Trans. George Boas. Bobbs-Merrill: Indianapolis, 1953.

Butler, Dom Cuthbert. *Western Mysticism*. Constable & Co.: London, 1927.

The Classics of Western Spirituality. In progress. Paulist Press: New York, 1978-   . 60 vols. projected.

Dionysius, The Areopagite. *The Divine Names and The Mystical Theology*. Trans. E.E. Rolt. S.P.C.K. Press: London, 1940.

_____. *La Hierarchie Celeste*. Traduction et Notes par M. de Gandillac. Etude et texte critique par G. Heil. Introduction de Denys L'Areopagite par R. Roques. *Collection Sources Chretiennes*. vol. 58. Paris, 1958.

_____. *The Works of Dionysius The Areopagite. Part II, The Heavenly Hierarchy.* Trans. Rev. John Parker. Richard Pub. Co: Merrick, N.Y., 1976, Reprint.

Dupre, Louis. *The Other Dimension*. Doubleday: New York, 1972.

Eckhart, Meister. *Meister Eckhart.* Trans. Raymond B. Blakney. Harper & Row: New York, 1941.

_____. *Meister Eckhart.* ed. Franz Pfeiffer. Trans. C. de B. Evans. Watkins: London, 1947.

Francis of Assisi, St. *Writings and Early Biographies. English Omnibus of the Sources For The Life of St. Francis.* ed. Marion A. Habig. Franciscan Herald Press: Chicago, 1972.

Griffiths, Bede. *Return To The Centre.* Collins: London, 1976.

_____. *Vedanta & Christian Faith.* Dawn Horse Press: Los Angeles, 1973.

Happold, F.C. *Mysticism: A Study and an Anthology.* Penguin Books: Baltimore, 1963.

_____. *The Journey Inwards.* John Knox Press: Atlanta, 1975.

James, William. *The Varieties of Religious Experience.* Collier-Macmillian: London, 1961.

Johnston, William *The Inner Eye of Love: Mysticism and Religion.* Harper & Row: New York, 1978.

_____. *Silent Music.* Harper & Row: New York, 1974.

John of the Cross, St. *The Collected Works of St. John of the Cross.* Trans. Kieran Kavanaugh, O.C.D. and Otilio Rodriguez, O.C.D. I.C.S. Press: Washington, D.C., 1976.

Jung, C.G. *Memories, Dreams and Reflections.* Trans. Richard & Clara Winston, Pantheon Books: New York, 1961.

Maloney, George A., S.J. *Invaded by God: Mysticism and The Indwelling Trinity.* Dimension Books: Denville, N.J. 1979.

_____. *Inward Stillness.* Dimension Books: Denville, N.J., 1975.

Masters, R.E.L. & Houston, Jean. *The Varieties of Psychedelic Experience.* Delta: New York, 1966.

O'Brien, Elmer. *The Varieties of Mystic Experience.* Mentor-Omega: New York, 1965.

Otto, Rudolf, *Mysticism East and West.* Macmillan: New York, 1970.

Plotinus. *The Enneads.* Trans. Stephen Mackenna. Faber & Faber: London, 1962.

Sharpe, A.B. *Mysticism: Its Nature and True Value.* Sands & Co.: London, 1910.

Teresa of Avila, St. *Interior Castle.* Trans. Allison Peers. Image: New York, 1961.

——————————. *The Autobiography of St. Teresa of Avila.* Trans. Allison Peers. Image: New York, 1960.

Van Ruysbroeck, Blessed Jan. *The Spiritual Espousals.* Trans. Eric Colledge. Faber & Faber: London, 1952.

Vanneste, J., S.J. *Le Mystere de Dieu.* Desclee de Brouwer: Malines, 1959.

Underhill, Evelyn. *Mysticism.* Dutton: New York, 1961.

Zaehner, R.C. *Mysticism Sacred and Profane.* Claredon Press: Oxford, 1957.

Orthodox Spirituality: An Outline of the Orthodox Ascetical and Mystical Tradition. anonymous. St. Vladimir's Press: Crestwood, New York, 1978.

Abraham, 13, 41, 63
Absolute, 2, 51, 56, 58, 64, 68, 86,   104
Absolute Beauty, 112
Absolute Beginning, 70
Absolute Community, 138
Absolute Essence, 114
Absolute Exemplar, 136
Absolute Existence, 113
Absolute Identity, 97
Absolute Knowledge, 125, 128, 132
Absolute Meaning, 100, 11, 118, 141
Absolute Mystical State, 84
Absolute Necessity, 145
Absolute One, 25
Absolute Reality, 63, 120, 143, 147
Absolute Standard, 112
Absolute Truth, 38, 72
Abysm, 144
Abyss, 71, 73, 74, 83, 144, 145
Abyss of the Godhead, 134
Act of Being, 68
Activity, 35
Actual Intellect (The), 142
Ad Extra, 77
Adam, 41
Aesthetic Mysticism, 7
Affirmation, 120, 130
Affirmative Theology, 106
Ageless Form, 53
Agnosia, 103, 105, 107, 116, 122
Albright (Foxwell), 15
Alexandrian School, 106
Anagogy, 100, 107
Ancient Wisdom, 4
Anderson (Bernard), 13
Angelic Hierarchy, 107
Angelic Intelligences, 105, 106, 107, 109, 113, 120
Angelic Knowledge, 121
Angelic Orders, 104
Angels, 101, 108, 114, 115, 121
Anthropocentric, 56, 59
Apophatic, 31, 50, 59, 87, 90, 99, 122, 124
Apophatic Method, 121, 128
Apophatic Theology, 105, 123
Apostolic Constitutions, 107
Arche, 109
Archetypal Ideas, 116
Archetypes, 4, 24, 112
Areopagite, 87, 100, 129
Aristotle, 113, 141
Armstrong (Hilary), 86, 97
Arnou, 97

Ascension, 18
Ascent, 105, 119, 122, 128
Aseitas, 10, 71
Aseity, 71, 78
Atman, 143
Attitude, 36
Auctoritas, 100, 101
Augustine, 108
Authenticity, 28

Beatific Vision, 34, 41, 51
Beatitude, 18, 85, 121, 132
Beauty, 53, 94
Becoming, 58
Being, 11, 22, 24, 25, 57, 58, 59, 60, 71, 72, 74, 76, 88, 105, 107, 112, 125, 131, 143
Beneficent Emanations, 109
Benficient Volitions, 116
Bergson, 2
Bernard, 45
Biblical, 104
Biblical Tradition, 106
Bilaniuk, 24, 25
Biological, 69
Blakney, 142
Blessed Trinity, 26, 37
Bliss, 54, 85, 141
Blissful Ground, 145
Boehme, (Jacob) 32
Bonaventure, 43, 51
Book of Mysteries, 107
Bottomless Sea of the Godhead, 134
Boundless, 126
Brahman, 57, 141
Brevard Childs, 14
Buber, 3
Buddha, 44
Buddhism, 43, 73, 111, 124

Caius, 103, 120
Cantica Canticrum, 45
Cataphatic, 122
Cataphatic Theology, 104,105
Catholic Church, 26
Catholicism, 124
Causality, 109
Cause, 112, 114, 118 119, 130
"Cave of the Heart", 28, 50, 66, 143, 147
The Celestial, 104, 117
Celestial Height, 53
The Celestial Hierarchy, 23, 106, 115, 116, 120
The Celestial Hierarchies, 105

Index

Eternal Bliss, 129
Eternal Center, 71
Eternal Glory, 129
Eternal Happiness, 131
Eternal Kingdom, 65
Eternal Life, 9, 18, 28, 49, 50
Eternal Meaning, 75, 137
Eternal Mystery, 138
Eternal Now, 62, 84, 130, 145
Eternal Torah, 63
Eternal Truth, 42
Eternal Word, 143
Eternity, 2
Eucharist, 85
Exemplar, 42, 116, 117
Existence, 11, 78, 84, 113
Existence Itself, 61
Existential, 43, 124
Existentialism, 2
Experience of God, 56, 147
Experiential, 147
Experiential Knowledge, 131

Faith, 9, 85
Father, 8, 18, 20, 21, 24, 25, 33, 34, 35, 36, 42, 62, 63, 64, 72, 74, 75, 77, 79, 80, 83, 84, 136, 137, 139, 140, 145
Fatherland, 89
Father-nature, 136
Fathers, 18, 26, 86
Fecundity, 72
Fichte, 134
Filiation, 137
Final Cause, 104
Final Purpose, 117
Finite, 69
First Clause, 69
First Epistle, 120
Flowing Fountain, 134
Forest Sages, 55
Forest Seers, 56
Form of the Good, 23
Formless form, 59
Formlessness, 141
Forms, 88, 107, 109, 116
Franciscan School, 42
Free Soul, 144
Fullness, 143
Functions, 74
Funkelin, 143
Ganges, 6
German Philosophy, 134
Gilson, 101
Glory, 92

Gnostics, 108
God, 10, 11, 13, 15, 21, 24, 25, 27, 31, 32, 33, 34, 35, 37, 38, 39, 44, 45, 46, 48, 50, 51, 57, 60, 61, 64, 66, 68, 69, 70, 71, 72, 76, 77, 78, 79, 80, 83, 84, 85, 86, 87, 89, 90, 91, 92, 93, 94, 96, 97, 98, 99, 102, 104, 105, 107, 108, 109, 110, 112, 114, 115, 116, 117, 118, 119, 121, 122, 124, 125, 126, 127, 128, 129, 130, 131, 132, 134, 135, 136, 141, 142, 143, 144, 145
God of Israel, 12
God-archetype, 4
God-consciousness, 26
Godhead, 8, 23, 24, 33, 34, 35, 38, 50, 57, 59, 60, 61, 62, 64, 70, 71, 72, 73, 74, 75, 78, 79, 80, 92, 100, 102, 103, 108, 109, 110, 111, 112, 113, 114, 117, 119, 120, 121, 123, 127, 130, 134, 135, 137, 138, 140, 141, 142, 144, 145
God's Esse, 16
God's Essence, 103
God's Holiness, 78
God's Name, 17
God's Nature, 77, 78
God's Personhood, 70
God's Presence, 103
Good (The Good), 38, 59, 87, 88, 105, 107, 111, 112, 115, 125
Goodness, 78, 79, 112, 115, 131
Gospel, 18, 34, 44
Grace, 31, 129, 130
Greek, 12
Greek Fathers, 42
Gregory of Nazianzen, 107
Griffiths (Father Bede Griffiths), 6, 41, 55
Ground, 33, 70, 73, 114, 134, 140
Ground of Being, 68
Guide, 86
Guru-disciple, 44
Habra (Georges Habra), 19
Haplosis, 91
Happiness, 141, 142
Hasidism, 3
Heaven, 54, 130
Heavenly or Celestial Hierarchy, 102
Heavenly Hierarchy, 107, 120
Heavenly Truth, 123
Hebrew, 12
Hegel, 57, 58, 95, 96, 134
Heidegger, 2, 134
Heisenburg, 2
Henosis, 100, 102, 104, 105, 106, 119, 121, 122

169